CW00971537

THE DREAM CAFÉ

Lessons in the Art of Radical Innovation

Duncan D. Bruce and
Dr Geoff Crook

WILEY

This edition first published 2015.

Registered office
John Wiley and Sons Ltd, The Atrium, Southern Gate, Chichester, West Sussex, PO19 8SQ, United Kingdom

For details of our global editorial offices, for customer services and for information about how to apply for permission to reuse the copyright material in this book please see our website at www.wiley.com.

Library of Congress Cataloging-in-Publication Data

Bruce, Duncan D., 1957-
The dream café : lessons in the art of radical innovation / Duncan D. Bruce and Dr. Geoff Crook.
pages cm
Includes index.
ISBN 978-1-118-97784-2 (hardback)
1. Strategic planning. 2. Branding (Marketing) I. Crook, Geoff, 1945– II. Title.
HD30.28.B78423 2015
658.4′063–dc23

2014043908

Cover Design: Mackerel Design and Art Studio
Cover image: (Wood background) ©K-Kwan Kwanchai/Shutterstock; (Black marker) ©iStock.com/sgtphoto; (Red pencil) ©iStock.com/WimL; (Notebook) ©Dragan Milovanovic/Shutterstock; (Coffee cup) ©Picsfive/Shutterstock; (Cappucino) ©Everything/Shutterstock

Set in 10/13.5 ACaslonPro-Regular by Laserwords Private Ltd, Chennai, India
Printed in Great Britain by TJ International Ltd, Padstow, Cornwall, UK

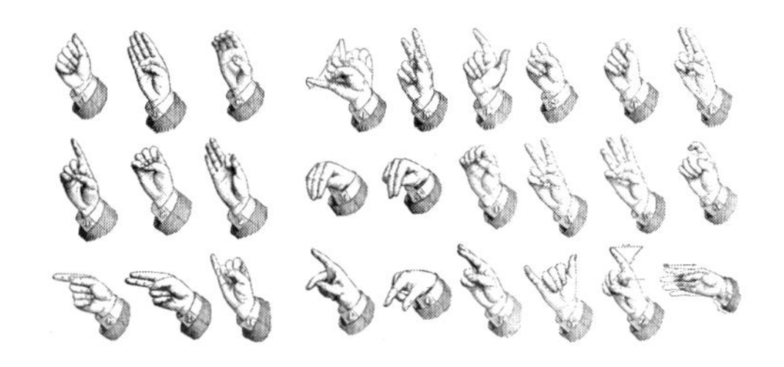

CONTENTS

PREFACE

The Dream Café offers an introduction to the lessons that brand owners can learn in a way that deliberately defies logic – that is, by emulating the way that the radical creative practitioners we commonly called avant-garde broke with convention, dismissed the naysayers and invented the future. The fact that artists and creative thinkers, from a wide range of backgrounds, could change the way we all think and do by initiatives that began with interdisciplinary conversations around a café table provides compelling evidence for a new way of engaging with the urgent task of brand innovation.

In order to practise what we preach we have avoided a conventional structure for our book and created an A to Z list of characteristics, actions and qualities that distinguish business that thrive from those that merely survive (and sometimes, don't), which is more akin to a series of 'Menu Cards'. We believe that in a 'time-short' world the insights we offer are best read on the run, much in the way that you would snack at a café. When the experimental French film maker Jean Luc Godard was asked about his apparent lack of interest in conventional narrative principle, he corrected his interviewer by pointing out that his films do have 'a beginning, a middle and an end', but 'not necessarily in that order'. It's much the same with this book: we want you to engage with it in 'bite-sized chunks'.

Despite innovation's ubiquitous nature nowadays – along with its profound and exponentially significant influence on our lives – we still tend to respond to new and disruptive concepts with a mixture of apprehension, disinterest and disbelief. Science fiction writer Arthur C Clarke summarized how our reaction to new thinking evolves from scorn to ownership without any awareness of our power to delay or indefinitely postpone innovation, as we undergo the following reactions to any given new concept:

1 It's completely impossible.
2 It's possible, but it's not worth doing.
3 I said it was a good idea all along.

Anyone who has read about, or was involved with, Steve Jobs' return to Apple will empathize with Clarke's summary. Jobs had to ignore the entire board in order to reinvent the business, but we doubt that many of those board members would now be wanting to own up to not seeing the future.

A number of the brand examples quoted in this book reference the tenacity that is needed to overcome the naysayers, or as in Kodak's case the danger of giving way to them. Our resistance to change provides a convenient alibi for those who see innovation as a threat to the status quo and act as gatekeepers against that threat. Not long ago, the cautious represented a key part of business strategy through their ability to perpetuate the maxim of: 'if it's not broke, don't fix it'. *The Dream Café* acts as an important reminder that THAT was THEN by enabling brands to live in the NOW and take ownership of THE FUTURE.

Businesses today operate in a context where the unpredictability of competition and customer loyalty has changed the rules of engagement – one where chaos rules caution and predictability becomes the enemy of economic sustainability. This is why companies need to do a lot more than simply re-educating their gatekeepers to create opportunities for inclusion that encourage everyone to participate in anticipating and owning the future. For most businesses, embracing disruption as an opportunity rather than a threat begins with a commitment to disrupt their own values and processes.

The Dream Café argues that business has a lot to gain from emulating the radical and edgy ways of thinking and doing that we associate with the avant-garde practitioners.

Places

Our research has led us to understand how the ad hoc informality that enables a café to become a location for brewing up extraordinary innovation can be emulated by business. This is why we've titled our book *The Dream Café*.

You'll see how café culture can provide a business with much more than a site for relaxation. We reveal how the unpredictable meetings between individuals who bring varying degrees of knowledge and experience will create greater value if you involve a café model. When we develop a Dream Café innovation opportunity we are always careful to find a location that will take our clients out of their everyday routine. We believe that the contemporary Google imitation obsession with creating a 'third space' in house misses the central point of innovation opportunity: to disrupt everyone and everything. We know that constructing your innovation strategy around what we call the 'fourth space' – because it's not familiar – will enable you to attract and develop the kind of unanticipated range of interactions and opportunities that are rarely attained by the type of rational planning that still dominates innovation culture. Psychiatrist and psychotherapist Carl Jung identified the power of the unpredictable encounters that a good café can facilitate: 'The meeting of two personalities is like the meeting of two molecules. If there is any reaction, both are transformed.'[1] Jung's focus on knowledge as a product of a dialectical process in which thesis and antithesis can lead to synthesis relates to our own work. He reminds us that there is an urgent need for an alternative to the cookie cutter approach to developing an innovation culture in which harmony is given more status than disruptive potential. No matter how well funded your innovation strategy may be, it ultimately depends on the interplay between the right (or the 'wrong') people in the right place and the level of permission that they are given to operate without rules.

For those prepared to scoff at the preposterous suggestion that business should organize its innovation culture around the notion of a café, it might be worth remembering that successful cafés are very good examples of high stakes management efficiency. Our belief that a café offers a perfect location for disruption is built on our understanding of the management difficulty of creating profit out of an open invitation to a broad and perhaps incompatible group of people. Imagine trying to get funding for a business concept that depends on creating and servicing a wide range of emotional and functional needs (from creative stimulation to basic refreshment). Add to that the idea of selling short-shelf-life food and drink to a demographic that ranges from people who appear to just want to sit and talk to others who want to smash the crockery and experiment in defining new levels of belligerence.

People

Even a brief study of the artists and other visionaries that have challenged and changed the world reveals the disruptive characteristics that the brand champions will need if they are to win the battle for the future. Author Robert Hughes described the avant-garde in the following way:

> *Ebullience, idealism, confidence, the belief that there was plenty of territory to explore, and above all the sense that (they) could find the necessary metaphors by which a radically changing culture could be explained to its inhabitants.*
>
> **(Robert Hughes, *The Shock of the New*, 1991)**

We at The Dream Café spend a lot of time and energy ensuring that we get the right characters to inhabit the cafés that we create for our clients. That said – our experience confirms that innovation is as much a product of place as it is of people. We believe that creating a culture of disruption is as much to do with changing the *ways* in which things are done, as it is to do with what people actually do.

Process

Our research has enabled us to synthesize a range of transferable strategies and attitudes that will help brands adopt the radical approach to innovation that characterizes disruptive practise in the arts. Compared to the typical 'scientific' approach to innovation, which still dominates traditional brand thinking, the often ad hoc approach of the avant-garde appears random and chaotic. But it is this ability to challenge conventional wisdom that lies at the heart of its attraction.

The following indicative summary gives a flavour of the open attitude that enables creative thinkers and doers to move beyond the known so effectively:

- Forgetting.
- No rules.
- Unpacking.
- Relaxing about how, where and when innovation opportunity is developed.
- Being open minded about the kind of people that you collaborate with.
- Embracing unpredictability as an opportunity.
- Understanding that rapid and risky decision making is safer that slow iterative evolution.
- Being at ease with any new strategy appearing to be counter intuitive.
- Assuming that anything is possible.
- Not always beginning with a definitive end in mind.
- Developing playful approaches to prototyping that emphasize metaphor rather than formal function.
- Celebrating the power of your imagination.
- Understanding that application is an open opportunity rather than a conclusion.

Expecting the Unexpected

Everett Roger's '5 Attributes: Diffusion of Innovations' model continues to define assumptions that a 'too much too soon' strategy of innovation may limit widespread adoption. The safety first approach that typifies conventional innovation strategy is the antithesis of the behaviours that enable avant-garde practice to redefine norms and values:

- Create an advantage over what's out there.
- Aim for compatibility with existing norms and values.
- Prioritize accessibility.
- Ensure that affordability encourages 'triability'.
- Makes results and benefits visible.

Implicit in the Everett approach is a commitment to iteration rather than disruption, which encourages middle of the road mediocrity that the avant-garde would see as part of the problem. The assumption that the present is the logical benchmark for any kind of innovation immediately removes the legitimacy of imagining what does not yet exist. The desire for 'compatibility' further reigns in an innovation team's potential to think beyond the conventional. The emphasis on obvious functionality eradicates the ability to invent new forms, functions and values. The concern for obvious benefits denies what the avant-garde would assume was a primary motivation, namely conceptual opportunity thought to be the evolution of intangible opportunities.

Being Avant-Garde

Our experience at The Dream Café has taught us that the art of radical innovation begins with some fundamental unpacking of the obstacles, inhibitions, habits and protocols that typically hinder change. Some of these obstacles are simply the result of becoming used to doing things in personal and particular ways – methods that we've inherited and/or unquestionably adopted. Others are the result of a much deeper conditioning process that has prompted our belief in rational deduction to dominate our strategy and the ways that we evaluate outcomes. Consider that, until recently, a lot of businesses believed it was possible to calculate which brands would sell and which would not, through a combination of strategic planning and market testing.

The Dream Café argues that we can no longer trust in the clockwork universe metaphor and that the only thing we can assume is that nothing is predictable. In order for our clients to learn how to succeed and prosper from a world in which everything is in a state of permanent flux, they need to forget what they thought they knew and embrace the possibilities of benign chaos.

The markets within which brands compete nowadays are changing every minute. There are no guarantees of success beyond a commitment to a permanent strategy of radical innovation. Disruption has emerged as possibly the best source of a sustainable future that we have available to us – and disruption is not for the faint hearted. It is deeply challenging. Much of what this book will reveal will appear to be counter-intuitive to our rationally conditioned mind-sets, but it promises the opportunity of leading rather than following.

Coming to terms with the benefits of unpredictability requires a whole new mindset, along with a reconnection between our heart and our head. We have to acquire the capacity to take risks based on hunches, rather than dodgy data dressed up as stats. And we have to discover the joy of trusting our instincts.

Recognizing and profiting from chaos begins by relearning the rules of logic. This requires that we do away with the faith in rational deduction that was instilled in us as we served our time in formal education. And the more 'formal' our education was, the more likely we are to believe that taking creative risks is counter intuitive; that collaboration is cheating; and that unprecedented ideas are the products of idle speculation. We need to unpack that experience and accept that our ability to dream is probably the one asset that makes us capable of creating the future.

Most of us grew up seeing the 'dreamers' in our midst as failures who were unable to cope with the intellectual demands of formal learning and the rigour of applying formulas. Yet these are the people that we need to learn from now – the ones dismissed because of their inability to cope with the culture of instrumental rationality. Hindsight shows us that their 'failure' is instead evidence of exactly the kind of traits that we now need to evolve. The dreamers instinctively resisted a system that was predicated on a belief that the only right answers were either ones that you regurgitated from 'facts' or deduced by measurable calculation.

We learned that scientific rigour provides a safety net of predictability – which has encouraged us to ignore the fact that the best science is very similar to the best art. As Einstein confirmed:

> *Imagination is more important than knowledge … When I examine myself and my methods of thought, I come close to the conclusion that the gift of imagination has meant more to me than any talent for absorbing absolute knowledge.*

Creating a Disruptive Culture

Businesses and institutions generally take a cautious approach to innovation. In comparison, the avant-garde reveals evidence that chaos can be a source of sustainable innovation. Chaos is indeed a fix for the creatively inclined, an opportunity in which a mantra of 'if it's not broken, break it' feeds our inquisitive minds, sustains the soul and inspires our dreams.

This inquisitive, risk-friendly approach enables the more creative of us to discover and sow the seeds of possibility beyond the edge of what we thought we knew, or could accept. The story of modern culture is one of disruption; throughout this book we reference the writers, poets, performers, makers, musicians and artists that have stretched and ultimately shaped our aesthetic and conceptual sensibilities. We have given priority to practitioners who have challenged rather than conformed to the status quo. It is also a story of an on-going relationship between the arts and big business that can be characterized by the words 'mutual dependency'.

History shows us that the divisions that now segregate the arts from business are a relatively recent phenomenon. A brief examination of the cultural response to the early phases of industrialization confirms that resistance to the emergence of the new was coupled with its critical co-option. This tendency for synergetic and catalytic engagement still lies at the root of cultural invention.

The Dream Café will encourage you to challenge the prejudices that have led you to believe disruption is only possible if you have the freedom from fiscal responsibility that artists appear to enjoy. We argue that the open minded and inquisitive approach typical of avant-garde practice will enable you to realize the kinds of opportunities for hybridization that the closed minded resist.

Gaining access to a more diverse landscape of possibilities is all about culture change rather than the absence of latent ability. Gaining access to The Dream Café is simply about deciding to enter.

Throughout the book, we will encourage you to work closer to the edge and will help you to understand that creating brands like an artist doesn't always depend on achieving total originality. Many of the lessons that we reveal suggest that there is a lot to be gained by re-imagining and re-assembling pre-existing components drawn for a variety of sources.

What follows is an A to Z of the attitudes and techniques that enabled the avant-garde to reshape our sense of what is possible.

A

AVANT-GARDE

The origins of The Dream Café's philosophy and processes are firmly rooted in an approach to the art of radical innovation, which started with café conversations. The informality of the café encouraged the development of interdisciplinary and transcultural discourses that led to a clear pattern of beliefs, practices and lifestyle habits that gave rise to the term 'avant-garde', which initially became clearly visible in France in the 1880s.

The coffee house forged the principles of the café as a fermenting pot for revolution during the eighteenth century. This meeting place informed unprecedented scientific breakthroughs and the industrialization of manufacturing. However, its impact on the arts did not achieve the same level of radical conceptual experimentation that occurred in France in the latter half of the nineteenth century and beyond.

The term avant-garde came into use in the early twentieth century, and was used to define a shift in emphasis from classical dependency to experimental challenge in which artist and other intellectuals redefined the parameter of the known, and effectively acted as the vanguard of modernity. Cafés became the catalyst and a crucial source of facilitation for a whole new way of thinking and doing that was fuelled by interdisciplinary and multi-cultural moments of connectivity around café tables.

We focus this brief introduction on the formative phase of the avant-garde (c. 1850s–1920s) including 'The Belle Époque' (beautiful period).

During the latter half of the nineteenth century, France – and Paris in particular – provided a heady context of revolution as volatile politics and energetic entrepreneurship combined to shape opportunity for innovation. Those parts of Paris that have become the major tourist attractions today were created during the 1850s through a process of massive urban disruption, which ripped out and built over the medieval core of the old city in less than a decade. Masterminded and managed by Baron Haussmann, the new Paris became the blueprint for the modern city. It created unprecedented social and economic opportunities that redefined how many people experienced urban life.

The artists, musicians, writers, poets, critics, designers and craftspeople who flocked to the city in this period of ferment were inspired and facilitated by a context in which unprecedented developments in science, technology, retail, entertainment and transport were emerging. While city dwellers had to accept tumult as a significant characteristic of contemporary life, the avant-garde embraced this flux as a source of inspiration and opportunity. The impact that the café had on intellectual and creative life is captured by the words of Irish novelist George Moore, in his book *Confessions of a Young Man*, published just after the turn of the century:

> *I did not go to either Oxford or Cambridge, but I went to La Nouvelle Athènes ... though unacknowledged, though unknown, the influence of the Nouvelle Athènes is inveterate in the artistic thought of the nineteenth century.*
>
> **(George Moore, *Confessions of a Young Man*, 1901)**

This urban upheaval acted as a magnet for artists and other experimentally inclined practitioners and theorists. Their desire to be where the action was led them to reinforce the development of an infrastructure that supported a bohemian lifestyle. New kinds of entertainment emerged, and benefitted financially by enabling the inquisitive access to its less orthodox customers. The infamous Black Cat Café (Le Chat Noir) in Montmartre, established in 1881, provided the blueprint for the decadent mix of cabaret, food and alcohol that fuelled the avant-garde. Montmartre was on the fault-line of the upheaval that reshaped Paris. Its mix of affordable rooms, galleries, cafés and brothels provided the context in which to found the Society of Incoherent Arts – arguably the first example of a deliberate concern to disrupt established notions of form and function in the arts.

By the start of the twentieth century, Paris had become renowned as a centre for disruptive experiments in art, lifestyle and culture. The kind of stimulating nurturing and facilitating context that it provided was essential for provoking and sustaining disruption. France was managing to encourage a process of reciprocation in which cultural innovation was inspired by the context of urban change, while helping to translate and define it.

The development of an avant-garde culture depended on the interaction between different personalities, stimuli and motivations. However, the courage to defy convention informed the evolution, and subsequently the influence, of the key practitioners who continue to give meaning to the term.

Learning to Ignore NO

One of the most important characteristics of the avant-garde is the refusal to heed when the gatekeepers say no. Being a pathfinder can be difficult, and requires people with an ability to override rejection. An avant-garde business is going to need to be confident and resilient to translate rejection into success. Fortunately, the history of innovation is littered with case studies of businesses that hung in there – and ended up owning the future.

One classic example of this is the problems that filmmaker George Lucas encountered in his attempts to sell his concept of a franchise for toys relating to the first *Star Wars* film. This was art trying to convert to business; according to *Wired Magazine* editor Chris Baker 'It's easy to forget that before Star Wars, licensed merchandise was a different, less profitable business. All the big toymakers turned down the rights to make Star Wars action figures; upstart Kenner didn't sign on until a month before the film's release.'[2] The *Star Wars* franchise opportunity's subsequent success redefined the toy industry, and continues to serve as a benchmark to this day, with annual sales in excess of $3 billion.

How Artists do Avant-Garde

Artists Charles Baudelaire and Marcel Duchamp played an instrumental role in defining the characteristics of the avant-garde through their capacity to challenge not only the status quo but also the nature and purpose of art itself. Though best known as a poet, Baudelaire also worked as an influential art critic, while Duchamp moved from painting to 'ready-mades' before giving up 'making art' to play chess.

Baudelaire demonstrated the symbiotic and changing possibilities of the artist's relationship with the urban landscape and the wider social and cultural context. At the start of his career he mourns the loss of the old city: that 'the old Paris is no more'. However, he responded enthusiastically a decade later to the new urban landscape in the dedication to his book *Le Spleen de Paris*:

> *Who among us has not dreamt, in moments of ambition, of the miracle of a poetic prose, musical without rhythm and rhyme, supple and staccato enough to adapt to the lyrical stirrings of the soul, the undulations of dreams, and sudden leaps of consciousness.*
>
> **(Charles Baudelaire, *Le Spleen de Paris*, 1869)**

Baudelaire defined the characteristics of the avant-garde as a way of life that was intentionally at odds with the mores of conventional society. He lived a life that would still be considered as provocative today, dressing and acting as an outsider.

Baudelaire also played a key role in establishing art as a force of disruption, by confronting traditional rules of grammar. He reframed how we understand language's metaphoric capacity, and opened up the aesthetic possibilities that lie beyond grammar's conventional frame. Much like a brand that establishes a new need by essentially discovering a latent desire, Baudelaire challenged a set of conventions that had effectively become culturally reinforced as a set of rules. In this respect, Baudelaire developed an essential maxim of disruptive behaviour: test, and then break the rules wherever they restrict innovative potential.

Compared to contemporary luminaries like Picasso, Marcel Duchamp had – publicly at least – a relatively brief career as a practising artist. However, the significance of his contribution has even more impact on art and life today than it did when he first exhibited his work. A clue to Duchamp's significance for development of the art of disruption lies in a famous quote: 'I force myself to contradict myself in order to avoid conforming to my own taste.'

Duchamp challenged himself as well as the mores of his time. Although his early work largely applied the traditional craft skills that remained central to the practice of many of his avant-garde contemporaries, Duchamp appeared to realize the contradiction inherent in utilizing traditional techniques to shape the future.

The formation of Duchamp's conceptual breakthroughs clearly owes much to his interactions with the Dada movements. The approach's common interest in disruptive practice simultaneously parodied the old order while developing new aesthetic possibilities that redefined art's form and function.

Duchamp instinctively understood that the scientific approach to innovation – one where the individual achieved objectivity through incremental steps framed by pre-existing rules, or repeated laws to prove a thesis – was at odds with the process that enabled the artist to trust in his or her emotions. Duchamp proposed that:

> *The artist goes from intention to realisation through a chain of totally subjective reactions offer business an insight into the value of gut reaction as a valuable source of innovation opportunity. In contrast to the tendency of the 'scientific' approach to minimize unpredictable outcomes artists are more likely to discover unprecedented potential by trusting in chance.*
>
> **(Marcel Duchamp, *The Creative Act*, 1957)**

Duchamp's transformation of everyday products into art works through the combination of signature and gallery display simultaneously disrupted the history of art, exhibiting, criticism, curating and collecting. His radical proposition was arguably the single most disruptive act in the history of art: 'My idea was to choose an object that wouldn't attract me, either by its beauty or by its ugliness. To find a point of indifference in my looking at it, you see.'

The Business of being Avant-Garde

The most important takeaway from Duchamp's contribution to the avant-garde is the need to challenge archetypes. This is equally true for brands, which waste so much time and money supporting tired propositions when they could be investing in game changing innovation.

The cafés of Montmartre did not just cater for artists; rather, they were part of a mix of individuals on a common endeavour to take ownership of the future. The crowd that came to cafés to converse and disrupt were inspired by the entrepreneurs, scientists and engineers who were challenging the very notion of what was possible. Gustave Eiffel's monumental Viaduc De Garabit, completed in 1884, had already signalled the potential for a new age of engineering transformation long before the Eiffel Tower opened for business in 1899. Pasteur had made the world a safer place through some extraordinary medical breakthroughs in the field of vaccination. Shopping was becoming a new form of leisure, ushering in the growth of the fashion industry as seasons emerged as a pretext for the notion of style redundancy. France had pioneered the department store concept of retailing in 1838 with the opening of Le Bon Marché.

Brand Dreams

The construction of the Eiffel Tower served as a contemporary icon to define a future-looking city. In the same way, the emergence of modern retail in Paris informed the evolution of the art of innovative branding. There was proactive serendipity between modern art and commerce as the aesthetics that emerged from café culture were quickly co-opted into the labelling and advertising of new brands.

There is a clear synchronicity between the conditions that gave way to the birth of the avant-garde in the late nineteenth century and the instability that brands are currently facing today. However, there are three essential differences that inform the rationale for The Dream Café. Specifically, today there is:

- Less opportunity for face-to-face interdisciplinary and cross-cultural discourse.
- An emphasis on efficiency that has devalued conversational discourse as a social opportunity not related to business.
- Increasing displacement of up-close-and-personal engagement with online conversation.

It is clear that the ad hoc and serendipitous opportunity that cafés provided for unanticipated connections was the secret of their success. Later in the book we will spend some time introducing our methodologies, and acknowledge the debt we owe to the pioneering spirits that informed and benefitted from a culture that valued time spent in meaningful conversation.

For the time being, we want to be clear that we will never claim to be able to compress the complex mix of time, place, people and context into a three or four day experience leading to an outcome as profound as the theory of relativity or cubism. Although more modest, however, we are still capable of creating a paradigm shift. By synthesizing and prioritizing the key ingredients that allowed café culture to stir radical Innovation, we can enable our clients to let go of the rules. This will enable them to reconsider everything they formerly saw as a challenge as an opportunity for themselves and the world.

Some of the Lessons that Contemporary Business can Learn from the Avant-Garde

Disruptions are always likely to incite resistance. Change typically involves upsetting people who feel that their values and knowledge are being threatened by people and principles that they do not understand. Robert Hughes captured the impact of disruption in his phrase 'the shock of the new'.

Creative individuals' ability to simultaneously respond to and drive change is a skill that many businesses today lack. The avant-garde's reputation was initially based on its capacity to challenge the status quo, and the conspicuous confidence its members displayed while doing so. While these individuals enjoyed a symbiotic relationship with the dominant culture, they also had a high degree of autonomy, effectively existing and operating as a subculture. While subcultures do exist in businesses, they are often and unfortunately a dysfunctional bi-product of a lack of effective discourse between different spheres of expertise, and/or management. The most obvious and most typical example of the battle between the quest for efficiency and the need for innovation is demonstrated by businesses that invest in efficiency enablers like 'Six Sigma' – only to find their innovation outcomes declining.

Bureaucracy has a tendency to prioritize processes that deliver predictable outcomes at the expense of ad hoc creativity. American multi-national conglomerate corporation 3M – a business that had built a reputation for innovation – saw a 9 percent fall in revenue from new products as a result of an efficiency (Six Sigma) strategy introduced in 2001. Although the drive for efficiency did achieve significant savings in manufacturing costs and other areas where people could be replaced by technology, it restricted the opportunity for unpredictable cross-cultural fertilization, which had flourished previously. The solution implemented in 2005 involved setting up teams, deliberately composed of people with different discipline expertise, who were given the freedom to operate outside of the Six Sigma regime. By 2010 innovation income was back up to 30 percent and rising.

Pivotal Locations

Art is frequently profiled as a solitary activity that emerges from a context of personal deprivation. Yet its history reveals another level of engagement focused on conviviality and discourse between different disciplines. The Black Cat in Montmartre was an iconic location that allowed artists and other creative dreamers to meet in an environment with which they could identify as a symbol of rebellion and otherness. The heady mix of food, drink and entertainment established The Black Cat as an engine of cultural revolution. It united different classes and interest groups in a place where they mixed freely and gained confidence in a world where rules matter less than ideas.

Dream Cafés

Picasso and others arrived in Paris too late to frequent The Black Cat, which closed in 1887. However, they sought out and founded their own equivalents. It is clear that food, drink and live entertainment facilitated and encouraged intellectual and artistic exchange. Development also played an important role in forming this culture of disruption. As Roger Shattuck confirms, in his illuminating history of the 'banquet years', creative practitioners and their patrons created their own banquets to deliberately foster opportunity for creative exchange and inspiration.

Context

Paris in the later nineteenth and early twentieth century became an important location for retail businesses focused on experience. As a result of the unprecedented explosion of entrepreneurial ambition, Paris became a world centre that attracted all types of cultural creatives. Revolutionary and iconic structures like the Arcades and the Eiffel Tower, together with the cabarets and cafés, helped to create an impression that Paris was the centre of the universe for fostering challenging and provocative ideas. The fact that many of the artists who became leading figures of the modern movement were attracted by this mythology, and then went on to actualize the myths, is an important factor in the creation of this self-fulfilling prophecy.

Investment

While many artists did indeed starve, Paris became a centre for the patronage and commoditization of culture that served to attract artists, audiences and investors. In many respects the modus operandi of the art investors who monetized the avant-garde is similar to the enlightened risk takers that grow disruptive businesses by aligning investment with ideas on the basis of instinct rather than precedent.

Style

Paris took the lead as a location for style and fashion in particular during this period. Along with the creation of the haute couture business of high-end fashion houses, Paris became a centre for the Dandy; and the Flaneur, bohemian style allowed artists and their followers to dress the part and gain recognition and sense of significance. This was a lesson that David Ogilvy, the Englishman who had a huge impact on the development of American advertising during the 1950s and 1960s, clearly absorbed. Many regard Ogilvy as the creator of the style and strategy of modern advertising; and he freely acknowledged that he used his penchant for distinctive sartorial style (including wearing kilts in Madison Avenue) as a means of drawing attention to his agency: 'if you can't advertise yourself, what hope do you have of advertising anything else?'

Paris became a blueprint for later cultural revolutions in which style and content played respective roles in reinforcing a sense of intentional and confident difference.

Critical Engagement

Paris attracted almost as many theorists and critics as it did creators, which helped develop a context for promoting, debating and evolving ideas. The twenty-first century seems to be full of theorists and critics who use others' creative endeavours as a platform for assuming ownership of art instead of working in the spirit of co-creation to evolve a constructive synergy between practice and theory.

Unquestioning obedience to tradition is the only thing keeping you from a more remarkable future. Considering the context that produced this work – and the mind-sets of the artists that created it – offers a useful introduction to the origins, characteristics and implications of disruption. The first phase of the avant-garde involved significant levels of daring innovation. However, the environment of conventional wisdom, risk-averse control and formulaic solutions that informed it is alive and well to this day. Responses to this context of constant change became a recurring source of the avant-garde's work. It is what enabled them to develop metaphors and new conceptual opportunities, which encouraged a reframing of the ways that we understood our relationship with the world.

It would be impossible to replicate the particular set of circumstances and personalities that enabled the radical challenges to the dominant canons of culture and aesthetics that defined the avant-garde. However, it is possible to emulate some of the characteristics of what constitutes a creative context and a disruptive practitioner.

B

BELLIGERENCE

Belligerence – whether through critical reactions to aggressive warmongering, hostile takeovers or bullying and ignorant responses to others – has fittingly earned a bad reputation. In the business context of culture building, belligerence ranks quite high on the HR list of 'don'ts' – and usually, rightfully so. But there is also a tendency to confuse belligerent behaviour with bullying. This can prompt companies to discourage or 'weed out' employees with qualities like individualism and passion, simply because they don't fit the 'preferred behaviour' for team members.

As Niccolo Machiavelli recognized, 'there is nothing more difficult and dangerous, or more doubtful of success, than an attempt to introduce a new order of things' (*The Prince*, 1532). As an arch strategist, Machiavelli often advocated patient diplomacy; however, he also understood that belligerent tenacity is sometimes the only way to deal with the aggressive denial that people tend to direct against the untried and untested. As he explained it:

> *whenever the opponents of the new order of things have the opportunity to attack it, they will do it with the zeal of partisans, whilst the others defend it but feebly, so that it is dangerous to rely upon the latter.*
>
> **(Niccolo Machiavelli, *The Prince*, 1532)**

Machiavelli's understanding that any level of change ambition needs to anticipate and negotiate access with the gatekeepers, whose primary motive is to maintain the status quo, is a useful reminder that innovation has not become any easier 500 or so years later.

The expression of personal angst at a slow or 'no' decision can cause us to dismiss an individual's passionate commitment to winning as aggressive hostility. But belligerence is part of what makes great artists and great brands succeed. Picasso acquired a reputation for being unreasonable when he railed against realism, but his courage to persist and ignore the naysayers of the world allowed him to create a unique brand.

In our current climate of political correctness overkill, 'telling it how it is' is often characterized as offensive, or at the very least insensitive. But a lack of robust critical response can lead to a culture of mediocrity. Hanging in there when the chips are down is a central theme of disruption.

How RIM Succeeded and Failed by Being Belligerent

RIM, or 'Research In Motion', is best known for the development of the smartphone market with the launch of the Blackberry. RIM's rise and fall has been attributed to the personality of its founding partner, engineer and former CEO Mike Lazaridis. Lazaridis created a business culture that favoured engineering over marketing. While this approach fuelled innovation, it also created a lack of sympathy for alternative points of view.

Blackberry's major innovation was the 1999 creation of a mobile email facility that would operate globally. As a result, the phone became the default choice for business executives and their key staff and by 2007, RIM was worth $42 billion. However, this was the year that Steve Jobs, another CEO renowned for belligerence, announced the iPhone, and by 2014 RIM's share of the smartphone market has shrunk to 0.6 percent. The difference in the roots of Lazardis and Jobs offers a tantalizing example of art versus science. Jobs had an ability to think and act like an artist and, because of that, he was prepared to bet the bank on the strength of an intuitive hunch. Lazardis, on the other hand, thought and acted like an engineer, relying on scientific method to test and refine the product in the understanding that performance was the main selling point. Lazardis is clear about his belief in process:

> *One of the things that we've really internalised here at RIM, is the belief in the numbers, belief in mathematics, belief in the limits imposed by physics, and the general understanding of physics. If you don't understand the limitations you can't design something that works well within those limitations.*[3]

Thinking Fast – Thinking Slow

Israeli-American psychologist Daniel Kahneman supports the theory that we rely too heavily on our conditioned ability for rational deduction. He argues that our tendency to make decisions slowly is informed by our mistrust of the new. Most of us get the future a bit later than the people who invented and promoted it – but as soon as we do get there, it seems natural and inevitable. The delay factor is not just informed by the predictable gap between our ability to come to terms with something that we have not experienced before; it is also influenced by our fear of being out of step. Someone who is emotionally and rationally orientated is effectively pulled in two directions at the same time. We find it difficult to comprehend or trust what's new; yet we have also been encouraged by our inquisitive minds to relish fresh opportunities. The conflict between our instinctive fascination with novelty and our conditioned reliance on logical deduction can lead to us to repress rather than encourage innovation, much in the way that we might try and suppress desires that the moral majority have deemed aberrant. We also know that once we are perceived as 'out of touch', redundancy looms – which is exactly what happened to Kodak.

Kodak: the High Price of Thinking Slow

The shocking disruption of Kodak's 100 plus year dominance of the photographic market represents the dangers of creating a hierarchical business that does not allow room for belligerent behaviour. Kodak's crisis was not due to lack of innovation; indeed, they were first off the block with the invention of the digital camera. They simply didn't have any team members who were belligerent enough to encourage the rest of the organization to let go of the past.

Unpacking

When we engage with a brand we always start with at least a morning of 'unpacking', during which we encourage stakeholders to announce their frustrations and anxieties and to identify the source of the gatekeeping that is stifling opportunity. This process provides insight into exactly what is holding the brand back from achieving its innovation potential. In the case of Kodak we are confident that the topic of a digital future would have been raised to the top of the agenda. We wish we could have gotten to Kodak at that key moment where someone was sitting in a lab with the world's first digital camera on a table while someone else sat in a boardroom looking at a Kodachome image of their future.

The Dream Café allows participants to harvest and respect internal initiatives, because we are able to locate them within a context of interdisciplinary wisdom that uncovers new ways of evaluating perceptions of possible futures. These projections include a respect for the brand's heritage. Additionally, much of what we do involves a rediscovery of attitudes that have simply been buried under decades of iterative innovation. Often, it's just the passage of time that has caused the root passion for the brand to be forgotten.

Ultimately aligning the brand vision so that it is future focused requires the reconciliation of the past with the present – and it does involve a lot of kicking and screaming for those who believe that letting go is an act of betrayal. But innovation never needs to be a fist fight. Belligerence can be constructive; it's all about providing a platform for alternative opinions.

The 'damned if you do, damned if you don't' syndrome can create the kind of indecision that leads to doing nothing for fear of doing the wrong thing. In the context of the arts, belligerence has been popularly associated with a tendency to over indulge in drink and drugs. The stereotype of the belligerent artist is someone who is vulnerable to schizophrenic mood swings, in which euphoric highs are countered by deeply depressed lows that can lead to a life of self-destruction. Welsh Poet Dylan Thomas, American abstract artist Jackson Pollock and American writer Hunter S Thompson are examples of the kind of raw material from which this stereotype has been hewn.

Creating the future is always going to be a painful journey that involves overcoming, or at least harnessing, self-doubt, misunderstanding, resistance and rejection. While there is often some innate condition that explains a self-destructive journey, the gap between self-belief and misunderstanding is often one in which the humiliation of rejection leads to rage. Despite some attempts at legislating against ageism, we continue to inhabit a world where disruption is still associated with youthful exuberance. In other words, many believe it should be something that we will 'grow out of'.

The conditioning that programmes our minds, and then our hearts, into tacit acceptance of the status quo is the enemy of disruption. There is absolutely no reason why older people cannot be as disruptive as anyone else. The mental and emotional slippage that leads us to accept that rebellion is the prerogative of the young is likely a by-product of what we have been taught, rather than a syndrome of what we can no longer do. Fighting against the obstacles in our way is simply a matter of passion.

Beware of Unquestioned Myths

The cult of youth has dominated the music business ever since Elvis started to shake his hips like a Harlem queen. As did so many industries, music assumed that older people were at best a minority market. It was not just the failure to notice the sheer scale of the grey demographic; it was the lack of understanding that the youth market was becoming increasingly influenced by the mythologies of rebellion associated with the counter-culture of the 1960s. Cue OAP belligerence as a brand opportunity; artists like Patti Smith and Scott Walker are currently demonstrating that disruptive creativity is not restricted to people under the age of 20. Others, like Bob Dylan and the late Gil Scott Heron, have consistently disrupted their established audiences as well as the mainstream by refusing to perform karaoke versions of their back catalogue.

In many respects, the belligerent older artist provides a multi-faceted exemplar of disruption. They do so by denying the formulas that dominate the music industry's approach to business, while continuing to challenge themselves as well as the audience. It is quite possible that somewhere out there the person who called Dylan 'Judas' for his disruptive adoption of a rock band is still feeling alienated – because, having adjusted to progress, he now has to listen while Dylan insists on doing weird versions of the electrified back catalogue.

The history of popular music currently offers ample evidence that a capacity for disruption is not limited to the young. The mythology that informed the evolution of popular music from the mid 1950s up until the early twentieth century was predicated on the ability of Rock 'n' Roll to alienate the older generation. The association of pop music and disruption fuelled the invention of the 'teenager' as a marketing category and an ability to disrupt became an implicit value judgement for qualities like 'integrity' that were used to promote new music and new artists that offer opportunity to alienate as much as they enraptured audiences. Bob Dylan's refusal to confine his imagination to the strict rules and regulations that had been imposed by a small coterie of self-appointed gatekeepers of the folk music tradition, which he had initially embraced, was regarded to as belligerent denial. When Pete Seeger tried to take an axe to the 'Band's' electric supply, he was doing what inevitably happens when disruption occurs: resisting change.

Fortunately, Dylan had the courage to resist the naysayers and become one of the most successful brands in the music history.

The music business offers numerous examples of the constant tension between creative free expression and business. It is generally conceded that the creation of the kind of 'talent shows' typified by television programmes like the 'X-Factor' has led to the unravelling of the trope of rebellion as a sales pitch in favour of mass market opportunity predicated on the buying power of the very young.

Technology has helped to alleviate this syndrome of market 'blandification' by providing opportunities to gain access to types of music making and listening that do not fit into the increasingly formulaic canon of 'pop'. There is a growing tendency for artists, including contemporary blues and country singer Valerie June, to take things into their own hands by using 'KickStarter' (a web based crowdsourcing fundraising solution for business, social and creative start-ups) to fund albums that the major labels are not prepared to risk. It is ironic that the current crop of disrupters, including June, demonstrates how circular the journey to the future can be.

With her 'Organic Roots Music' and interest in 'perfect imperfection', June draws on the roots that Dylan appeared to challenge 50 years ago when he strapped on an electric guitar and introduced the 'Hawks' as his band. Music offers an important example of the fact that the art of radical innovation is often a process that begins in NOTICING new and contemporary relevance for strategies that have been overlooked or neglected. Much of the music that is currently challenging the synthetic norms dominating the contemporary marketplace is as much a product of rediscovery and reimagining as it is of unprecedented origination – but that does not prevent it from being full of disruptive potential.

Social networking opportunities presented by platforms like YouTube are freely available to everyone. As such, they allow artists who are belligerent enough to dare to build and market their brand outside of the conventional channels to create traction and profitable success.

Businesses need to disrupt themselves before another organization does it for them.

The music business appeared to enjoy the same opportunity as fashion with its ability to constantly replenish desire by emphasizing the value of 'what's next.' Thanks to the apparently inexhaustible supply of aspiring artists, the music business has never been short of new talent. However, this may have bred the complacency that allowed them to miss the fact that the profit lay in distribution – not production. The music business's obvious dependency on, and vulnerability to, the digital age offers a crucial learning opportunity for other brand led businesses. This age of DIY offers opportunities to an increasing range of start-ups to build their own brand traction – posing some serious competition for the corporate giants who are still grimly clinging to their traditional formulas.

Music is one area of the arts where creativity and profit have always enjoyed a problematic and dysfunctional relationship. Despite its myriad spheres of engagement, the music industry remains notoriously prone to sticking with the formulas. As Mark Hornsby stated when paraphrasing Hunter S Thompson:

> *The music business is a cruel and shallow money trench, a long plastic hallway where thieves and pimps run free, and good men die like dogs. There's also a negative side.*
>
> **(Mark Hornsby, *Music Business*, 22 September, 2012)**

We can understand the industry's tendency towards caution, because businesses with a reputation for radical innovation tend to have earned it by accident rather than intention. The maxim of 'if it's not broken, don't fix it' tends to dominate; but because of the mythology of youth in the music business, this was traditionally coupled with the logic that 'if it's old, replace it with a new one'.

Some of the Lessons that Contemporary Business can Learn from Belligerence

Learning the Art of Disruption in a Dream Café

Dylan's break with the stifling constraints of heritage came about during his immersion in avant-garde that had evolved in the café culture of Manhattan's Greenwich Village. His encounters with the beat movement cafés in New York City and San Francisco introduced him to a very different aesthetic universe from the one that dominated the world of folk music. Dylan's sense of what was possible was dramatically extended by mixing with poets, artists, philosophers and writers who refused to be bound by convention.

This learning curve is an inspiration to The Dream Café's strategy of enabling brands to challenge and extend their norms by connecting them with creative minds from other disciplines. Just as Dylan opened up a whole new world of opportunity for the music industry by transcribing the esoteric into the mainstream, the Brand Visions that we reveal and release are all about the belligerently constructive potential of daring to think and do differently.

Don't be Your Own Gatekeeper

It is obvious that disruption requires breaking the rules a bit. In this way, brands need to remember to break their own rules as well as the ones that others are concerned to impose upon them. Unfortunately, most brands tend to act as their own gatekeepers – continuing to behave as if a rigid set of 'dos and don'ts' continue to inform our perceptions of right and wrong.

Even brands that have managed to break free and embrace disruptive alternatives still operate according to the rulebook of conditioned belief. This happens particularly wherever the business is dominated by a rule based culture that sees its purpose as one of protecting and perpetuating the 'truth' of what used to be. In May 2014, *The New York Times* took a bold step and published a self-critical report about its failure to competitively innovate:

> *The New York Times is winning at journalism. Of all the challenges facing a media company in the digital age, producing great journalism is the hardest. Our daily report is deep, broad, smart and engaging and we've got a huge lead over the competition. At the same time, we are falling behind in a second critical area: the art and science of getting our journalism to readers. We have always cared about the reach and impact of our work, but we haven't done enough to crack that code in the digital era.*

The report identified numerous examples of resistance from sections of the business that tried to cling to the old rules but were now ready to embrace the reality that the future could not afford to rest on the past without questioning and challenging everything: 'The newsroom, once resistant to change, is energized by these recent successes and eager to tackle difficult questions and try new things.'

Employing People Who are Old Enough to be Strategically Belligerent

The self-reinforcing nature of conditioned belief presents a greater barrier to disruptive change than the belief itself. This is particularly true of people who tend to act according to the role expected of them, rather than challenging that restrictive stereotype.

Belligerent older people can act as useful roles models, because they show business and society that the RULES are simply an outmoded fiction. By defying established cultural stereotypes, they can reassure others that the art of disruption is simply a matter of attitude, instead of the prerogative of young rebels. In this respect, the 'senile delinquent' provides brands with a timely warning: live life backwards by learning from your mistakes, rules are there to be tested.

Serial investor Warren Buffet provides a perfect example of an older person as a source of disruption. Even though the popular mythology proposes Buffet as the personification of the wisdom of age, his true strength lies in his belligerent ability to takes risks and invest in areas where others fear to tread (until they follow Buffet's lead, of course). The irony of Buffet's influence on the market lies in its close resemblance to the tendency for fast moving brands to trust in the 'wisdom of youth'.

Let the Heart Rule the Head

'Belligerence' is clearly a by-product of passion – and, occasionally, a characteristic that others tend to define as an 'attitude problem'. Impatience is not necessarily the best source of disruption, as the process of shaking things up tends to take time. The qualities inherent in impatience are informed by the crucial ability to not take 'no' for an answer.

Indeed, some evidence has emerged of brands that are begging to incorporate belligerence into their value system. Consider the Brazilian football team Vitoria, who decided to uses its distinctive 'kit' as a call for compassion. Vitoria are known as the 'Red and Blacks' because of their choice of red and black striped shirts. The team effectively blackmailed their fans into giving blood by refusing to don their traditional shirts until they'd achieved a target donation. Football is all about passion – and passion is catching. By being belligerent with their fans, Vitoria demonstrated that passion can achieve positive outcomes – energizing themselves and their community.

Don't Get Drunk; Get Control

While a substance abuse lifestyle is often a subtext of the history of creative belligerence, it is by no means a prerequisite of belligerent disruption. Good art, like a good brand, anticipates and gains strength from the kind of opposition that may require a degree of belligerence before it is overcome. A passionately belligerent brand raises everyone's commitment to winning. If you know that you are swimming against the tide, you work together to tap into those extra energy reserves that eventually allow you to prove that you were right. That is what we call Constructive Belligerence.

C

CHAOS

The word 'chaos' tends to be associated with a negative stereotype of disruption, which casts it as the enemy of strategy and profit. If you have witnessed the disintegration of your best laid plans because of the unpredictable intervention of the 'hand of fate', you will find it difficult to accept the possibility that chaos has a benign side.

The evolution of the Ancient Greek scientific method was born out of a quest to comprehend and ultimately manage the random or chaotic character of nature, in order to make life more predictable. This ambition, and the methodologies that supported it, became part of the post-enlightenment quest to use scientific method as an engine of sustainable economic growth through industrialization.

It is because we have been conditioned to trust in logic that we find it all too easy to mistrust our intuition. This prompts us to view chaos as the enemy of progress. However, this brief defence of chaos as a vital source of disruptive opportunity will appear completely counter intuitive to the belief that progress is forever rational. And we can easily correct this misunderstanding by looking back into history. There, we discover that many of the ideas, inventions and brands that have shaped our sense of human progress have emerged from unpredictable, chaotic and ultimately magical coincidences. As the philosopher Friedrich Nietzsche put it:

'You must have chaos within you to give birth to a dancing star.'

Honda founder Soichiro Honda offers a key role model of 'purposeful provocation' – a strategy of internal disruption that was born out of his observation that business was more inventive at times of chaos. Honda was the victim of a series of dramatic crises, ranging from steel rationing to the destruction of the factory by fire. However, each recovery encouraged substantial enhancement of the manufacturing and marketing strategies, which made the company a global brand business.

This concern to introduce chaos as a catalyst for creativity was developed into an innovation management strategy that became known as 'kick out the ladder'. Just at the point where a team thought they had reached a conclusion, the means and rules of a project were deliberately changed. The result encouraged the team to review their progress and would often lead to the discovery of a better solution, because they were able to look and think outside of the trajectory that they had locked themselves into as they progressed their thinking.

Inspiration is much more likely to emerge if we trust in the power of serendipity and chance. Allowing chaos to help shape disruptive intention requires us to radically adjust, or temporarily abandon the formal methodologies that typically inform innovation strategy. The history of avant-garde art reveals important clues to the ways in which chaos can provide the source of spectacular and sustainable progress. When a brand disrupts the market, it allows us all to redefine the landscape from a gridded depiction of 'NO-GO limitations into an ANYTHING-ANYWHERE opportunity.

The Art of Radical Innovation

Turning chaos to your advantage requires a high degree of courage. You must be prepared to gamble that the alternatives your instinct is proposing will work for others once they are able to form empathy.

The collapse of many of the proofs that used to determine our expectations – from economic theory to climate change – has encouraged us to seek out alternative models and processes that will offer some way of managing unpredictability productively. The exponential influence of technology on our contemporary habits and values alone should be enough to convince an arch rationalist that intuition may well offer more hope than scientific method.

Chaos and The Dream Café

The Dream Café does its absolute best to engender conditions in which chaos can flourish. We create scenarios where unpredictability and its outcome improbability are allowed to rule. We know that inviting chaos into the room encourages the kind of playful engagement that liberates conditioned hearts and minds to abandon their need for order long enough to reveal the power of the unfettered imagination. The human capacity for imagination is an engine of productive chaos because it allows us to operate outside of the rules.

Once you are able to liberate participants to work against their conditioned expectations and step beyond the exclusion zone, you enable them to experience their latent potential and recognize the opportunities that they typically ignore. Being avant-garde begins with giving yourself permission to think and act differently and the rest is all about applying your imagination. For example, Andre Breton was the principal architect of the Surrealist Movement and key advocate of chaos as a strategy rather than an accident. Breton's stance still seems, to many brand managers and CEOs, to be the enemy of progress. Granted, he was a deliberate provocateur – but that should not prevent business learning the art of taking advantage of chaos from the Surrealists.

Sending our delegates into the environment on a journey of unpredictable discovery is an important part of our strategy of disruption at The Dream Café. We call this brief adventure opportunity 'The Surrealist Perambulation', because it is based on a technique that Breton helped to pioneer. In short, his approach sought to ensure that Surrealist practitioners reframed their conditioned behaviour by deliberately and provocatively resisting opportunity for their experiences of the environment to be constrained by logic. A typical example of the technique involved going to different cinemas for brief periods of time in order to allow the visitors to create their own narrative from the bits of films that they viewed.

Our experience of utilizing this technique has enabled participants to return to The Dream Café at the end of their journey armed with ingredients for a collage of possibilities that typically proves to be a potent source of new thinking and doing. Whether it is images, sound, objects or random detritus, the source of disruption lies in their ability to make connections between stuff that would not normally be considered as having any logical relationship.

Some of the Lessons That Contemporary Business can Learn from Embracing Chaos

All that is Solid Melts into Air

Karl Marx's critique of capitalism famously addressed the replacement of tangible engagement in the creation of goods by mechanization. In his quest to maintain sensorial immersion in the manufacture and use of goods, Marx anticipated our contemporary need to come to terms with the rise of digital experience as a primary definition of our perception and experience of what we understand to be our reality.

Because of his belief in cooperative endeavour, Marx would have probably ignored the potential profit opportunities from a more imaginative exploitation of the complexity of our relationship with today's virtual/physical landscape. Most people now accept that buying, consuming and storing our possessions is as much to do with the digital domain as it is to do with physical objects and access.

The heritage of the majority of brands is still located in the world of physical goods and services. For them, the emergence of digital commerce summoned a reaction roughly the equivalent of the rationalist's response to chaos: dismissal shortly followed by fear and loathing!

Currently the jury is out on the potential of effective combinations, but there is some tantalizing evidence around suggesting that in the near future we will all be able to benefit from the best of both worlds through a strategy of hybridization. This is likely to result in much of our experience being amplified focus on cathartic rather than calm modes of engagement. If this is true then chaos, as symbolized by the adventure of becoming involved in the joy of unpredictable outcomes, will rewrite the rulebook of what creates brand empathy.

Gaming offers an obvious example of a location for hybridization that has already helped to spawn the phenomenon of 'cosplay'. In this situation, obsessive identification leads to the consumer's adoption of costumes and lifestyle habits that are based on fantasy rather than conventional reality. The development of 3D printing interaction with gaming opens up a wealth of brand opportunities that requires established brands to start thinking much more radically about relevance in a hybrid space.

Science Shaped the Twentieth Century, but Biology will Define the Twenty-first

Creating disruptive art forms requires that we trust in the discovery that the organic process affords us. This trust depends on our ability to understand that unpredictable outcomes are often more important than predictable ones. Designing an organic development process within your business will encourage the emergence of different iterations. These will provide you with a range of alternatives, which you can then use to verify and set your agenda – while immersing you and your team in the excitement of tangible creative discovery. There are a number of very successful businesses that advocate and practise organic innovation, ranging from Tiffany & Co, the fine jewellery and luxury goods design, manufacturer and retailer, to Harley Davidson, an American motorcycle manufacturer that has acquired cult brand status. Despite the difference in their brands, these businesses appear to share some common strategies that begin and end with making sure that employees at all levels become stakeholders. By challenging the traditional 'divisions of labour', a business that innovates will organically benefit from the fact that everyone is able to make a contribution to the system of feed-in and feedback loops that operate without the exclusions of hierarchy. Harley has extended its strategy of inclusion to involve its customers in its stakeholder culture.

The Mind of the Beholder

If art adopted the same excuses that so many brand managers rely upon, then there would have been no disruptive art – because 'the customers are not ready for it'.

It is rarely the case that people are not ready for change; it is almost always the case that they are not given the choice, because of the timidity of those that supply them with goods and services. Artists have always been very good at acting first and thinking later. Indeed, any kind of innovation that eventually disrupts the status quo emerges because someone has dared to engage in new thoughts and new actions. Inspiring new needs is entirely dependent in the availability of new stuff.

D

DREAMING

Formal education tends to teach us that our dreams are merely a distraction from the priorities of learning how to comprehend and apply logical methods of deduction. Dreams were exorcised from our curriculums, and anyone who continued to do so was given the none-too-desirable label of 'Day Dreamer'. Fortunately, a few individuals discovered that their inability to succeed in the narrow rut that continues to define educational norms allowed them to see their dreams as a source of inspiration, rather than distraction. Indeed, many of the artists and scientists whose work and ideas have reshaped the world are proud and grateful for their ability to trust their dreams. The list of lucid dreamers includes Andy and Lana Wachowski, the brothers who created the hugely profitably and mould breaking *Matrix* film franchise. They informed the basic premise of the *Matrix* from their own experience of dreaming: 'How do I know that my reality is not an illusion?' American physicist Richard Feynman – perhaps drawing on Einstein's use of dreams – has explained how his ability to pose and resolve complex mathematical problems is informed by his capacity to dream:

> *I also noticed that as you go to sleep the ideas continue, but they become less and less logically interconnected. You don't notice that they're not logically connected until you ask yourself, 'What made me think of that?'*
>
> **(Richard Feynman, *Surely You're Joking Mr Feynman*, 2014)**

Surrealist artist Salvador Dali pioneered dream incubation strategies that enabled him to develop the potent synergy between technique and subject that enabled him to achieve a hugely successful career as artist and 'brand'.

The scientific verdict on how and why we dream is still out. Much of the twentieth century was caught in the thrall of Freud's categorization of dreams as repressed longings that we were not able to express in public life. Carl Jung's 'theory of dreams' has and continues to influence our understanding of their power and function. Both men have had a profound influence on the arts' exploration of dream imagery and their psychological implications.

Our role at The Dream Café is to enable our clients to acknowledge their capacity to dream as a magical antidote to the inhibitions that rationality encourages. The history of innovation in all sectors has emphasized how necessary it is to take our ability to dream seriously. The examples that follow are drawn from a brief but fairly wide ranging selection of the inspiration derived from dreams over the past two centuries. The list is designed to demonstrate how dreams can unravel and/or inspire original solutions or inventions that are by nature destined to be disruptive.

Product Invention: The Sewing Machine

Elias Howe invented the sewing machine in 1845 – following a five year period of frustration. His many attempts to design a needle that would carry cotton through material and return it without knotting and breaking failed to create a workable solution. Howe's breakthrough came from a dream in which a threatening crowd of natives brandishing spears surrounded him. On recalling the dream, he remembered that the spears had a hole near the tip –and the rest, as they say, is history.

Patent Medicine: Hair Restorer

An invention by Madame CJ Walker (1867–1919) seems to have been a solution for alopecia rather than male pattern baldness. Walker, who became the United States' first self-made female millionaire, was active as an African American social activist and philanthropist during her lifetime. The recipe that allowed her to graduate from cotton picker to multi-millionaire was conceived in a dream:

> *He answered my prayer, for one night I had a dream, and in that dream a big, black man appeared to me and told me what to mix up in my hair. Some of the remedy was grown in Africa, but I sent*

for it, mixed it, put it on my scalp, and in a few weeks my hair was coming in faster than it had ever fallen out. I tried it on my friends; it helped them. I made up my mind to begin to sell it.[1]

Physics: The General Theory of Relativity

Albert Einstein claims to have conceived of his 'General Theory of Relativity' (1916) during a dream in which he was sledding down a steep mountainside at the speed of light, causing the stars in the sky to change their shape. It took Einstein eight years to develop the mathematical skill to translate his dream into theory but his accomplishment transformed our understanding of time and space. The relationship between art and science is ongoing – and has arguably become more critical in the last two decades. During this time, science has become more conscious of the mutual learning opportunity from disciplines that have more in common than conventional discipline stereotypes suggest.

Einstein was a cultural traditionalist with no obvious affiliation with the breakthroughs occurring in the arts that appeared to anticipate or draw on his innovative approach to the space and time continuum. The gap between Einstein's own taste for the 'old masters' and the aesthetics of modernity does not deny the need to address the possibility of understanding how a common context of technological and social innovation can fuel new and disruptive thinking. The difference in perception and response that science has begun to grasp still appears to be little understood by business. This resistance may well be informed by a conditioned suspicion of the creative's tendency for intellectual promiscuity in which aesthetic excitement is just as likely to be a source of inspiration as a rigorous interrogation of theory.

At The Dream Café we are excited to discover that Einstein's inspiration came in the form of a dream because this makes him a Surrealist physicist and we need more of them.

Human Biology: The Chemical Transmission of Nerve Impulses

Otto Loewi (1873–1961) won the Nobel Prize for medicine in 1936 for his work on the chemical transmission of nerve impulses. The insight that led to the development and proof of his thesis came in a dream in 1903. According to Loewi:

The night before Easter Sunday of that year I awoke, turned on the light, and jotted down a few notes on a tiny slip of paper. Then I fell asleep again. It occurred to me at 6 o'clock in the morning that during the night I had written down something most important, but I was unable to decipher the scrawl. The next night, at 3 o'clock, the idea returned. It was the design of an experiment to determine whether or not the hypothesis of chemical transmission that I had uttered 17 years ago was correct. I got up immediately, went to the laboratory, and performed a single experiment on a frog's heart according to the nocturnal design.[5]

Standardization at Ford

In 2002 Phil Martens, head of Ford's new product development group confronted the dilemma that every business now faces: cutting the cost of manufacturing. Marten's solution for vehicle design teams to share designs and technologies among similar vehicles came to him in a dream: 'Copy with pride. That's our mantra.' According to Martens, 'The flaw in Ford's previous approach to design was that each new project was prone to "free-wheeling" … [The system] was expensive and we had no focus ... We had to simplify our culture.'[6] His solution involved connecting previously discrete initiatives.

Searching the Entire Internet: Google

Google inventor Larry Page had the idea for 'downloading the entire web onto computers' in a dream when he was 23 years old, in 1995. He claimed, 'I spent the middle of that night scribbling out the details and convincing myself it would work.'[7] The back story suggests that Page was a beneficiary of 'lucid dreaming' – a situation where you are either enabled or unintentionally go to sleep primed to dream as a problem solving activity. Page was enrolled on a PhD programme at Stamford University's Computer Science Faculty. His background was informed by a father who studied and taught computer science and his own lifelong enthusiasm for inventing. His solution effectively reframed the problem by defining digital content as a collection of 'citations' that could be captured and shared.

These moments of inspiration placed dreamers into the creative territory that is familiar to avant-garde practitioners – namely, trusting in illogicality. Although the majority of the examples led to the evolution of extremely pragmatic products the moment of gestation was led by the brain's captivity for origination when in its free-form mode.

Some of the Lessons That Contemporary Business Can Learn From Daring to Dream

Sometime Symbols are Better than Words

Novelist Stephen King offers a compelling insight into the relationship between dreams and creative inspiration:

> *That's what dreams are supposed to do … [dreams] are a way that people's minds illustrate the nature of their problems. Or maybe even illustrate the answers to their problems in symbolic language.*[8]

King clearly understands that creativity is a business. His prodigious output is informed by his ability to develop disciplined habits that enable him to continually refresh his imagination and ensure that the time and facilities for writing his dreams in accessible form are available. The parallel between King's business-like approach to writing offers important lessons for contemporary brand business's, because it respects the fact that efficiency of the means of reproductions is entirely dependent on the ability to evolve products (dreams) that are worth reproducing.

Day Dreaming

Taking time out to dream would be perceived as pretty radical in a traditional business structure. However, it's vital in today's competitive environment to recalculate the economic value of daydreaming. Developing disruptive brands, as Google amply demonstrates, can literally be the stuff of dreams if a culture of creativity is fostered and supported. To its credit, Google has invested in the assumption that its staff is its greatest asset and encourages employees to spend 20 percent of their paid time pursuing their own dreams. While this will seem to be counter intuitive and profoundly inefficient to a Six Sigma culture, it makes complete sense in a business environment where tomorrow's profit is dependent of today's dream.

The Google founders' understanding of the power of dreams includes an awareness that our capacity for dreaming is likely to be at its most lucid when we are allowed the creative space to dream and be paid for it.

The opportunity for irrational solutions that dreams provide lies at the heart of the creative process. Breaking our conventional habits requires us to suspend our tendency – at least temporarily – to seek the logical route to a creative outcome. As the inventions identified earlier confirm, the solution often lies outside of the rational bandwidth that constrains our imagination.

Pragmatism Can Always Come Later

Re-imagining the creative process to include time and respect for dreams will alarm the pragmatists in your business. Predictable concerns about risk, guarantees, timeframe, and budget will rain from the iron ceiling. The irony is that there is never a guarantee with any creative process. However much practitioners and theorists try to create protocols and processes, serendipity will always play a greater role than logic if the idea is intended to be disruptive. When we hear innovation managers expressing their inability to comprehend the triumph of competitor innovation in markets where their focus group insight investments have confirmed the superiority of their brand's taste, or functional efficiency, we wonder how long it will take them to understand that empathy is driven by more than conventional definitions of function.

Wired or Wireless?

Dreams offer a crucial metaphor through their capacity to depict ideas without the constraints of conventional boundaries. The activation-synthesis hypothesis identified earlier follows the contemporary trend to explain brain function through the language and conceptual framework of twentieth-century computing. As the evidence cited here amply demonstrates, dreams are too organic to be strung with wires. Perhaps it is this capacity that will allow dreams to become a crucial source of disruption in the world of brands. It is clear that brands need to be able to let go of the wires that limit them. When a brand disrupts the market it confirms the Surrealists' concern to redefine the landscape. They understood that dreams can liberate you from a gridded depiction of NO-GO limitations into a NO-RULES-ANYTHING-ANYWHERE opportunity.

E

EXPERIMENTATION

Experimentation is at the heart of every great disruptive brand strategy. Insight can only ever tell you where an opportunity for innovation might exist; experiments are where you create opportunities and the site where the space for serendipity resides.

The classic approach to setting up an experiment – known as scientific method – involves the utilization of a strict protocol of testing and retesting a hypothesis. In this way, experiments become a means of proving a conclusion that has already been reached. The focus on achieving a self-fulfilling prophecy will sound familiar to anyone who has operated in the brand business. Perhaps it's got something to do with the fact that marketing tends to be taught like it's a science – but there is a clear tendency to reiterate the known in almost every industry. Holding onto the comfort blanket of old formulas can only ever provide temporary relief from the need to acknowledge the truth – that it's time to let go and begin to innovate.

Innovation can and does come from the application of scientific method. However, in A world where taste, need, values and definitions of function are constantly shifting, we need a more open approach – one that offers opportunity to not only discover but actually create the future of need.

Don't Wait for the Future, Because it Won't Wait for You

The radical and disruptive impact of the first waves of avant-garde creativity was established by an unprecedented series of experiments that spewed out a deluge of concepts, aesthetics and functions that challenged conventional wisdom. Café culture was an important catalyst for the disruptive activities of the avant-garde and in many ways we can regard the unplanned and largely uncoordinated development of the café as an open and creative forum as an experiment in cross-fertilization.

Writing the Future

We can understand the energy and unanticipated outcomes that emerged from these café encounters as part of the set of influences and opportunities that reframed the status – as well as the forms and functions of cultural output. The development of the modern literature was closely intertwined with café culture as Emile Zola's self-referential celebrations of the themes that he spends his evening debating with his coterie of fellow creatives like Manet. The novel evolved from its linear narrative focus into a form that played with the randomness of chance and the knowledge that life only made logical sense if you allowed yourself to live it that way. The authority of formal grammar was challenged and replaced by experiments in chance that came to be celebrated for their ability to encourage provocative and unpredictable connections in the reader's mind.

James Joyce's *Ulysses* is widely regarded as a novel that disrupted literary tradition through its use and celebration of language. Joyce used a technique of word combinations supported by his assistants, including Samuel Beckett, in order to construct a library of random but complementary juxtapositions of words. These combinations were assembled in a way that was closer to the construction of musical compositions than conventional narrative form. Joyce's approach was deliberately experimental and appears to have been influenced by the perceptual transformations that innovations in technology, travel and social discourse allowed.

The Vanguard Effect

One way of understanding the potential of avant-garde thinking is to juxtapose the term with vanguard to confirm the power of being first in to a situation. Too many brands take the 'wait and see' approach, believing that they can let others test the waters. This strategy is full of risk; it not only leads to lost opportunity, but it is likely to breed a culture of risk aversion. Creative strategy is all about early response. That is why creatives have been so successful in predicting the future – because they have created and/or signposted it.

Joyce's self-conscious and highly informed experiments with narrative can be seen to disrupt how we communicate in much the same way that texting and twittering and other social media have captured, informed and evolved shifts in our understanding and use of language. Joyce was responding to and helping to create a new reality that was forming in the cracks revealed by the impact of modernity. Like a proactive brand culture, he created a shift in the way that we understand our lived experience and enabled us to renegotiate and extend the limits of what we thought possible. Joyce's attempt to capture and define the rhythms of NOWNESS anticipated a significant experimental opportunity for today's brand leaders to take the pulse of the now and give it dimension.

Past–Present–Future

In the rush to be contemporary, we frequently neglect the opportunity to learn from history. But we have ample chance to correct this mistake in an age of easy access. The Dream Café is self-consciously a product of the kind of insight into the past that enables you identify and formulate opportunities for the future. We have made much of the attitude of risk taking that shaped the avant-garde's pioneering potential, but there is also a potent history of method in the madness that can demolish convention.

Creating Creative Process

While serendipity and the art of the unanticipated are essential components of the art of radical innovation, so too is pragmatic process. We have no interest in creating a café culture for the twenty-first century that depends purely on chance. The emergence of a disruptive culture is likely to benefit from some careful planning and a methodology or two that evolves from an understanding of the connection between location, activity, aspiration and involvement.

The Art of Developing Dream Scenarios

The history of cultural innovation has benefited from some notable examples of catalytic educational strategy ranging from the Bauhaus to Eindhoven. However, one of the most relevant to the theme of this book was created in America in

1933. The Black Mountain College (closed in 1957) represented a remarkable experiment in liberal arts education that enabled a series of radical cultural breakthroughs to evolve in areas including engineering, design and performance. The college was inspired by the educational theories of the pragmatist philosopher John Dewey and was notable for its pioneering recognition of the potential of interdisciplinary cross-fertilization.

Evidence of the power of experiments designed to catalyse radical outcomes is to be found in the long list of disruptive outcomes of this remarkable college. A short list would include the 'geodesic dome' that was first created in the grounds of the college by the revolutionary thinker and doer Buckminster Fuller; the experiments in composition that enabled John Cage to redefine music; and the 'drip-art' of Jackson Pollock that enabled the USA to steal the crown of the 'epicentre of cultural disruption' from Europe.

The impact of these three creative practitioners continues to resonate in the twenty-first century through their ability to provide a case history of precedents that have enabled developments in architecture, aesthetics, strategy and performance to be signed off.

Dreams Can Come True if You Have the Right Process

Evaluating the impact of the Black Mountain College on contemporary innovation requires a wide-ranging audit of impact and influence. The following list of key examples is intended to be indicative rather than comprehensive.

Interdisciplinary Practice

The collaborations between John Cage and the dancer Merce Cunningham revolutionized the relationship between composition, choreography and performance.

Time–Space–Movement

Cage and Cunningham's collaboration also introduced new modes of thinking and practical experiments that have yet to be fully recognized for their significance in our own time.

Back to the Future

Cage and Pollock informed their own disruptive strategies by drawing on established cultural traditions that acted as a repository of aesthetic potential that enabled them to break with classical preoccupations with symmetry and sequential development. For Cage, Indonesian Gamelan music offered breakthrough inspiration. For Pollock, the sand painting traditions of Native American artists offered evidence of technique and form that were radically different from Western tradition.

Art for Our Sake

Fuller's various experiments in re-engineering the ways in which we thought about the relationships between form and function anticipated a number of our contemporary concerns around environmental impact, bio-feedback, lightweight structures and new materials.

Experiments Breed Experiments

One of the best lessons the Black Mountain College offers is the fact that creating a location and a culture based on the concept of open-ended experimental exploration will give its inhabitants collective and individual permission to challenge and break the rules that typically limit innovation to the same but slightly different iterations.

The relationship between a culture of experimentation and brand success is well established. It appears to have meaningful impact where the brand business understands the concept of learning by failing.

The Art of Innovation by Imitation

Renowned serial entrepreneur Richard Branson's restless desire to monetize opportunity for plugging gaps in existing markets has achieved the trick of sustained profitability by limiting the scale of its experiments and narrowing the odds against failure.

Branson's Virgin mainly focuses its brand extension strategy on emulating what others have already done – but with a twist. It's a strategy that has been successful in sectors where others fail, like airlines and banking. Some other areas – ranging from cola to jeans – have proved to be less profitable, and were therefore discretely abandoned.

Despite the occasional failure, Virgin has developed the ability to treat new ventures as experiments that confirm rather than undermine the brand's credibility. In this sense Virgin has the capacity to behave like a radical artist who deliberately sets out on a quest with the primary motive of learning. Rather than containing his or her quest for new understanding within the safety net of prescribed boundaries, the artist will back a hunch. If it fails to achieve anything of merit in terms of tangible evidence the artist knows that their personal learning curve will more than compensate for this failure. Virgin's ability to behave like an experimental artist, and its resilience, has been enhanced by the decision to base the brand on Branson's own predilection for high-risk adventures. His strategy of personal experiment enables Virgin to construct failure as an outcome of a valiant attempt to win against the odds, and thus support and encourage the positive connotations of daring to fail. While there are obvious downsides to brands that are based on one personality, the interplay between Branson's mythology and the brand has a calculated similarity to the legends that have informed the rising status of the arts as a source of disruptive potential.

Old Dogs Can Learn New Tricks

We are reassured that Virgin Galactic finally represents a new phase of confidence. Rather than feeding off other brands' failures, Branson is truly 'Going Where No Brand Has Gone Before'. Space travel has an interesting relationship with the brand's experimental persona. The decidedly great risks involved in this venture require the reassurance of tried and tested scientific method to convince early adopters of the safety factor. The brand's success in running an airline with an exemplary safety record undoubtedly helps in this cause; however, upping the adventure stakes raises an interesting question about the dangers of disruption bullishness.

The Digital Dreamscape

Technology is a hugely competitive brand arena dominated by an elite group of wealthy players. The majority have come from the kind of start-up standing start that anyone is capable of achieving – including the juggernauts. Brand leaders like

Apple, Google and Facebook have all influenced each other, and have taught and learnt from more established technical driven brands like Samsung. They are now in a position to use their global reach to consolidate their brands in established territories while they work to invent the future. Yet they still remember that their initial success was determined by the ability to experiment with ideas, concepts and the courage to 'hang in there' long enough for that innovation to stick.

Knowing about the opportunity for innovation and making it happen are two completely different types of engagement. The reality and the need are best reconciled by bringing these modes into a more productive configuration. This is often the location for disruption dismantling, particularly when one individual becomes the source and the champion (see references to Steve Jobs in the B = Belligerence chapter).

The gap between inspiration and execution opens a whole range of opportunities for the 'Gatekeepers' to resist change. Their negative role in sabotaging – or, at best, needlessly delaying – disruptive strategy tends to create a faux culture of experiment in which risk is relegated to lip service.

We have identified four categories of motive that can inform brands' experiments.

Disruptive

Disruptive experiments are intended to find a solution to a perceived gap in a market or the invention of a new function/need. They require a high level of risk to be signed off at the front end, as it is rare that the solution will arrive quickly or the adoption will be rapid. Amazon offers a good example of a strategy of perpetual disruption at all levels. Perhaps more importantly, it has evolved a long-view approach to profit and persuaded investors to back it. Much in the same way that its strategy of selling books online challenged, and was dismissed by, the bricks and mortar book sellers when it launched in 1995, Amazon has grown by questioning accepted norms in ways that has redefined normal. Its latest move, using drones to deliver products to the doorstep, demonstrates that Amazon's capacity for disruptive thinking and doing has not abated.

Perception Building

Virgin's creation of a mythology of adventure is largely belied by its history of innovation, which the company has achieved by tweaking established market strategies. However, the brand's success suggests that disruption can be about gaining acceptance for its ability to represent the spirit of change rather than necessarily delivering measurable evidence of innovation. The contemporary responsibility of being seen to be eco conscious offers a good example of the concern to reconcile sustainable business opportunity with a reputation for being a BENIGN BRAND. McDonald's and Ikea are role models for the ability to change perception.

Incremental Enhancement

Experiments that are aimed at updating existing brands are typically driven by degrees of caution. The decision to update rather than replace or re-imagine betrays a level of commitment to brand heritage that would not allow radical innovation. The incremental approach is likely to achieve demonstrable results but it is unlikely to ensure sustainability in a market that is driven by new thinking. Applied Materials – a precision materials and engineering business that specializes in the semiconductor, display and solar sectors – provides an example of the attempt to create a 'risk-free' strategy of balancing caution with new product development. Gary Dickerson, the CEO, explains:

> *We develop 40 or 50 new products a year, so having a framework for innovation is very, very important. We have a process we call the Product Development Engine ... Part of this we call architectural analysis, a way of measuring whether our products are differentiated and valuable to customers and if this is sustainable. At the same time it is important to have specific goals and metrics to measure product development across the company and focus on the right areas.*[9]

Going Through the Motions

Faux experiments are typical of the kind of camouflage exercises of risk-averse brands in which businesses engage. The object of the faux experiment is to create the impression of a commitment to progress while at the same time delaying it. The banking sector have demonstrated skill in claiming to be engaged in culture change without really offering significant evidence of how their new found commitment to ethical and customer-first strategy is delivered. The Dream Café has a passionate belief that the banking sector has a huge potential for leading the future of BENIGN BRANDING, once one of them breaks ranks and reimagines its market opportunity and the business that it could be in.

Since Steve Jobs' death in 2011, Apple's brand equity has been continually questioned due to a lack of visible disruptive innovation. Various media and social networking autopsies have commented on the post-Jobs era emphasis on incremental enhancements rather than new thinking. While Apple's recent track record reveals a failure to truly disrupt, we need to compare this to the fact that Apple stimulated its competitors to raise their game from cloning to competing at the disruption end of the innovation spectrum.

Google is currently the brand that we would most immediately associate with disruption – ironically, because of its evident ability to 'think differently'. Although there is little evidence of Apple-level profit from take up of disruptive innovations like 'Google Glass' or the 'driverless car', the brand has managed to create the kind of buzz about its ability to author the future that was once reserved for Apple.

At a business level, Google appears to have created a culture of experiment, designed to maximize sustainable income from its established networking software and services. It does so via incremental developments with a commitment to newsworthy disruption. Although Google is wealthy enough to not bother with pundit bad mouthing, it has created a win-win business opportunity through disruption investment that most businesses should envy and emulate. The Google approach to experiment keeps analysts happy while maintaining shareholder dividends.

Some of the Lessons that Contemporary Business Can Learn from Experimentation

Forging the Future

At face value, we notice some crucial differences between the scale of innovation engaged in by big brand businesses and those that are typical of the individual creative practitioners. Budget is clearly a major factor that enables big organizations to afford experiments that are prohibitive for smaller-scale enterprises. The large numbers of people, products and services that typify corporate endeavour also distinguish it from more modest enterprise. This said, the scale of innovation success is entirely dependent on the scale of ambition and the scale of risk. At this level, smaller scale enterprise is likely to have the flexibility and commitment – and a degree of 'madness' – that enables them to succeed against the odds.

Exceptionally creative people often aspire to make things ranging from novels to spaceships that redefine everything that we thought we knew. They do so by developing prototypes that enable them to give dimension to their concept and test its worth. Compared to many of the tentative experimenters that personify brand innovation, serious disrupters generally start as far out as their imagination will allow them to reach. People who possess radical ambition know that it is easier to challenge the status quo if you start by breaking with convention.

The businesses that are currently successfully developing innovation cultures are more likely to draw on the precedents established by avant-garde practice than they are to emulate other big businesses. The growth of brands like Innocent, that have managed to demonstrate that you can reconcile ethical practices with profitability, offers a good example of how start-ups benefit from the absence of the baggage that big businesses find so difficult to unpack.

Lib-Lab

Although it may smack of political expediency rather than meaningful experiment, a liberal laboratory culture that is free from the narrow protocols of scientific method is an essential part of disruptive culture. A lab for disrupters (like a Dream Café) is a playful, open and discursive space in which experiments do not need to be wholly owned by science, or budget forecasts. In the context of a supportive and non-formal culture an experiment can be a site for inquisitive and playful exploration where serendipity rules.

Process or Outcome

Scientific Method is all about belief in testable outcome through rigorous process. The scientifically inclined continue to argue that rigorous procedure is the only way to achieve meaningful outcomes. However, in a Dream Café culture of experimentation, we keep finding that amazing outcomes tend to pop up when and where we are least expecting them. The world of innovation needs both possibilities, the regime and the playground, and both strategies can only gain form greater correspondence and sympathy. Wherever the inspiration for your brand innovation comes from, it will need a lot of science on the journey to market. But even during that journey, unanticipated outcomes need to be harvested, celebrated and generally taken seriously, because they may actually represent the germ of a better question or even a better answer.

E for Essence

Brand innovations often derive from relatively small degrees of iteration that open up slight shifts in the experimenter's perception of what is possible. In our search for disruptive opportunity, it is important to question everything and be prepared to progress in a haphazard way. It's a bit like motorway journeys – you often shoot straight past the really interesting bits that lie beyond the hard shoulder. Your focus on the destination rather than the journey encourages you to concentrate on efficiency of time rather than the inspirational possibilities of the landscape you are located within. You may call this 'progress'; but we at The Dream Café regard it as a missed opportunity. These pockets of possibility that fall outside of the grid are exactly where we are likely to find the essence of what we really need to discover.

Seed now Discover Later

Patience is often a primary necessity for serious innovators. However, it is not regarded as a serious asset in a world where a fast forward mode of engagement is the dominant reality. The slow food movement has helped us understand that efficiency is sometimes a dish that is prepared and consumed with patience, where the priority is less about instant gratification and much more about sustainability. Seeding now to harvest later may not appear to be a natural fit with the urgency of the disruption agenda, but it can work as a strategy that fits particularly well in a culture of co-creation. Imagine an innovation scenario where everyone contributes to seeding ideas and works together to develop a culture of patient nurture that is rewarded by the shared discovery and propagation of a new species.

F

FUSION

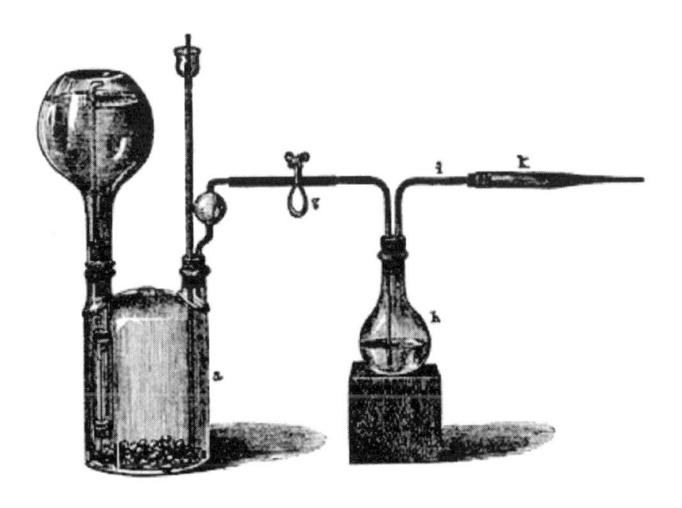

Café culture has undeniably played a huge role in enabling the art of radical innovation. One opportunity that quickly becomes evident lies in the unfettered creative mind's ability to repurpose words as descriptions of a whole new way of thinking and being. 'Fusion' is one such word that has become a metaphor allowing access to a different way of thinking about innovation.

Until recently, business – by comparison – appears to have a very limited grasp of the potential of fusion as either metaphor or process. This is evidenced by the fact that the dominant use of the word is limited to a plethora of worthy 'fusion' theory that focuses entirely on the need for more integration of IT into business management thinking and doing.

The Art of Fusion

'Fusion power' is readily available now for any brand that wants to tap its latent potential to transform awareness of future opportunity. Fusion is a basic component of The Dream Café's strategy of interdisciplinary and multi-cultural interaction. It represents one of the key learning outcomes of our research into the connections between cafés and avant-garde disruptive innovation.

Switch On–Turn On–Transform

At the simplest level, historically the café worked as a fusion opportunity for creative practitioners purely through its ability to attract and engage a diverse and eclectic range of individuals. The context of conviviality enabled cross-fertilization, which helped to catalyse new thoughts – that in turn, led to new actions.

Numerous examples from the arts demonstrate how fusion can create new and hybrid forms and functions. Performance art typically requires collaborative engagement between different disciplines – ranging from dance to painting – as part of a search for a multi-faceted aesthetic experience. Perhaps the greatest evidence of fusion as a source of origination is to be found in music. The results of combining musical styles are increasingly defined by relatively safe and polite collaborations between musicians representing different cultural traditions. Pioneering fusions like jazz trumpeter Miles Davis' embrace of rock music in the late 1960s (*Miles in the Sky*, 1968) were radical in nature. They achieved relatively unprecedented new sounds, rhythms, performance styles and themes that disrupted the sensibilities of traditional audiences, who resisted the challenge of his new direction.

While many contemporary experiments in fusion music remain safe and bland, there are exceptions – notably the development of Icelandic musician Bjork's concept album *Biophilia* (2011), which developed a fusion between science and music and multi-platform access. According to *Wired* magazine, Bjork's album had the ambition to 'define humanity's relationship with sound and the universe' but also to 'pioneer a music format that will smash industry conventions' (August, 2011). The hugely ambitious *Biophilia* project involved collaboration with leading physicists, biologists, neuroscientists, technology developers, including Apple, educationalists, filmmakers, instrument makers, animators, conceptual artists and documentary filmmakers such as David Attenborough – to create what was effectively a multi-dimensional fusion.

Bjork's project was both a response to and an anticipation of the development of business opportunity in the virtual realm. Fusion as a brand challenge has moved from avant-garde disruption to a mainstream agenda, as the combination of sound, image and multi-platform access has become a primary location for any brand that wants to appear to be in touch with contemporary modes of access and expectation.

Fashion Fusion or Confusion?

Fashion is one of the obvious examples of a design strategy that depends on fusion. At its best, fashion achieves this by remaining open to mixing different cultural references into new and provocative combinations. Fashion has recently become more radical in its preparedness to set up dialogues between different disciplines including science and technology.

Sharing and Caring

As awareness of ecological responsibility has grown to include growing clothes, the need for interdisciplinary collaborative fusion between biologists, botanists, technologists and fashion designers will become increasingly normal. Incorporating the kind of innovative recycling strategies that allow plastic bottles to be transformed into smart materials opens up whole new definitions of form and function. However, achieving this will require more than fusion at a creative level; at the very least, it will demand innovative long-term investment from retailers and education.

How Mash-Ups Can Make for a Win-Win

Sports shoe manufacturing is leading the way in fusion, with Nike playing a leading role. According to Nike president and CEO Mark Parker:

> *Nike succeeds because we're obsessed with innovation. We are relentlessly curious about our world and how we can make it better. We apply that curiosity to our sustainability efforts, and we continue to learn what is required for real, meaningful progress.*[10]

Nike's commitment to curiosity means that it understands the need to establish conversations and collaborations that push it beyond its comfort zone of conventional expertise. Operating in a domain where the demands of function and style offer a constant push and pull on innovation, Nike needs to maintain a total commitment to perpetual innovation that is informed by the principle of interdisciplinary fusion.

Moving Beyond Mono Mania

The emergence of increasing awareness of the power of fusion opens up a whole new set of opportunities for collaboration with other disciplines. Brands' successes are increasingly defined by their ability to set up locations and scenarios that enable and inspire multi-disciplinary fusion. We've yet to realize this high ground of disruption, however – partly because the average creative practitioner is still ill prepared to take advantage of this level of collaboration, and partly because brands tend to be cautious about investing in challenging concepts, which leads to multi-dimensionality. The collision of different perceptions, spheres of knowledge and values is always a latent opportunity for evolving more than the sum of the parts. Unlike the polite intentions that underpin collaborative strategies, fusion has the potential to define disruptive as its modus operandi. The new thresholds that will lead to the new brand landscapes are more likely to evolve out of the sparks of cultures clashing rather than the subtlety of mutual sympathy.

Some Lessons that Contemporary Business Can Learn from Fusion

Flux is Fun

The Dada and Surrealists' playful approach to creativity was facilitated by the fact that they spent time together in social situations where good food and drink encouraged conversations that led to spontaneous actions. The Surrealists embraced the cinema as a medium in which the kind of improbable juxtapositions that typify our dream experiences could be rendered; however, they also found that the constraints of formal narrative structure inhibited magical outcome. Their solution was to visit several cinemas in the same day so that the film they experienced was composite of several different movies that their strategy allowed them to randomly assemble into a new and less linear narrative.

If brands were imagined and marketed in the same way, they would suffer less from the problems of predictability and might discover that – as famed composer and lyricist Stephen Sondheim said in 2005 – 'Art ... is an attempt to bring order out of chaos.'

Chief Collaboration Officers

The Motley Fool – a multimedia financial services company that provides advice on stocks and personal finance – prides itself in thinking and acting differently. As such, the company has invested in management innovation to try and ensure that it practises what it preaches. Founder Todd Etter has helped to forge an inclusive strategy of collaborative participation and has taken on the title of Chief Collaboration Officer to confirm his company commitment. Etter has devised game-play scenarios to ensure that collaboration is a regular habit rather than an aspiration and the Motleys Fool's employee retention results suggest that his workforce is happier than that of his competitors.

Collaboration does not Guarantee Fusion

Collaboration has become a buzzword amongst government and business managers. The British Civil Service – an organization not particularly noted for its innovation record – announced in 2012 that it was 'introducing a new competency framework to support the Civil Service Reform Plan and the new performance management system.' The goal was to achieve objectives including 'Collaborating and Partnering', which is focused on the need to 'create and maintain positive, professional and trusting working relationships with a wide range of people within and outside the Civil Service to help get business done.'

The British Civil Service has long held a reputation for drowning any innovation in a quagmire of bureaucratic protocols. The organization should be applauded for its concern to employ members of staff who are 'innovative and seek out opportunities to create effective change'. However, it seems to miss the point. The statement of ambition is an exemplar of bureaucratic speak. The ambition to create 'a culture of innovation ... and take managed risks' is set in a context of deliberating telling employees exactly HOW they should innovate. A failure to trust the individual's initiative is a prevailing problem of organizational culture. It's one that appears to relate to the fact that business is still heavily influenced by the kind of top-down control systems that were evolved and institutionalized by the self-sustaining alliance of military and state. This influence is still evident in the perpetuation of phrases like 'storming and norming' and the belief that employees need to be educated rather than learnt from and with.

The prevailing tendency to flatten hierarchies severely inhibits the potential for evolving fusion cultures in which mutual learning and achievement is allowed to benefit from the kind of unanticipated outcomes that emerge from unpredictable fusions. Our experience at The Dream Café tells us that fusion is more likely to occur in a culture that is not highly formalized, prescriptive and obsessed with the metric of measurability.

Letting Go

There is a great deal of ambiguity around the notion of fusion as a component of a productive innovation culture that centres on efficiency and power rather than unpredictability. There is little point in fusing two similar things together unless your ambition is to make a longer thing; but fear sets in once we move beyond that level of ambition.

Unpredictability is the enemy of formal management systems because it implies lack of control; but of course, unpredictability is the friend of innovation. So how does a business learn to accept that future advantage is never likely to come from repeating the past? The answer lies in building trust and understanding that uncertainty is an adventure that allows work to be more like play. Using the analogy of play enables us to understand that competing with clones will result in tedium and predictability, while pitting ourselves against the unknown raises our game and encourages us to learn quickly.

Head Banging

The force of collision is crucial to the fusion process – and that could be painful unless we understand that your force of engagement does not have to directly involve bodily collision. Bringing different skills, values and perceptions into an innovation culture is likely to prove challenging and will require some degree of management to avoid standoff levels of negative conflict. This is where café culture provides important lessons on how to ensure that fusion leads to positive benefits. The kinds of cafés that acted as midwives to disruptive force were designed to reap the rewards that can accrue from combining different personalities and persuasions. A great café mixes the old with the new, attracts different disciplines and interests, and serves as a location where everyone feels welcome and free to be him or herself. The only rules required are focused on ensuring a degree of respect for difference, and this is enough to encourage cross-cultural fertilization.

G

GUT REACTION

Business appears to be dominated by two distinct personas: risky and risk averse. The dominant stereotype created by business commentators and creative souls who find their concepts blocked by tiers of risk-averse bureaucrats and middle managers proposes that, the bigger the business the more risk averse it is. While there is enough research and empirical experience to reinforce a self-fulfilling prophecy that BIG = CAUTIOUS, it is important to note that there is a lot of caution in the sphere of small to medium enterprise zone as entrepreneurs try to avoid failure by limiting their risk exposure.

We look to creative hearts and minds as sources of inspiration, because creatively inclined people have a very different way of working. It is a process that involves making instinctive judgements, which are either informed and/or evolved by a process of reflection. The classic stereotype involves the artist who makes a mark on canvas and them stands back to ponder the implications of his or her gesture on their ambition. This reflective process is very different from the more systematic approach employed by the scientifically inclined. It relies on intuitive insight, which is likely to include consideration of a relatively wide range of thoughts that are just as likely to extend beyond the next step to embrace decisions about purpose and alternative possibilities. So next time you see an artist apparently doing nothing, except to stare into space, realize that they are in fact working really hard.

Reflecting on the Bigger Picture

American pragmatist philosopher and educational theorist John Dewey promoted reflective practice as a way of developing understanding that knowledge was not just a product of studying and memorizing pre-existing theory; it was also an outcome of experiential immersion. Dewey passionately promoted embodied participation as a source of creative insight that is not accessed by keeping one's nose firmly pressed into a textbook denies. His view that, 'while we cannot learn or be taught to think, we do have to learn to think well, especially acquire the general habit of reflection' (Dewey, 1933) has helped to inform an on-going respect for reflective practice.

American educational theorist Donald A Schön helped to evolve our understanding of the implications of reflective practice. His study of various disciplines ranging from surgery to architecture had to cope with – and, in many respects, gain advantage from – operating in a context of unpredictable terrain and uncertain outcomes. His description of the 'swamp' as a location for higher level insight resonates with us at The Dream Café:

> *In the varied topography of professional practice, there is a high, hard ground where practitioners can make effective use of research-based theory and technique, and there is a swampy lowland where situations are confusing 'messes' incapable of technical solution. The difficulty is that the problems of the high ground, however great their technical interest, are often relatively unimportant to clients or to the larger society, while in the swamp are the problems of the greatest human concern.*
>
> **(Donald A. Schön, *The Reflective Practitioner: How Professionals Think in Action*, New York: Basic Books Inc., 1983)**

Schön understood that reflective practice begins 'where practitioners are problematizing their practice and learning afresh about both the knowledge and skills and attitudes that their practice demands' (*The Reflective Practitioner*).

When Less Becomes More

Individuals and teams who achieve the art of radical innovation understand that narrowing the scope of vision and eradicating disruption from the process is likely to lead to predictably bland outcomes. Successful filmmaker Robert Rodriquez has pointed out how small scale can offer a major incentive to avoid doing the predictable: 'Low budgets force you to be more creative. Sometimes, with too much money, time and equipment, you can over-think. My way, you can use your gut instinct.'[11]

Corporations tend to limit risk due to their shareholders' concern for short-term reward. They have traditionally appointed CEOs who are not perceived as risk takers. However, the shift in the context in which profitability is managed has begun to become so unpredictable that proactive prediction has limited usefulness. The future seems to be owned by individuals or cultures that are able to balance the voice of reason with a preparedness to trust in their gut, or intuitive perception of potential opportunity for innovation. Compared to their business counterparts, creative practitioners tend to rely on their gut reaction or intuition to verify the validity of their insight or inspiration. It appears that the more trust that people place in their intuition, the greater the probability that they will reach the best conclusion.

To Boldly Go?

In the context of big business, buccaneer types are associated with an ability to bet the bank on their gut instincts. As discussed in the chapter on D = Dreaming, Richard Branson has managed to build the Virgin brand by creating a myth of his ability to spot a gap in the market:

> *I never get the accountants in before I start up a business. It's done on gut feeling, especially if I can see that they are taking the mickey out of the consumer.*[12]

While the Branson myth suggests a twenty-first century swashbuckler who dares to go forward while others hesitate, Virgin is relatively cautious and relies for its profitability on its ability to minimize its exposure to risk by focusing on gaps in already established markets. Virgin also leverages its cash flow by involving other shareholders in the funding of its major brands like Virgin Atlantic, Virgin Money, Virgin Media and Virgin Trains license deals, which allow the brand to be used by other businesses that are all wholly owned and managed by other owners, such as Virgin Mobile USA, Virgin Mobile Australia, Virgin Radio and Virgin Music.

The excuse for risk aversion strategy is frequently the claim that management gains credibility from their emulation of science's testability rigour. But the truth of science is that the gut plays a major part in the creation of paradigm shifts.

Do Blinking Black Swans Think Fast or Slow?

Despite a wealth of evidence to the contrary, it is still common for those who promote and practise scientific method to cast intuition as a very questionable approach to deduction. Their problem with the 'gut reaction' is informed by its challenge to the very tenets of their training. A superficial reading of the theories promoted by Daniel Kahneman (*Thinking, Fast and Slow*, 2011), Nassim Nicholas Taleb (*The Black Swan*, 2007) and Malcolm Gladwell (*Blink*, 2005) have cast doubt on the professed rigour of established rational methodologies that have been designed to verify the validity of outcomes. But the best conclusion we can read is the right methodology for the right circumstances.

Kahneman's conclusions about gut reaction do not fully square with our experience at The Dream Café. According to Kahneman, gut reactions are informed by the information that is readily available at the moment of decision WYSIATI (what you see is all there is). The other system is based on rational deduction in which all the salient information that relates to the decision that needs to be made is reviewed and factored into the conclusion. This suggests to us that he has a limited experience and knowledge of the way in which radical creativity happens.

However, Kahneman does argue that luck plays a significant role in the success or failure of rational decisions. This point has been well illustrated by Gladwell's *Blink*, which identifies numerous examples of intuitive and rapid deduction that had led to insights that rational method failed to provide. Gladwell identifies what he calls 'analysis paralysis' – a kind of information overload in which analysts are simply confronted by too much information for them to be able to sieve the patterns of probability that they need to identify to reach a valid judgement.

The Case for Emotional Intelligence

The status of intuition received a boost from Carl Jung's (1875–1961) psychological theory and its influence on psychometric profiling (The Myers-Briggs Type Indicator (MBTI)). Jung identified the importance of intuition for certain typologies, including entrepreneurs who recognized the value of their creative inclination. He proposed that an 'extraverted intuitive type' was 'the natural champion of all minorities with a future', because of their tendency to keep moving on in search of new levels and types of challenge and sources of stimulation and gratification. While there is evidence that extroverted entrepreneurs get things done and show others the way, this stereotype tends to overshadow those individuals, like Bill Gates and Charles Schwab, who have enjoyed significant success without conspicuous evidence of extrovert behaviour.

The tendency to perpetuate leadership myths ignores and continues to undermine the potential for the synergetic fusions of skill and personality that happen during effective partnerships. It is often the participation between complementary personalities that acts as a catalyst for the productive application of emotional intelligence simply because maintaining an effective collaboration requires that all of the participants work to achieve maximum empathy. It is worth noting that Larry Page and Sergey Brin did not like each other on first meeting, but developed and continue to run Google together.

The ways in which we continue to priorities IQ in our assessment of intelligence has the significant impact of inhibiting the potential of developing the various other forms of intelligence that Howard Gardner has promoted with and post his 1983 breakthrough book *Frames of Mind: The Theory of Multiple Intelligences*. Gardner proposed various categories of embodied intelligence: musical–rhythmic, visual–spatial, verbal–linguistic, logical–mathematical, bodily–kinesthetic, interpersonal, intrapersonal and naturalistic. Later he extended his theory, with the suggestion of existential and moral intelligence hinting at, but not pursuing, a whole new way of defining how decisions are made when we are operating outside of the constraints of instrumental rationality.

In the creative sector, the role of the visionary intuitive occupies an aspirational status for many who see the arts as primarily a lab for innovation. Funding and income statistics tend to suggest that the arts are well populated by the risk averse, particularly in areas where state funding dominates investment and access. But like every other area of human endeavour, the occasional example of spectacular success offers a potent opportunity for belief.

A Sense of Possibility

The ability to trust and nurture instinct is crucially important for creative practitioners who are involved in disruptive purpose or outcome. Creativity involves bringing new combinations of thought and function together in order to discover what purpose they could anticipate.

Openness to degrees of chance and risk, and an ability to trust in intuitive judgements, can facilitate a relatively rapid and playful process of speculative iteration. In the creative context, one's gut reaction becomes a source or insurance of the likelihood of spontaneity. It draws on the range of awareness that constitutes our embodied intelligence. Instinctual recognition of latent opportunity is informed by our sensorial capacity to touch, taste, smell, hear and see subtle connections.

Band of Joy

A recent success story comes in the form of a small plastic loom that enables purchasers to weave bracelets, clothes and decorative items from rubber bands. This product's popularity exemplifies the power of gut reaction while also confirming Edison's maxim of 1 percent inspiration backed up by 99 percent perspiration. 'The Rainbow Loom' inventor, Cheong-Choon Ng, aged 45, was a senior crash-test engineer for Nissan Motor Co in Detroit who simply created the prototype to amuse his daughters. Encouraged by the reaction of his own and neighbourhood children, Cheong-Choon drew out his savings of $10,000 and developed a marketable design solution in 2010. An order was placed with a Chinese manufacturer – then the hard work began. The stress factor became acute as Cheong-Choon experienced rejection from tradeshow and retail buyers. Two years after he bet his savings the first major orders were achieved from an educational toy retailer brand, 'The Learning Express' in Alpharetta Georgia. Success was informed by the retailer's decision to organize classes and these quickly led to viral take up among local children who caught the bug. The Rainbow Loom has gone global and by August 2014 Cheong-Choon's business was valued at $131.7 million dollars.

Some of the Lessons that Contemporary Business Can Learn from Gut Reaction

People Matter

The chance nature of The Dream Café encounters allows serendipity to inform disruptive strategy. Creating a culture of innovation begins and ends with an open-minded approach to the potential for productive discourse between different cultures and disciplines. The creative's ability to trust strangers is informed by an inquisitive approach to not yet known people, things and experience. The excitement of discovery from encounters with the unanticipated is a major factor in the successes that have evolved from chance meetings. Rationalists often fear to tread where creatives rush in; or, find they are too late to take advantage of an opportunity that has evaporated by the time they have finished weighing up the evidence. People are regarded as either the font of or the threat to new knowledge, depending on the brand, the inclination and independence of the key decision makers. So while some brands like IKEA, Virgin and Apple proclaim disdain for focus groups, others – the majority – are constantly trying to check the consumer pulse through a never ending slew of focus groups. At The Dream Café we worry about companies' reliance on sampling without bothering to check how many times they have paid for the same conclusions or really doing anything with the information. Our own involvement over the years with traditional focus group research has made us cynical about its value, but at the same time we despair at the waste of resources, particularly when the data gathered are so often shelved. While we despair of the limited power of traditional focus group research, we are passionate advocates of the need to invest in trying to understand consumer perceptions.

It's shocking that some of the brands we have worked with that specialize in person-to-person or business-to-business communications do not understand the value of talking to consumers. The worst examples treat their customers as dumb profit units who need to lead into predictable behaviours in order to maximize efficient income opportunity. Our approach to gathering knowledge of customers is predicated on our understanding that we can all learn from intelligent discourse. The people that we talk to are all engaged in CAFÉ CONVERSATION mode, so that the brands we work for can learn from our ability to set up respectful discourses with their customers in which meta narratives of emerging need are able to evolve alongside, and often out of, short-term frustrations.

Emotional Intelligence

The way that we are educated to resolve problems or identify opportunities logically restricts our ability to evaluate potential by responding to the way that our hearts lead us. Although debates about the validity of the theory of EI (emotional intelligence) remain unresolved, it seems plausible that people who are in touch with their emotional response to experience are at an advantage. They are more likely to recognize and react to quality and opportunity with more commitment and alacrity than those who always weigh the options carefully before making a decision.

Just Do It

Spontaneity lies at the heart of gut reaction – thinking fast is arguably less important that acting fast. One of the traits that separate creative minds from rationalists is their ability to engage in rough prototyping. Rationalists have a tendency to want to complete the calculations before they commit to their conclusions. While the rationalists hold back, creatives have a tendency to roll their own, or others', sleeves up – and this can allow them to literally feel the solution.

Speeding Up

Photography is an immediate reaction, drawing is a meditation.

(Henri Cartier-Bresson)[13]

Cartier-Bresson – a French photographer considered to be the father of photojournalism – acknowledged the instantaneous promise of photography that alerts us to the increasing speed that defines the digital age. Our ability to download ready to use images is a major factor in the failure to invest in creativity. The 'why would I bother when I can get it for free' syndrome enables the short sighted to achieve dominance in a culture where time is also money. The question of whether we are dealing with laziness, cost cutting or speed is central to a future where the 'access anything-anywhere' assumption informs many of our personal and business investments.

Learning to Fail

Kahneman has verified that the consequences of rushing in can indeed lead to failure. However, while there is much to be said for caution there is also much to be learnt from understanding that each failure provides a significant learning opportunity. Meridith Valiando Rojas, the co-founder and CEO of DigiTour Media, claims that: 'The greatest lesson I learned was that mistakes will not end your business.' DigitTour Media was founded on the back of failure when an artist Meridith was managing on Capital Records was dropped because of lack of 'exposure to social media (which is) the secret to breaking talent in this new world order.'[14] DigiTour Media clearly has potential to be a player in the new brand spaces that the hybridization of the digital-physical worlds is revealing.

Evaluation Criteria

Two levels of achievement dominate the way in which we can define innovation success in business. The first level – to simply get a new idea out of the door – is a vital precursor to the second, which is predicated on profit and brand perception.

In risk-averse businesses, ideas are evaluated by their ability to deliver short-term profit. This tends to lead to a damping down of gut reactions. Intuitive hunches are not the stuff that statisticians tend to favour, and so they create evaluation criteria that generally pre-empt the need to reject the unprecedented – because it is unlikely that anyone would be stupid or brave enough to suggest it.

Knowing When to Quit

The Rainbow Loom's success story illustrates the earning power of a viral craze. However, there is a long history that stretches from Yo-Yo's to Croc Shoes that suggests that viral crazes are rarely sustainable. Planning the exit point as soon as a craze catches fire is crucial. In fact, failure to do so has cost large and small businesses, who suddenly find their warehouse full of unsalable stock. It can happen overnight – and while there is no formula, there is an obvious downside when gut reaction leads to an obsessive passion that is hard to let go of. There are three tried and tested solutions:

1. Take the money and run by trusting your gut (in reverse).
2. Continually develop new features; this will prolong the lifecycle of your original innovation, but not indefinitely.
3. Invest as much as you can in developing new products that will produce new income as the original source goes into decline.

H

HABITAT

We named our agency The Dream Café because we believe that the places and processes that determine where and how you work have a crucial impact on the quality and relevance of your contribution. Moving on from the definition of socialization and collaboration locations as the 'third space', we have designed The Dream Café innovation strategy around our theory of the 'fourth space'. There can be little doubt that the spaces in which we work, rest and play have a profound effect on the quality of our engagement.

The concern to encourage innovation activity in business has led to the prioritization of people and processes rather than investment in thinking about the way that places can revolutionize the way that people and think and create. The lack of intelligent and usefully innovative thinking in the design of the spaces that we occupy to develop the art of radical innovation may well be a by-product of the fact that many businesses are still unable to abandon their traditional assumptions about efficiency as an outcome of distraction minimization. This legacy has a tendency to undermine the achievement of breakthrough innovation and that is why we have evolved the concept of The Dream Café as a distinctive fourth space strategy. We deliberately encourage our clients to augment their internal strategies by externalizing their need to dream and prototype innovation into processes and places that are very different from the ones that prevail where they normally work, socialize and strategies their future.

A Brief History of Production Places

During the first phases of industrialization new typologies of buildings, such as the factory, the office and the shop, were created with the intention of organizing, predicting and controlling human behaviour. These spaces were designed to maximize output rather than enable imaginative participation. Various commentators and critics, ranging from Adam Smith to Karl Marx, identified that the control of efficient productivity through a division of labour led to high degrees of alienation and a stifling of personal creativity. The history of transforming humans into automatons in the name of profit has begun to reach a logical conclusion, as robots replace humans as the primary mode of production.

Unfortunately, the mechanized formulas that worked to maximize the productivity of employees on a production line during the first phases of industrialization are still part of the DNA of contemporary attempts to organize creative labour. Even in relatively sophisticated employment contracts, some very old fashioned ideas of 'value for money' prevail – including rules like physical attendance at the corporate workplace and fixed hours.

A Brief History of Creative Places

The shift to creativity as a priority for the employment of human endeavour in business has ushered in the need for a serious rethink about why and how people are employed. The first phase of the shift to a creative economy in the 1980s and 1990s provoked a quest for new building and space typologies that could accommodate and facilitate creativity. But, for many businesses, 'rethinking the working space' involved little more than stripping out the walls that used to demarcate individual offices to create the 'open-plan' office of today.

Early adopters of the open-plan approach tended to be creatively led businesses. During the design boom of the 1980s, the dismantling of individual office space tended to be accompanied by innovations intended to encourage and promote the company's brand. Suddenly, workspaces incorporated pool tables and other style led additions like slides between floors. Pioneers including Advertising Executive Jay Chiat learned to regret their investment in style and tech led innovation:

> *The US advertising agency Chiat Day … tried to do away with cubicles and desks in favour of absolute freedom and flexibility … the technology simply didn't exist to support founder Jay Chiat's dreams of a virtual office. People … resorted to sending their*

> *assistants in to claim (one of the few desks) at 6 in the morning. Within three years, the grand experiment had been scrapped, and Chiat himself had sold up and left.*
>
> **(Archie Bland, *The Independent*, 6 July 2013)**

Another creative pioneer, Manifest Digital, a creative agency based in Chicago, literally embraced the concept of openness and lived to regret it:

> *CEO Jim Jacoby describes his previous office at 600 W. Chicago as 'one giant open room … I thought, this is what I wanted the whole time,' he said earlier this year … The issue is, in one giant open room with, let's say, 60 to 80 people, you have so many different emotions and communication styles mixing that it just didn't work. If you had somebody upset, that would just wash over the room. You had line of sight to everything and everybody. It just did not work.*
>
> **(Get In Touch: @Grid_Chicago | grid@suntimes.com, 22 July 2013)**

The latest solutions developed by forward thinking businesses like Google and Ifbyphone are informed by a hybridization strategy, so that open areas are complemented by other spaces that are bookable or simply available on a drop-in ad hoc basis. The 'mix-n-match' solution is summarized by Ifbyphone's Executive Vice President of Customer Experience Cindy Pogrund: 'Make it eclectic … There's a place for open, but there's also a place for doors.'[15]

Collaboration has become a key word for the development of creative spaces. American psychologists Leon Festinger and Stanley Schachter, together with sociologist Kurt Back, developed an influential research project in the late 1940s that was designed to investigate how friendships form and evolve. They concluded that:

> *friendships are likely to develop on the basis of brief and passive contacts made going to and from home or walking about the neighbourhood.*[16]

Much of their research was conducted by interviewing students of the campus where all three worked, Westgate West. Their proximity helped them to notice that the campus mix of residential, cafeteria and relaxation spaces were important facilitators in the socialization of these students.

Embracing the idea of innovation as a product of a creative environment has led to the co-option of terms like 'campus' that were hitherto mainly utilized by academic institutions. Google's commitment to creating 'creative' spaces has clearly been informed by Steve Jobs' Pixar development; and its realization of 'campus' and 'lab' spaces has attracted a lot of media interest. Google's Manhattan 'campus' or London 'lab' are designed to facilitate a relaxed and collaborative mode of working, including their insistence that no employee is ever more than '150 feet from food'. Google's New York City campus has even slowed down its lifts in the hope that they will encourage workers to 'casually collide'.

The Third Place

Google's incorporation of food and socialization into its innovation strategy reflects insights revealed in 1989 by urban sociologist Ray Oldenburg, who drew attention to the trend for dividing our lives between home, work and the 'third place'. Oldenburg's book *The Great Good Place* 'argued that there are a number of attributes that make a third place a third place: It has to be convenient, inviting, serve something, and have some good regulars' (Dolan DA, *ForbesWoman*, 29 May 2012). He suggested that it functioned more effectively as a catalyst for socialization:

> *People have had third places throughout history [that have] ranged from taverns to coffee houses to barbershops … Third places are different from first or second ones because we go to them in our in-between time – their voluntariness is what makes them so special and unique.*
>
> **(Ray Oldenburg, *The Great Good Place*, 1989)**

Oldenberg's Theory of Three Places

The First Place: Home

- Place for rest and retreat.
- Place for family.
- Not a good place for friends to gather and socialize.

- Not everyone is comfortable in the setting.
- Usually not adequate furnishing and seating.
- Damageable personal objects are present.

The Second Place: Work

- The setting is productive, structured and competitive.
- This is where people earn a living.
- Inappropriate for leisurely, informal socializing.

The Third Place

- The core setting of informal public life.
- Leveller.
- Low profile.
- Full of friends, character and conversation.

Oldenberg identified a range of examples of 'third places', which included 'German Beer Gardens', Main Street USA, The English Pub and Le Bistro (French café). His analysis of the French café is particularly relevant to our concept of The Dream Café: '[It] Encourages visits of longer duration, it is scenic, inviting, and never a far walk from [one's] residence' (*The Great Good Place*, p. 163).

Oldenberg cited a number of key socialization advantages to the third place that ranged from opportunities for friendship to intimacy. His conclusions all point to his belief that a great café or hostelry encourages its inhabitants to feel secure and trusting of the habitat and each other.

Why the Right Place Produces Profitable Outcomes

It's generally accepted that Starbucks can claim credit for the development of a contemporary 'third place' that attempts to deliver on the parameters Oldenburg established. Starbucks' success has profoundly influenced what we currently expect in the way of service, choice and facilitation from a coffee shop. Yet despite its 'open door policy', Starbucks and contemporary café culture in general are a long way from the cafés that played a catalytic role in the development of avant-garde culture.

Are Creative Places Trying too Hard?

The verdict is still out on the success of the 'fun' office approach. Tim Sullivan, Editorial Director of the Harvard Business Review Press and co-author with Ray Fisman of *The Org: the Underlying Logic of the Office*, explains how these environments often work:

> *They strike a … cautionary note, drawing a distinction between changes that make a workplace more efficient and those which are mostly to do with retaining employees tempted by the trampoline in the foyer down the road … And there is some evidence for that serendipitous theory. But there's not a lot of evidence to support the idea that happier workers are more productive. It's making small steps towards a concrete goal that makes workers feel satisfied.'*
>
> **(Archie Bland, *The Independent*, 6 July 2013)**

Behind the major investments made by businesses like Google, Razorfish and Innocent, some of the failing experiments that currently dominate the 'open-plan' strategy have been led by cost-cutting rather than creativity.

Archie Bland, senior writer for British newspaper *The Independent*, conducted an analysis of the work places that are designed to encourage creative engagement in collaborative endeavour. His profile of strategy versus outcomes effectively balanced history with current practice and suggests to us that we've learned very little, and that style still trumps content. According to Philip Ross, a consultant and author on the future of workplace design who has worked with many major corporations: 'We're seeing the application of these ideas in almost any industry, anywhere. We are just at the inflection point.' Bland's profile of starting the week at smoothie brand Innocent may sound seductive until you ask the question why?

> *On a recent Monday morning, as office workers across Britain crawled to their desks and wished fervently that it was still the weekend, about 200 freshly tanned employees of Innocent were*

gathered in an astroturfed canteen, overlooked by a plastic sheep, standing with their eyes closed and remembering their favourite moments from the minibreak they had just spent together in Marbella.

(Archie Bland, *The Independent*, 6 July 2013)

The triumph of style over content suggests some fundamental gaps in the 'creative places – create creative engagement' strategy. Building spaces that create a buzz is a good thing; but it's important to remember that the makeover approach can nurture underachievement by encouraging people to spend too much time in the office. Our experience at The Dream Café tells us that it is the brands that encourage their employees to get out of the office and have conversations and collaborations with people who are not doing the same thing that have the best hope of developing new thinking. We advocate rewriting the Google algorithm of **'DISCOVERY + COLLABORATION + FUN = INNOVATION'** as **GETTING OUT AND ABOUT = DISCOVERY = UNANTICIPATED COLLABORATIONS + FUN = INNOVATION'**. As Angela Benton, Founder and CEO of NewME Accelerator, says: 'It's easy to miss a potential piece to your innovation puzzle when it's right under your nose if you aren't there.'

Part of the intention of the redesign of a creative space is outwardly looking at a way of communicating the brand image – and there is nothing wrong with this ambition. If it becomes part of a self-fulfilling prophecy that fuels the brand empathy of employees as well as customers, then it can have a positive impact. The real problem of the contemporary fashion lies in the simplicity of the strategies that inform its self-conscious style affectations. Although collaboration is an important part of an innovation process, it is no more important that the need for individuals to be able to isolate themselves and grapple with something that is personal to them.

The assumption that you will ever be able to employ all of the personalities and knowledge owners that you need to create the kind of dialectic that is combustible enough to provoke genuinely radical thinking and doing is both arrogant and naive. The belief that people who work caught in the glare of a digital screen are simultaneously capable of forming meaningful rapport with others is bizarre. The idea that conversations are best left to start on their own misses the crucial contribution of the maître d' character that provides the catalyst for unanticipated connection.

The Fourth Space

Oldenburg's research suggested that regulars provide the social catalyst and 'anchor' for a café. However, there is compelling evidence that the great cafés helped to facilitate the birth of the avant-garde; that waiting staff with attitude and the maître d' (the literal definition = 'front of house') who acted as Master of Ceremonies played a crucial role in orchestrating and evolving the heady atmosphere that fuelled creative revolutions. There is a significant difference between a café primed for revolutionary ideas and an in-house catering facility, however integrated, inclusive and funky its décor and intentions might be. There is also a real difference between the kind of regular who persuades everyday conversations and the unknown conversations that strangers might bring to the table.

> *A great café is effectively a theatre waiting for a performance in which staff and customers act out unscripted scenarios that rehearse yet to be realized futures.*

From the Black Cat to the Village Gaslight

The Black Cat Café (Paris, 1881) has a mythical role in the history of the avant-garde because it became a venue that attracted and thus brought into proximity pivotal figures in its development and dissemination. The same is true of the role of the Village Gaslight, the Greenwich Village café that connected beat poets together with musicians, writers and artists, and helped to launch the counter culture that shaped many of the values and initiatives that we now take for granted.

The connection between these two legendary venues lies in the motives of their respective founders. The Black Cat founder Rudolph Salis self-consciously set out to attract an intellectual and culturally ambitious clientele. The same is true for Village Gaslight creator John Mitchel – who, like Salis, was a performer in his own right and created a venue that he would have liked to frequent. Both of these entrepreneurs had a clear vision of the opportunity to disrupt the status quo of their time and were thus able to attract the kind of clientele and performers who represented the vanguard of the next big thing. The public realization of Mitchel and Salis' disruptive visions allowed others to action their own dreams. For performers and audience alike, the heady atmosphere of 'there's something strange going on here tonight' (REM) was empowering and enabled them to return home and create their own innovations.

Why the Fourth Space is Important

The Dream Café's 'fourth space' disruption strategy is so effectively able to radicalize your realization of innovation opportunity, because it's not a familiar part of your workplace. The fourth space encourages you to separate yourself from the corporate conventions that hinder one's ability to do things differently – something it does by creating (at least for a few days) a situation of liberation:

- A lack of distractions.
- Playful participations.
- A lack of predictable expectations.
- Inclusive engagement.
- Naivety is taken seriously.
- A lack of rules.
- Passion on tap.
- New and evolving agendas.
- Interdisciplinary engagement is always available.
- The atmosphere is inspirational.
- The menu is focused on feeding the heart as well as the head.
- Seductive conviviality.
- Entertainment is part of the menu.
- Challenging and inspirational guests.
- Activities that encourage you to think and do in different ways.
- A lack of prescriptive intentions.

Some of the Lessons that Contemporary Business Can Learn from Investing in the Right Habitats

The Tyranny of Style

There is no doubt the fashion for intelligent building design, quality food and socialization opportunities enhance opportunities for 'unplanned collaborations'. The 'buzz' of employees connecting with each other is seductive; but acting out creative rituals can absorb more energy than their tangible contribution to innovation appears to achieve. There is intriguing evidence that the new order of endless interaction is as doctrinaire as the modular determinism that it has attempted to replace. The controlling influence of investment in a process brings expectations of compliance and leaves very little room for exceptions. An innovation process requires the inclusion of all kinds of idiosyncrasies including, for example, people who work better in isolation in the middle of the night. The history of innovation is informed by examples of atypical engagement and individuals who have created the exceptions that become the new norms by challenged the existing norms. At The Dream Café we believe that an innovation process needs to include space for quirky individualism.

Innovation as Performance

Beyond the fashion for enabling 'buzz', the tradition of café culture suggests that innovation can be facilitated by benign disruption of the individuals or teams who are charged with delivering new opportunities. The contribution of great cafés to the history of innovation was informed by their ability to establish an atmosphere in which the heady mix of eccentric and passionate individuals created the kind of theatre that inspired participants to up their game. The hosts developed (or have learnt) the ability to act as choreographers of meaningful rituals that challenge and involve everyone in equal measure. Scrutinizing the contemporary relationship between design, food and experience, it is clear that theatre is often missing without trace.

Something Strange

Exceptions should always be the rule, and every day should promise an encounter with something or someone that challenges your expectations. The culture of unanticipated encounters in the context of a large or small corporate business is contained within a high degree of predictability, in which open plan encourages familiarity with most people who work in the business. The chances are that there are only so many productive versions of the 'unanticipated encounter'. Once the range of permutations that define your version of trans-disciplinary and inter-cultural discourse have been exhausted, you will tend to make sure that you are sitting next to people who you have rapport with – and that may well come down to the people who you work and socialize with. This means that the 'shock of new people' will not be a daily opportunity and therefore becomes a deliberate catalytic opportunity. As Freud pointed out in his 1919 essay on the 'uncanny', it is those aspects of experience that disturb and extend our sense of normal that influence and ignite our imaginations. An 'uncanny' encounter is more likely to happen in a habitat that welcomes strangers.

Beyond Legacy

The DNA of industrialized process is in serious need of a fundamental exorcism. The promise of new technologies and new working modes must be effectively planned without compromise. The most obvious example of this is the growing influence of alternative food culture, in which every sector from production, processing and retailing to serving is now led by alternative non-industrial strategies. From organic growing to artisan food, individuals and collaborative practices have demonstrated significant demand for alternatives. These initiatives have encouraged corporate brands to think and act differently, but typically they are late to the party and this suggests a reactive rather than pro-active learning curve, which is indicative of a failure to initiate radical innovation. Ironically, there is plenty of evidence to suggest that the alternative food and drink agenda setters are reacting to the same data that are accessible to their mainstream competitors, and that is the evidence of the three principal habitats where food agendas are confirmed: the kitchen, the shop and the restaurant.

Get me out of Here

Two common syndromes of immersion appear to be getting in the way of innovation progress: immersion in digital screens and immersion in our workplaces. Both limit the very contact with the world that is needed for innovation. The innovation process must therefore include more opportunities to apply imagination in a real world that is not limited by the perimeter walls of your building. At The Dream Café we believe that the great 'outdoors', whether it be gritty urban or sublime rural, is all part of the innovator's habitat. We use the jump-leads' metaphor to confirm the value and function of the atypical habitat. On getting out of the office, if you choose or stumble into an inspirational habitat you will have that moment when 'the shock of the new' will hit you like a 'bolt from the blue'.

I

IMAGINATION

The Age of Imagination

We have coined the term 'the age of imagination' to describe the paradigm shift that has moved the purpose of brand participation from practical functionality to inspiration opportunity. We believe that 'the age of imagination' is the latest in a long line of zeitgeist shakes that periodically change the way that we think about the world. Each moment of realignment profoundly influences how we create and consume the stuff that gives our lives meaning and momentum.

Applied Imagination

We call The Dream Café an 'Imagination Agency'. As such, the term 'applied imagination' summarizes the core of our strategy for empowering our clients to participate in and benefit from the art of radical innovation. Our embrace of the imagination is designed to contradict and compensate for the overwhelming dominance of rational and incremental process in the business world. We encourage and enable our clients to enter the age of imagination so that they reap the benefits of their latent ability to think and do unpredictable things in unpredictable ways.

A Gap in the Market

Although the age of imagination's impact is already being felt, there is little evidence that business is investing in the kind of radical innovation that will enable it to keep pace let alone driving the agenda. This may well be because imagination is not a commodity that has formal status in the majority of brand businesses. At worst, it may be that imagination is suppressed.

Why Imagination Matters

Albert Einstein succinctly captured the significance of our ability to imagine in a world that has been locked down by logic when he said that 'Logic will get you from A to Z; imagination will get you everywhere.' Einstein evolved and tested the hypothesis that led to his theories of relativity by creating 'thought experiments' (*gedankenexperiments*) that were effectively a 'flight of the imagination' that enabled him to imagine what it would be like to travel at the speed of light. Indeed, he appears to have been more interested in Renaissance art than the disruptive strategies that redefined the forms and functions of the arts in his own time. However, he was also acutely aware of the artist's role as a pathfinder: 'I am enough of an artist to draw freely upon my imagination. Imagination is more important than knowledge.'

Although the two men do not appear to have met, Picasso created art that redefined the ways in which we understand the world in similar ways that Einstein did. He broke the logic of the rule-based system of perspective and learning and was more concerned with ritual engagement than literal representation. Picasso was a confident iconoclast who refused to be bound by convention. He had a gift for giving dimension to the state of flux. He was acutely aware of the ways in which the tyranny of reason limited our capacity for radical innovation: 'If only we could pull out our brain and use only our eyes.'[17]

Picasso was one of an elite group who picked up the baton created in the Parisian cafés in the latter half of the nineteenth century. He used it to challenge and change the way we thought about the world we thought we knew. His passion for rejecting prevailing conventions in favour of exploring the imagination reflects the insight of the avant-garde pioneer Victor Hugo, a habitué of the French café culture, who perfectly captured the limitations of rational deduction: 'Reason is intelligence taking exercise. Imagination is intelligence with an erection.'[18]

The Tyranny of Logic

> *Imagination, a licentious and vagrant faculty, unsusceptible of limitations and impatient of restraint, has always endeavoured to baffle the logician, to perplex the confines of distinction, and burst the enclosures of regularity.*
>
> **(Samuel Johnson, *Rambler*, no.125, 28 May 1751)**

Samuel Johnson wrote these words at a time when the first phases of industrialization sparked a backlash that ultimately became the Romantic Movement – a development comprised of individuals with a relatively common interest in challenging the increasing dominance of instrumental rationality. Across Europe and America, poets, artists, musicians, writers and philosophers used their work to share and promote a belief that nature was a source of inspiration that needed to be *celebrated* – rather than tamed. Although the movement attracted scientists and others who sought to understand how the mind worked, they remained a minority. The post Descartes view held that the supremacy of the mind was predicated on its capacity for reason, not aesthetic excitement, to inform intelligent evaluation of experience.

Why Business Needs a New Brain

Advances in neuroscience during the twenty-first century have made great strides in understanding our ability to take imagination seriously. During the past two millennia, awareness of the significance of the human capacity to construct intelligence through emotional response to experience has increased. Additionally, it has required people to break ranks with the orthodoxy that inhibited the development of alternative perspectives. It was not a question of a 'new brain', per se, just a different way of noticing how it works. Theory had become dogma and that created a culture of institutionalized myopia – and some of you reading this book may find a parallel in your sector of business.

Our advice at The Dream Café would be:

> *Challenge any orthodoxy, anywhere, anytime! And if it's more than your job is worth, then move on. Life is too short to dance around other's limitations.*

Our own experience of gatekeepers generally begins with the PA who has been trained to avoid time wasters – who doesn't usually have the experience or ability to differentiate between time wasters and people who can generally bring something new to the brand. The best way to bypass the PA is to find a direct number – something you can resolve by making an early morning call to the switchboard operator. Once you are inside the business there are a range of gatekeepers and the larger the business the more there will be. These will range from middle weight brand managers who believe that their careers will be best served by avoiding radical thinking at all costs, to senior players who have been trained to think analytically and view people who start quoting avant-garde precedents as anathema.

As Jeff Bezos of Amazon suggests, there is always an: 'expert gatekeeper ready to say "that will never work!" And guess what – many of those improbable ideas do work, and society is the beneficiary of that diversity.'[19] Others, perhaps more cautious souls, advise massage; Sean Asset defines the skill of overcoming interdepartmental gatekeeping as a 'boundary spanner' recalling his experience in the global compliance office of Gap Inc. he identifies a range of key skills including: 'empathy, open-mindedness, active listening, strong communication skills, strong abilities to synthesize information, emotional maturity and integrity.'[20]

Some of the Lessons that Contemporary Business Can Learn from Investing in Their Capacity for Collective and Individual Imagination

The Rationalist's Dilemma

Despite branding's ability to tap into our irrational desires, many business managers still seek to leave irrationality at the door. For rationalists, irrationality is, understandably, something that is peculiar to consumers but should be kept firmly out of business. BP, the global oil brand, challenged convention by creating a cultural change strategy that was based on enabling frontline managers to get in touch with their imagination and narrative ability. The managers were given the brief of 'designing their own lottery ticket'. The programme introduced a major re-evaluation of the role of irrationality as a change agent and has led to further role out of narrative strategy in a business that was almost entirely rationally focused.

Many 'reasonable' types perceive our captivity to flex our imagination as behaviour that borders on the irrational, because it appears to lack logical process. But eliminating this prejudice is a priority for any business that wants to stay in business. However, it will require a substantial programme of re-education. We always tell our clients that if we are going to help them to break out of their rational progress into oblivion, then they have to take their imagination seriously.

Reprogramming

Releasing a business's capacity to be imaginative is analogous to reprogramming computer software. Imagine if Google search did not just auto-suggest the right spelling for your question – but went further and asked you if this was even the right question to be asking, or suggesting some alternative questions based on its knowledge of your interests. Pretty amazing, huh? But as long as left brainers dominate your business, your view of the future is likely to be pretty *un*imaginative.

Mapping the Gatekeepers and Breaking Down the Barriers

Every time you read the history of a business failure, it is shocking to discover how obvious the answer to survival was. And it's usually tied up with a resistance to imaginative thinking. It is very likely that your business ethos has created a powerful group of 'imagination gatekeepers' who may well feel personally empowered by the apparent complete lack of imagination on the part of the CEO. If *you* are the CEO, then it is your job to circumvent those who are preventing progress. There are some pretty obvious places to find the imagination gatekeepers; the first place to start is HR, who will primarily be concerned with toeing the line. As such, they will unthinkingly recruit and develop staff members who show a potential to occupy their own, or others', time in pursuits of the imagination. The early evidence is revealed by all those super successful innovators who started their businesses or careers after getting fired. The list extends from Thomas Edison through Walt Disney to J K Rowling. Abtin Buergari was one of the most recent graduates of the perverse learning curve of being fired by a gatekeeper. Buergari specializes in 'electronic discovery' for lawyers who specialize in litigation. His first experience of data mining and sieving was gained by working for a legal practice while still studying law at school. He quickly realized that the process could be streamlined by some relatively simple programming. His approach to the firm for support was roundly rejected as it threatened tradition in which a lawyer's status was informed by their ability to engage with a mechanistic task. Instead of funding and permission Buergari was given the sack and the threat of being sued. He quit law school and started his own business, which is now achieving $18 million in sales and has a listing on Inc.'s 5,000 fastest-growing companies.

J

JEST

Deciding what to cover in this book involved careful choice and lots of discussion. We agreed that humour was essential, but H was already allocated to Habitat – and we were not going to miss out on the opportunity to introduce one of the primary opportunities for any brand business to innovate. So here is H = HUMOUR thinly disguised as J = JEST.

The Dream Café is full of jest. We know that creating the kind of rapport that enables our clients to trust us with being the midwives to their brave new future requires a substantial sense of humour. That said, we never want to introduce the process by saying, 'sit on your bean bags and get ready for FUN' – since this often kick-starts those buttock-clenching ideation events that are created 'to empower you to RELEASE your INNER CREATIVITY'.

Humour, jest, wit, jokes, satire, comedy, pastiche, irony and absurdity are a crucial part of the palate of possibilities that artists, writers, filmmakers and brand marketers use to connect with others. The motive for employing humour covers a wide spectrum of needs and intentions that include seduction, undermining power, negating competition and creating positive empathy. Additionally, humour has a powerful ability to connect. Consider that comedy films consistently rank second in the most popular genre stakes in annual film box office success across the world (http://www.bfi.org.uk). A brief perusal of YouTube, particularly those uploads that have achieved viral success, will confirm that comedy also wins in the DIY movie world.

Humour remains a dominant trope in the world of branding, because of its ability to bond consumers to almost any product or service sector. It has proved particularly useful in exploiting the viral surge potential of social media. Evian has demonstrated significant ability to exploit the power of viral connectivity with its

'Roller Babies' (2009) and 'Baby and Me' (2013) videos that achieved in excess of 69 million downloads each.

Of late, tweeting has become the media of choice for connecting customers to brands via humour. This has led to the establishment of creative departments and agencies that engage in 'instant' response to 'live' situations – something now known as 'agile marketing'. Oreo cookies have demonstrated how to use humour and social media for competitive brand advantage in the USA. Oreo's 'live' response to a 34 minute blackout during the 2013 Super Bowl was a tweet that read, 'You can still dunk in the dark'.[21] In the UK, Golden Wonder Crisps achieved a the same level of agile tractions with their response to the announcement of Sir Alex Ferguson's retirement from his long-term role as manager of Manchester United Football Club, featuring a pack-shot with the 'Golden Handshake' logo.

Above line marketing relies heavily on humour. It is able to create positive connections that overcome negative perceptions, ranging from health concerns to insignificance. Consider the McDonald's 'Baby' commercial that appeared at a time when McDonald's was feeling the pressure of the health lobby. The ad portrayed a scenario where a father is driving his baby around to try and persuade it to sleep. The sympathetic response to his repeat visits to a drive-through service checkout presented McDonald's as a brand that understands families and cares for them.

The Science of Humour

The American Advertising analyst P S Speck has identified three kinds of 'humorous processes' that summarize the range of choices available:

1. **Arousal–safety.** This creates arousal concern and concludes with the viewer being made aware that the situation was in fact harmless. Toothpaste, mouthwash, toiletries and the majority of brands that promote protection from infection tend to depend on the arousal–safety. Both above and below-line marketing typically exploit humour as a means of encouraging the customer to identify with the brand as a trusted friend who comes to your rescue in a moment of panic and solves your problem with a knowing smile. This is most obvious in the promotion of brands that deal with household germs, which are typically represented as cartoon characters, albeit with malevolent intentions.

2. **Incongruity–resolution.** The audience is presented with a scenario that does not add up and are left to puzzle the reason for the incongruity. A recent commercial for Tide to Go stain remover drew on the familiar stress of a job interview. It featured a familiar and empathetic situation in which the interviewer notices a stain on the candidate's shirt. The stain starts to talk nonsense and its babble drowns out the candidate's attempts to convince. The strap-line 'Silence the Stain' appealed to anyone who has been through the ordeal of a job interview by connecting with a range of paranoias about appearance, coherence, connection etc. – all of which allowed the commercial to make a mundane product achieve 'water-cooler-conversation' currency.

3. **Humorous disparagement.** This is the basis of satire, in which the audience is invited to share the joke with the teller at the victim's expense. Stella Artois has used satire recently to great effect in a series of promotions that draws on the 'mad-men' era to promote fashionable retro style as a promise of up-market lager. The brand has extended the strategy to specifically target women who are seen as a growth market for lager. 'The Perfect Serve', directed by art house German Director Wim Wenders, features a pool side bar man who appears to spend his day anticipating the demand for the perfect head of foam by a stylish female guest. His concern to get it right is never acknowledged until he get it wrong and she returns to the bar with froth on her nose and smiles.

(Referenced in Charles S Gulas and Marc G Weinberger, *Humour in Advertising: A Comprehensive Analysis*, 2006)

There is general agreement on how the three 'processes of humour' (identified here and summarized as 'Relief-Incongruity-Superiority') service three primary functions:

- **Relief**: benign confirmation + identification.
- **Incongruity**: clarification + differentiation.
- **Superiority**: identification + enforcement = differentiation.

The human capacity for humour is also a major factor in our ability to socialize and build trust and empathy. This is what makes jest so attractive to brand communication.

Learning to Laugh at Yourself

Perhaps it simply comes down to the fact that scientific research is not renowned for its investment in fun. However, the cognitive/neural processes that inform our sense of humour remain as one of the great imponderables of neuroscience. But we do know that we are apt to find the kind of humour that is likely to encourage and facilitate the art of radical innovation in individuals and businesses that have mastered the ability to not take themselves too seriously.

An inspirational example of the value of learning to laugh at yourself is provided by Kevin Plank, the CEO and the founder of the Under Armor brand of moisture holding athletic shirts. Plank was ridiculed for his profuse sweatiness by other players during football practice and his response was the creation of a sweat preventing t-shirt. The man was flat broke when the orders started coming in for his new athletic wear. Plank funded design, manufacturing and distribution with $20,000 cash and a credit card debt of $40,000. The bank that he 'laughs his way to' now holds an account worth nearly $500 million dollars.

Businesses that lack a sense of humour can have a tendency to laugh at others, as Steve Ballmer, Microsoft's business manager, revealed when he scoffed at the iPhone launch and laughed at the lack of a keyboard.[22]

Art, Cafés and Comedy

The development of humour in art has been informed by a variety of agendas that may, at first glance, appear to have very little to do with the traditional values that art represents. Yet we at The Dream Café argue that the business of brands has much to learn about humour from art. In fact, art has been the tail wagging the dog for the past century.

When Marcel Duchamp proposed and eventually exhibited a standard production urinal as a work of art, he effectively invented the future of that to which brand innovation should aspire. His work criticized and extended the process and function or creating, selling, buying and displaying art. Perhaps more importantly, Duchamp's 'Readymades' challenged and redefined everything that the world in which he lived thought it knew about what art was and could be. Duchamp argued, 'An ordinary object [can be] elevated to the dignity of a work of art by the mere choice of an artist', creating a work that was 'in the service of the mind ... as opposed to a purely "retinal" art, intended only to please the eye'.[23]

Duchamp's influence continues to shape what art and artists aspire to; for example, the majority of artists who have been associated with the label YBA (Young British Artists). Damien Hirst – possibly the world's most financially successful living artist – and his contemporaries owe much of their initial success to advertising guru Charles Saatchi. Saatchi astutely collected and marketed their work and the YBA brand, which provided a convenient label for what was effectively a fairly disparate group. Hirst's approach to art leads us to believe that he understands what Duchamp meant when he said: 'People took modern art very seriously when it first reached America because they believed we took ourselves very seriously. A great deal of modern art is meant to be amusing.'

So *Why* Aren't Brands More Fun?

Our ability to make brands acceptable to a broad range of consumers through the portal of humour is mainly focused on the post rationalization of their relevance through marketing. In other words – very few brands consciously intend to bring humour into their users' lives. While fun may be a frequent value, it is much more likely to be value ambition rather than a deliberate feature or function. There are two important reasons why most brands lack a sense of humour:

1. They are constructed by individuals conditioned by education and profession to think of design as more akin to science than comedy.
2. The majority of brands are hatched in corporate environments that do not prioritize humour; they see innovation as a *serious* business.

Some of the Lessons that Contemporary Business Can Learn from Jest

The Joke's On You

The use of humour is likely to backfire unless you have clear brand values and tangible integrity. We can readily see a recent example of how the culture of post rationalization can lead to a pratfall with British supermarket giant Tesco. In 2013 a widespread concern about the undisclosed use of horse meat in prepared supermarket products led to the discovery that nearly a third of the meat content of Tesco's 'Everyday Value Burgers' was derived from horses. Tesco was quick to minimize brand damage but neglected to brief its customer service to avoid embarrassing tweets resulting in a message that read: 'It's sleepy time we're off to hit the hay'.[24]

Joining up the Dots

Make humour integral to the brand's form and function: in an age of insecurity we need more opportunity to laugh. Additionally, jest can provide a great sense of empathy. Humour has a powerful socialization and security potential. We can always do more to connect consumers to these primal desires through design and functional attributes that enable users to feel more secure and relaxed about their lives. The development of new opportunities for integrating brands into customer lives that social media presents offers a platform for the kind of knowing strategies that once were available to local retailers with a small customer base. Taking advantage of digital media's ability to track users gives brands the potential to customize dialogue and build rapport by exploiting and sharing consumer behaviour. 'Tex-Mex' fast food brand Taco Bell has developed a knowing strategy for Facebook and Twitter that invites customers to laugh with it and sometimes at it. The success of brands like Taco Bell in social media is informed by their ability to understand that digital discourse is driven by speed of response and tone of voice. The brand's ability to share in, but take ownership of, humorous comment is exemplified in their response to a Twitter feed that read: 'If Taco Bell thinks that they're revolutionary by putting nachos inside of a burrito, then they've never met a drunk person'. Taco Bell responded: 'Where do you think we got the idea?'

Fun = Fun

Creating a transformational innovation culture may be a serious need for any competitive business – but that does not mean that an innovation process needs to be *too* serious. It may just be that, if you temporarily delete the bean counters from the equation, then a FUN IN = FUN OUT formula may provide your brand with the key to effective disruption. And as we all know, there is no point in trying to disrupt the market unless you disrupt yourself.

K

KINETIC

Art that Moves

Simply put, kinetic art is art that involves or engages with physical movement, or the illusion of movement. Kinetic art has its roots in the late nineteenth and early twentieth century cafés of Paris and Zurich. At different times and places, artists and intellectuals began to question the old orders that insisted art was limited to a style that followed classical tradition and was predicated on stasis. The context of rapid technological progress has fundamentally changed most people's ability to conceive of the relationship between time and space by making rapid movement and mechanized facilitation a part of everyday experience.

Mechanization provided a major source of inspiration for the arts. While dystopian scenarios were relatively commonplace, the excitement created by the new technologies of transport and communication proved to be inspirational for artists in all spheres. Pace was possibly more important than product, as witnessed by the excitement of the Italian Futurists: 'We will sing of great crowds excited by work, by pleasure, and by riot; we will sing of the multicoloured, polyphonic tides of revolution in the modern capitals' (F. T. Marinetti, *The Founding and Manifesto of Futurism*, 1909).

Another key source of avant-garde challenge was the DADA movement. This approach was more politically motivated and exploited the potential of pseudo machines to criticize a world that was increasingly relying on machines as a source of salvation. Art that drew on and extended the concept of kinetic engagement began to feature in the work of a number of emerging artists in the first three decades of the twentieth century.

Mechanization is a Way of Being

Machines have become so much a part of our everyday lives that we fail to notice them except when they are new or they break. The syndrome of familiarity breeding indifference presents a dilemma for technology brands – one that's exacerbated as technology becomes increasingly invisible.

During the first phases of the mechanization of our lives, new technology was presented as a source of liberation. Although there were influential sources of political and cultural descent, these tended to focus on the mechanization of life rather than fantasizing about the freedom that machines could achieve for us. However, as machines moved out of the factory and established themselves in the home and office, we welcomed their ability to provide efficiency. At the domestic level, machines were portrayed and perceived as aspirational saviours. People looked forward to their ability to convert existences that would otherwise be limited by the drudgery of performing repetitious tasks into lives filled with leisure opportunities.

Creative Thinkers and Doers Notice and Respond Rapidly

Celebrating and deriving inspiration from the speed of transition and access that mechanization allowed was not unique to artists. However, their response typically transformed technological progress into a whole new set of ways of thinking about progress. Early twentieth-century artistic experiments in reimagining the way that we depict the world had a profound effect on the ways in which business and customers began to evolve, apply and exploit the concept of movement. Influence can be found in every form of brand engagement from transport to fashion to those contemporary kinetic wands called mobiles. As the British Vorticist artist and writer Wyndham Lewis (c. 1930) said: 'The artist is always engaged in writing a detailed history of the future because he is the only person aware of the nature of the present.'[25]

The most significant implication of kinetic art for the contemporary world of branding lies in the artist's ability to embrace movement as a function and an aesthetic form. In this respect the kinetic avant-garde anticipated much of the experience and expectations that have become normalized by the exponential influence of digital intervention in our lives.

We understand technology through the metaphors that creative thinkers construct to make sense of the world. Digital technology has raised the bar; it is able to locate us in a hybrid universe where we're as likely to undergo experiences in the digital realm as in the physical. The difference, at least for the time being, is the power to defy the space–time continuum that our digital world affords us. This skewing of our conventional kinetic limitations has left all of us in a permanent state of mobility expectation – which is a major opportunity for brands to exploit. We can only define those opportunities via a mix of insights and inspiration capable of evolving a level of conceptual engagement that flies free of the rational precepts that typically limit visionary engagement.

The other significant problem we have – after being conditioned by our education and employment to think in terms of a gridded world – is that it makes it much harder to imagine collapsing those artificial boundary lines. But that's the only way to release the kind of space–time blurring that artists have been so good at anticipating and now represent the new landscape that more of us are able to recognize.

It is the stuff of dreaming and cafés – and that is where we come into our own.

Higher Function

The exploration of the kinetic landscape was and remains an ideal topic of exploration for the artists, thinkers and doers from other spheres of practice who sit around café tables discussing the meaning of the stuff that surrounds them. During the first phase in Russia, kinetic explorations became a primary concern for the Russian Constructivists: they offered metaphoric opportunity to give dimension and create immersive experiential engagement. This concern to enable a sense of dynamic participation opportunity with the spirit of change that fuelled the revolution has many parallels with the contemporary hybrid lifestyle that is increasingly shaped by a search for cathartic opportunities in the physical world that simulate the dynamism we experience in the digital realm.

Positive and negative responses to technological determinism and its impact and potential became key themes of art. Eventually, the term 'Kinetic Art' evolved into an umbrella label that encompasses a variety of motives, techniques and technologies involving the exploration of movement, and/or the illusion of movement. Notable practitioners include Victor Vaserly, who did much to evolve interest in the perceptual illusion of kinetic activity through his sculptures and images. Jean Tinguely created auto-destructive machines, 'metamechanics' that deliberately satirized the mechanization of mass production of consumer goods. Tinguely also organized auto-destructive events that did much to develop the concept of art as a 'Happening'.

Kinetic Applications

It is clear that creative thinkers and doers had recognized creative potentials before the rest of the world caught up. They were able to develop perspectives that, even when overtly critical, contained the seeds of the kind of thinking that could revolutionize our relationship with technology and industrialization. The existence of faster and cheaper technology opens up endless possibilities of developing new distinctions and interconnections between work, rest and play including the ability to slow down, which is as much the province of kinetic opportunity as frenetic speed.

Yet at a time when the pace of change has a potential to be counterproductive, investing in some 'inefficient machines' may be a prescient brand opportunity. The opportunity to develop 'slow commerce' for online shoppers may seem to be a retrogressive strategy, but some online brands are beginning to understand that a reflective opportunity is likely to lead to deeper engagement and empathy with the brand. Patagonia, the outdoor clothing and technical apparel brand, was a pioneer of the strategies of 'funnelling' and 'stickiness' in which visitors to a website are engaged in a variety of invitations to view or read about anything from usage tips to technical specs, which encourages them to 'linger longer' and builds trust and rapport. Obviously, if you are trusting a brand to facilitate your and your family's safety and security in an extreme sports participation zone then trust is important, but Patagonia's journey narratives should not be unique to an outdoors, or clothing, brand.

It is clear that we need to slow down and reflect on whether we need, want or will continue to pledge our unquestioning allegiance to technological determinism as an answer to everything. There are already compelling indications of the kind of a groundswell of interest and support for 'slow' agendas from the 'Slow Food movement'[26] to The Long Now Foundation[27] to suggest that there are several million individuals with lingering doubts about the 'fast forward agenda' whose needs are not being served by business. It is no coincidence that the founder of Slow Food, Carlo Petrini, and the founder of The Long Now Foundation, Stewart Brand, were both people who had counter-culture history and reputations for constructively questioning the status quo.

Stewart Brand is perhaps best known for producing the *Last Whole Earth Catalogue* (1971), a self-help manual for those who wish to operate outside of the norms of industrialized society. Carlo Petrini was a member of the Italian Communist Party who worked as a journalist, challenging the logic of industrialized mass culture. The Long Now Foundation's website reveals: 'The Long Now Foundation was established in 1996 to creatively foster long-term thinking and responsibility in the framework of the next 10,000 years.' Slow Food's website confirms: '[it] was founded to counter the rise of fast food and fast life, the disappearance of local food traditions and peoples' dwindling interest in the food they eat, where it comes from, how it tastes and how our food choices affect the rest of the world.' Both movements offer compelling evidence for the power of alternative thinking and disruptive strategy in an age where conformity to industrialization is increasingly questioned and rejected.

We will begin to see the possibility of alternative functions as time frames begin to evolve. With this, a range of opportunities may finally redefine our conditioned need for a faster future into a more balanced strategy that combines fast, slow and something in between. A contemporary example of the inheritance of art by science that really plays with time, space and technology is represented by an evolving research project by scientists at the University of Bristol who have bubbles that act as a screen for images and release a scent when burst. Lead scientist Professor Sriram Subramanian described how his 'chrono-sensory mid-air display system' creates bubbles that are tracked so that images can be projected on them. Subramanian anticipates an ambient notification system making our interactions with machines such fun that the technology just disappears.[28]

The relative silliness of Subramanian's concept of bubbles as a communication device project is precisely what makes it significant. This is the kind of thinking that is very likely to happen when you gather around one of those mythical tables with a group of individuals who do not have common expertise but share a passion for reimagining the world. The bubble project is more like art than science, because it explores some very relevant but latent themes. As such, it is likely to make some kind of contribution – no matter how small – in terms of redefining how we think of and utilize technology.

The significance of that opportunity should be alerting brands that currently have no real role in technological access to start thinking about the possibilities inherent in the bubbles concept. For example – the key theme of ephemerality is very relevant to food and drink brands. The kinetic agenda that movement (floating bubbles) plays in this project alerts us to a significant space for any brand that engages with motion and that ranges from transport to clothing.

Kinetic Intelligence

There are countless advantages to bringing different forms of intelligence into different kinds of interaction in a Dream Café context. One obvious opportunity is revealed by the research into intelligence developed by Howard Gardener who defined eight distinct modes: musical–rhythmic, visual–spatial, verbal–linguistic, logical–mathematical, bodily–kinesthetic, interpersonal, intrapersonal and naturalistic.

Gardener later proposed existential and moral intelligence as potential extensions of these categories (*Frames of Mind: The Theory of Multiple Intelligences*, 1983). Gardener's theory has been criticized as subjective and unscientific. Yet anyone with enough self-awareness to respect their own, or others', embodied skill will instinctively empathize with Gardener's perspective.

Brand Opportunities to Apply Our Kinetic Intelligence

We consider it imperative to acknowledge that different kinds of intelligence exist. This opens the door to our Dream Café process of using different intelligences to stimulate the development of new and alternative perspectives that enable a brand to imagine territories and products and services that do not yet exist. From a brand business perspective, we can activate opportunities using Gardener's definition of intelligence as 'biopsychological potential to process information'. We at The Dream Café see potential for this kind of intelligence to be facilitated in a cultural setting where the latent ability to solve problems or create valuable products offers a whole new landscape ripe and ready for colonization.

Frenetic Kinetic

Kinetic indicates frantic engagement but as our allusions to the 'slow movement' suggest, our conditioned assumptions about value and purpose are merely the tip of an iceberg of possibilities that are waiting to be exploited.

Here are three of the possibilities that our research at The Dream Café has identified:

1. **Moving pictures.** The rise of social media has encouraged us to record our lives and broadcast them to others. This has created an opportunity to connect our physical to our digital existence. It will therefore not be long before our digital personality will begin to influence how we interact with physical space in all kinds of ways – including the full spectrum of sensorial engagement.
2. **Up close and personal.** Kinetic interaction is much simpler to achieve in the digital realm than it is in the physical realm; there, we are currently limited by our mobility and the obstructions that stand between us and potential opportunities. Google Glass is a sign of kinetic thinking's ability to blur that boundary. There will be many more as this hybrid space becomes a landscape for the imagination.
3. **Time travelling.** Well-behaved software has the ability to allow you to revisit and recapture stuff that you accidentally deleted or thought you no longer needed. It is also evident that it takes much longer to recapture lost experience in the real world. A decade or so ago, many would have argued that reassembling lost experience would have been impossible; but at The Dream Café, we suggest that you watch, or start to invest urgently in, that kinetic space.

This is already compelling evidence of kinetic opportunity all around us. The only thing to do now is reassemble it and develop brand opportunities that enable an eager public to take advantage of it. For example, we are already being tracked, because we carry gizmos that are satellite connected. At the moment that seems to work to the service providers' and surveillance motors' advantage more than it does to our own. Therefore, a significant brand opportunity here lies in our ability to reconnect with physical experience in much the same way that we can endlessly flit between time and space in the digital realm.

Some of the Lessons that Contemporary Business Can Learn from Kinetic

Think Like an Unfettered Creative

When you compare the scenarios that the creative intelligentsia has laid out for us over the decades, it makes the state of contemporary brand development look pretty bland and predictable. The ability of science fiction writers like H G

Wells, Arthur C Clarke and William Gibson to imagine a future leaves brands like Google looking pretty pedestrian. The ongoing influence of *Star Trek* continues to surprise with its ability to anticipate what will become reality. From Kirk's communicator (smartphone) to transparent aluminium and spray-on inoculations, *Star Trek* confirms the ability of fiction makers to achieve the level of liberation that conventional innovation strategies fail to reach. 'Google Glasses' and smart watches look like something that belongs to the thinking of the 1940s, designed for gumshoes like Dick Tracy who need to compete against superhuman powers with toy gizmos.

The only way to reach the future is to go beyond it. Forecasting's power of creative engagement lies in its lack of conventional parameters. Yet it is also informed by fiction's ability to locate inventions in a context that allows them to become familiar. It is no coincidence that a television series as universally popular as *Star Trek* shaped the ambitions of generations of inventors by insinuating an expectation of extraordinary technology into their sub-conscious.

To Virtually Go

The exponential enhancement of technological opportunity is continuously opening up new possibilities for engaging the public in the narrative. *Advertising Age* writer Cotton Delo argues in a recent article that:

> *'The mistake every new medium makes is trying to take what the old medium was. They read books on the radio at the beginning of radio; in the beginning of cinema, they shot plays. There's a completely new form of storytelling that has to evolve for this new [VR] canvas,' said Chris Milk, a filmmaker and music-video director. Last year, Milk shot a short film of a Beck performance for automaker Lincoln's rebranding campaign. He also created a rendering of it in 360 degrees with six GoPro cameras. Consider Coca-Cola's approach. Last month it staged a VR experience at the World Cup, where participants entered a replica of the locker room at Brazil's Maracana Stadium; then, after putting on VR Oculus Rift goggles, they moved from the locker room to the pitch and played on the field, all without getting up from their seat. Matt Wolf, Coca-Cola's head of global gaming, said there's branding within the experience, but the more valuable aspect is that viewers are getting access to something that wouldn't otherwise be possible. 'It's about the authenticity of being inside that stadium,' he said. 'Yes, thanks to Coke.'*

(*Advertising Age*, 27 July 2014)

One of the useful aspects of kinetic opportunity is the necessity to remind us that motion tends to be focused on frantic need. We argue that a life spent in perpetual motion is simply a habit; as such, we urge brands to encourage rather new definitions of motion and to understand that fast is only one mode. We all need the brand equivalent of a 'PAUSE' or 'DIM' button to create vital moments of calm in our over active lives.

Feeling Better

Howard Gardener's theory identified opportunities for kinaesthetic learning: that is, learning by doing. Kinaesthetic experience is all about the sensation that enables our body to engage (or not) with physical experience and much of it is semi-subliminal partly because we are not taught to be in touch with our bodies. Yoga practitioners, for example, will understand how subtle energy is an amazing source of the feel good factor that we all need, but most brands fail to tap into this sphere of opportunity. The development of fashion and technology mash-ups and the increasing integration of technology in sports ware is the first major indication of the potential for brands to connect with humans' capacity for kinaesthetic feedback. As the science and creative thinking evolve it is certain that a kinaesthetic dimension will become a crucial aspect of interface design and physical and digital experience, from car design to furniture.

Portable

Using personal or mechanical movement to collect energy is hardly a new idea. There are numerous examples that are waiting to produce profit once energy storage ability is enhanced. That said, there are numerous small-scale opportunities that are waiting to be developed, or enhanced, and it is clear that every future technology brand will have portable energy generation built into it. It is also extremely likely that all clothes, footwear, buildings and transport solutions will have to address this opportunity and will profit from doing so.[29]

L

LOVE

In 2004, Saatchi & Saatchi CEO Kevin Roberts attempted the ultimate takeover with his proposal that BRANDS in the future would be replaced by his concept of LOVEMARKS. Roberts argued that LOVE was more than an idle emotion; rather, it was the source of connectivity that cements consumers to the products, services and experiences that they love. He asked the question: 'What builds loyalty that goes beyond reason? What makes a truly great love stand out?'

Robert's answer proposed 'Lovemarks' as a source of multi-faceted connectivity opportunity that would deliver three critical elements:

- **Mystery**: great stories: past, present and future; taps into dreams, myths and icons; and inspiration.
- **Sensuality**: sound, sight, smell, touch and taste.
- **Intimacy**: Commitment, empathy and passion.

Though Roberts cited Nike as an example, consumer research has failed to find evidence of higher than normal brand loyalty for Nike. However, lack of tangible confirmation of the theory has not stopped Roberts – along with numerous imitators who are gaining clients by investing in the possibility of 'feeling the love' on their balance sheet.

Is Everyone Looking for Love?

Humans are clearly focused on finding love – so much so that they spend a great deal of their lives engaging in experiences that simulate or reinforce their infatuation with an idealized version of it. Most of us have been raised with the expectation that, somewhere, there is the right someone for everyone. Although the narrative conclusion may confound the desire for a happy ending, the thrust of the narrative is generally based on the search for fulfilment of the dream romance.

Looks Aren't Everything

The music business is just one example of an industry that has made a lot of money by investing in love. Love songs feature heavily in the all-time big earners charts. Music performers are marketed as brands, and 'stars' of the love genre emerge because of their ability to conform to the stereotype of attractiveness that is part of the ideal version of love. The same is true for the 'romance' genre of film – one that is permanently successful due to its ability to recompile the classic narrative of need → search → fulfilment. Romantic leads come and go, but once they find success, like Richard Gere or Julia Roberts, they tend to be typecast to the point that they continue to play out variations of the stereotype throughout their career. Richard Gere, for example, established his credentials as a romantic lead in 1982 with *An Officer and a Gentleman* at the age of 32, and was still portraying a contender at age 63 in *Arbitrage* in 2012.

The publishing industry derives significant income from romance as well – and as publishing moves into the digital realm, the visual imagery and symbolism that are vital components of the genre are beginning to play a greater role in reinforcing our association of love with looks. The growth of online dating has confirmed that love is a primary agenda for the digital generation. Social media sites offer evidence of the priority role that love plays in the image of ourselves that we want to present to the world. See how many images your Facebook 'friends' have featuring them in cuddles or clinches with a significant other.

The Science of Love

Biology and neuroscience research tells us that when people fall in love they feel better about themselves and the world in general. It is largely accepted that there are two stages to a loving relationship: attraction and attachment. The chemical response is remarkably similar amongst all cultures; it's not different for particular individuals or couples. Tangible increases in testosterone and dopamine levels have been recorded. They confirm a pattern of arousal leading to a steadier and, eventually, permanent enhancement of positive and benign feeling of connection as the relationship matures. The main difference in our chemical response to these stages is marked by the greater production of oxytocin and vasopressin in response to long-term attachment.

Brand Love

So how does business tap into this connection? From a brand perspective, the need to develop loving relationships is crucial. The two-step engagement process from instant attraction to long-term bonding is an obvious aspiration for any brand.

The quest for brand loyalty trumps early adoption any day of the week. However, this is where the weakness in the love equation begins to disappear into the romantic mist in which it was formed. If we accept a premise for which there is plenty of anecdotal evidence, then many of us have similar expectations of brands as we do of romantic partners. We expect loyalty, empathy, understanding and sensitivity to our needs and feelings. However, we also want contemporary relevance because the person or brand that we are seen around with is an expression of who we are.

When we apply these simplistic criteria to a number of brand sectors, the brands we can discount as partner contenders become immediately apparent. Banks, for example, tried to morph from paternalism to flirtatious trendies without realizing that the values that we used to grudgingly respect – like forcing us to beg for an overdraft – were and remain appropriate. The last thing you want from a bank is a no-commitment-one-night-stand (unless you are breaking into it!). In much the same way as relationship choices and tastes have expanded, brands need to come to terms with the fact that there is no longer a one-size-fits-all formula. They must work harder to woo and maintain the romance. The British budget airline EasyJet provides a good example of the potential to develop a lasting relationship while still being flirtatious and even promiscuous. Its initial incarnation was flirtatious but cheap and cheerful, yet continuous innovation has enabled it to attract a much broader demographic. Most recently it has begun to allow customers to book seats in advance and was quick to realize the potential of smartphone boarding passes and tickets. It has achieved these without recreating the potential for alienation that is perpetuated by traditional price structures and seating arrangements that juxtapose luxury with 'cattle-class'.

Fickle Feelings

The title of Zygmunt Bauman's 2003 book *Liquid Love* says it all. Bauman argues that Freud got it right when he theorized that we are all caught between the increasingly irreconcilable push and pull of our desire for freedom and our need for attachment. Placing this dilemma in the context of brands' endless search for lasting love has indeed fuelled the promiscuity from which they now suffer by trying to give us too much of everything on the first date.

Imagine your average BRAND posting itself on an internet dating site using the nickname INCLUSIVE-B:

> *INCLUSIVE-B: Are you looking for the answer to your dreams? I'm really contemporary, full of good taste with a carefully designed wardrobe and I come well recommended. Loyal and dependable, but I can be a bit frisky as well. I'm also cheap and I am not put off by cultural differences. I'm really into all the latest politically correct agendas and I'm not averse to the bi-thingy! I really think I can empathize with almost anyone, including people who don't share the same values as me. So if you are looking for someone who can combine affordability with luxury experiences and PC credentials, then let's connect right now.*

It is probably not difficult to imagine that INCLUSIVE-B does not form many lasting relationships. The three main British political parties – The Liberal Democrats, Labour and the Conservatives – need to think very carefully about their desperate attempts to construct brands that appeal to everyone while failing to communicate the truth and potential for integrity of their value system. Trying to be all things to all people is a classic brand error that big players like Tesco, the British supermarket chain with global presence, are now suffering from.

The paranoia's and ambitions that drive this self-defeating strategy of pluralism are typically informed by the twin negatives of cloning your competitors' strategies and spending too much time listening to focus (consumer research) groups and knee-jerking to provide them with a version of what they say they want. If the main political parties looked closely at what is happening to other brands that want to be liked by everyone, they might notice that a perception of a lack of integrity is often the Achilles heel of trying to deliver to the conflicting and confusing short-term whims of the public at large.

Love at The Dream Café: a Brief Fiction that Could be Your Reality

The popular stereotype of artists and intellectuals is that they are volatile, given to multiple affairs and absolutely rubbish at long-term attachment. However, our belief that art has a lot to teach brands is not based on personality; rather, it is predicated on the creative thinkers' and doers' insight into the human condition. The value of the outsider and the rebel is their ability to comment on and make visible the kind of stuff that most of us never even notice.

That's why The Dream Café knows that sitting disparate but extraordinary creative minds around a table will throw up the kind of perceptions of possibility that will change how you understand everything you thought you knew about your brand. Imagine your brand is a Robotic home help called H T– and imagine further that we have gathered together a few intelligent and talented artists and intellectuals around the table to create new insights and persuade customers to love it.

Here's how the conversation might open:

> *H T CEO Christine: OK let's cut to the big issue. We've got to find a way of persuading people to trust this thing, we are getting a lot of focus group feedback that respondents don't trust it enough to bond. We need to work out exactly what the core brand values should be and how to communicate them. So tell me your thoughts?*
>
> *H T Brand Manager Dan: The closest we have got is 'LOVABLE' and that seems to promise a positive experience. Maybe it's all about downplaying the science and upping the ART? There is a real danger in getting too caught up in the emotional bonding agenda. We have put a lot of work into making H T really helpful and people need to understand how much time it can save them. If they want a friend, or a cyborg lover, then we are talking a very different brand.*

So imagine you were at our table. How would you draw on your knowledge and experience to respond?

This imagined conversation raises the opportunity for new perceptions and challenges, a chance to extend the brand owner's perception of what is needed and what is possible by bringing different perspectives to the process of applying imagination. Our imagined introduction represents what The Dream Café calls the 'UNPACKING' phase in which concerns, questions and aspirations are revealed. We deliberately allow (and if necessary encourage) free ranging responses. A principal objective of The Dream Café is to open rather than close the potential for new understandings.

Fast forwarding to the insights that we might gather from our fictional CAFÉ CONVERSATION then, we would anticipate discovery of the obvious issue: the difference between the starting point of designing an efficient domestic 'home-help' machine and creating a machine that is capable of establishing trust. The misunderstanding of the touch-points that will enable the brand to establish empathy is a common problem that is by no means restricted to robots. Brands that are failing to connect are often ones that either misunderstood the needs that they were created to serve or have not adjusted to the reality of new needs beyond attempts to create opportunity for traction by dressing up in contemporary style.

What does a brand need to do to encourage customers to move from instant attraction to a long-term relationship?

Our fictional client would learn that the function of a brand is defined by a range of criteria and that efficiency is only one of those. They would develop a much deeper insight into what a brand needs to do to encourage customers to move from apprehension, to inquisitive and flirtatious to love and then to a long-term relationship.

The insights would almost certainly include:

- Love is something that you have to work hard to maintain.
- Love is rarely sustained if it is based on face value appearances.
- Lasting love and mystery are closely connected.
- Love begins with understanding our own need.
- Clichés are not a good place to start a love affair.
- Love is volatile; you either learn how to dance or get off the floor.
- Love allows you to discover yourself.

These kinds of insights can enable a brand to move beyond the predictable into a place where they evolve a much more sophisticated approach to creating the love affair they aspire to. The Dream Café 'slam' is not as neat as Kevin Roberts' 'Lovemarks' formula; but we argue that it's infinitely more realistic.

Dreaming of Everlasting Love

If you want to know how to create love for your brand, there is little point in starting with an idealized version – because, like so many relationships, that may soon dwindle into habit. Our aim is to create sustainable opportunities for our clients and that requires being realistic. Confronting the difficulties of maintaining the sparkle of first encounter requires a completely different starting point from the position of 'all-things-to-everyone'.

We all kid ourselves that we are perfect and that a prospective partner would be lucky to get us. That touch of arrogance is important to some degree, because success needs self-belief; but it there is a fine line between narcissism, complacency and the kind of delusion that tends to fester in brand businesses that spend too much time locked into a circle of self-congratulation. This inevitably prompts a resistance to outsiders who might challenge their assumptions. Insularity so often limits the vision that creates the clarity of every great brand that we fall in love with.

The Dream Café understands the need to maintain and support confidence; but we also know that real confidence comes out of knowledge. Our strategy of assembling luminaries with our clients in our Café is informed by our concern to widen the information base that will lead to a new and relevant knowledge base.

Black Swans or True Love?

Nassim Nicholas Taleb's theory of 'Black Swan Events' utilizes the metaphor of a black swan to define how we often have to rely on hindsight to enable us to realize that events that we predicted would achieve a happy ending (the perfect romance?) actually conclude with unpredictable outcomes (the end of the affair?).

Taleb concluded that:

- The high proportion of unpredictable outcomes to carefully planned strategies suggests that we confuse narrative assumptions about happy endings with reality.
- Scientific method is a highly inefficient way of predicting outcomes because of the small number of probabilities that are available.

Our tendency to preload our assumptions about what our strategy will achieve with positive (or negative) psychological biases can lead to individual and collective myopia. However, creative thinkers understand that nurturing an ability to challenge prediction begins with unpredictable conversations and leads to unforeseeable perspectives – and that is why you need them at your Dream Café table.

Some of the Lessons that Contemporary Business Can Learn from Love

Even before the advent of the Internet, the computer played an important role in matchmaking. Respondents were required to list all of their preferences, and the computer's job was to sift through likely matches among people who fitted that profile due to shared interests. Unfortunately, the theory promised more than it could deliver and ideal matches often proved to be less than successful. The history of sustainable love seems to be defined by those remarkable examples of divergence that foster mutual independence rather than hybridization. Complementary difference creates the potential for two individuals to become more, rather than less, than the sum of their parts. Brand businesses often tend to become self-reinforcing by recruiting people who can demonstrate unquestioning loyalty to the brand. So it's a welcome sign to read recently that Sandy Douglas, President of Coca-Cola North America, only drinks 'one-a-day'; this suggests a concern to engage in a conversation in which absolute loyalty is not the starting point (*Businessweek*, 31 July 2014). The divergent relationship always has the potential to be unpredictable because it has two sources of the unanticipated opportunity.

In other words – brands need to learn that love can begin and continue with unpredictability as its main source of attraction.

Love in a Foreign Language

As the business of brands becomes increasingly global, the subtleties of cultural differences can quickly escalate from 'lost in translation' bemusement to full-on divorce. Brands must develop a fully informed export strategy and communicate their core values in ways that respects the host culture to sustain the love affair. The need for understanding and respect is of course mutual, as the reason why brands are exportable can be due to their specific cultural heritage. This also has to do with the fact that this is perceived as something desirable, not least because it is absent from the host country. The history of love has always been informed by the attraction of the exotic, and the fascination for people and things that are from outside the dominant culture has always provided an important source of cultural and personal innovation. Love in a foreign country is always going to suffer from gatekeeping and this is particularly obvious in cultures with a high degree of centralized power.

In 2014, Volkswagen found itself the target of Chinese state broadcaster CCTV's 'name and shame' day on 15th of March. This is the channel's 'Consumer Rights Day', when it takes on multi-nationals. Volkswagen was effectively caught with its 'gearbox out' as the channel exposed a fault. Volkswagen's response offers an exemplar of how to overcome the first public spat, recover and strengthen the love affair.

Volkswagen:

- Relied on its local expertise even though the damage repair task fell on Catherine Peng, VP of PR, who had only been in post for two months.
- Wasted no time in owning up and apologizing.
- Opened the doors to the media and demonstrated its concern, but communicated the strength of its resolve.
- Wasted no time in turning words into action.
- Established a very efficient solution.
- Gifted a software update to respect China's gift culture.

Following the recall, Volkswagen was rewarded with a 17.5 percent increase in sales, making it the leading automobile brand in China. This is surely confirmation that if you work on a relationship it has a high chance of surviving and growing.

Love is Where you Find it

The Internet was still at a relatively embryonic stage of development and application when Kevin Roberts proposed his theory of 'Lovemarks'. Agendas that featured sensuality and intimacy as meeting points have proved difficult to sustain in our evolving age of digital encounter.

It's not that media is incapable of simulating these opportunities online; they simply have to learn from the wider media expertise in packaging and selling romance.

Sustaining the relationship happens when instant attraction turns into work and mutual commitment.

Meeting a brand in the flesh that has pressed your buttons on screen is potentially the equivalent of meeting a 'star' that you idolize and finding that somehow they do not measure up to the airbrushed illusion. Reconciling the journey from digital fantasy to tangible reality is one that requires a whole new way of thinking about love stories and happy-ever-after-endings.

Love Does Not Need to be Blind

Raising the odds in favour of long-term amour is usually delegated to research that result in lots of predictable questions – followed by even more predictable answers, that are then dressed up into 'statistical evidence'. It's rarely surprising that research fails to support transformational innovation. However, we are not convinced that this is simply due to people's limited vision. Rather, it is mainly the limited imagination of the people creating, asking, analysing and presenting conclusions that restricts potential. Our response to the collective myopia called INSIGHT was to create a process that we call CREATIVE INTELLIGENCE. We'll talk more about this later – in the 'J' section – but its starting point is a quote from Alexander Fleming. When asked how he connected some mould on a test tube to the invention of penicillin, Fleming defined his flight of imagination by saying:

> *'Everyone sees but very few people notice.'*

We respect the power of the creative eye and mind at The Dream Café. They are able to encourage scenarios that involve new things to notice and new conclusions to be drawn. Whether you buy it from us or someone else we really do encourage every brand to start involving creative people in their research.

Long-term Love

Moving from lust to a lifetime love affair requires constant but appropriate refreshment. While that becomes harder in an age of instant everything, it is not impossible. Sustainability is mainly down to integrity and integrity is all about the right kind of core values.

Psychologist Barbara Killinger's definition may sound idealistic, but we need to set the bar high: 'Integrity is a personal choice, an uncompromising and predictably consistent commitment to honour moral, ethical, spiritual and artistic values and principles'. She argues that 'integrity is undermined and lost as a result of obsession, narcissism, and workaholism' (Killinger, *Integrity*, 2010). Could this explain why we become bored with brands that we fell in love with a few weeks earlier?

Big Love

Sustainable relationships are substantially dependent on the promise that was identified at the start. A lot of brands make the mistake of promising more than they can deliver on a long-term basis. At The Dream Café, we look for the narratives that are going to continue to fascinate – and that requires us to do some editing of a number of seriously overly ambitious promises.

M

MULTI-SENSORY

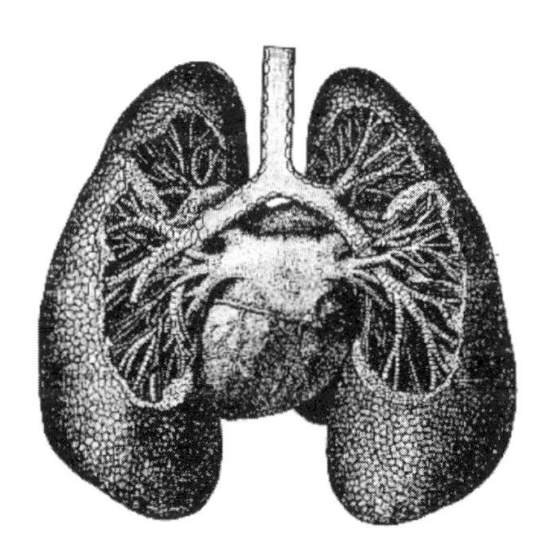

Sensing an Opportunity

Multi-sensory branding has become a constant theme over the past 15 years. However, we are still at a point where the theory is promising more that the practice seems to be capable of delivering.

The origins of multi-sensory brand communication have been influenced by academic and philosophical reflection on empirical practice; including the insights of John Dewey (mentioned in more detail later in this section). Unfortunately, the translation of theory into brand practice – particularly by branding agencies desperate for a new edge – has often led to a diminishment of potential. At The Dream Café, we call this the 'scratch 'n' sniff' school of brand sense. We think the worst kind of promotions try and reduce luxury experience – for example, a good perfume on a strip of paper that comes 'free' with a magazine, which you have to peel open and then scratch with your finger. It is difficult to imagine anything further removed from a luxury experience, apart from a journey on a budget airline that has not moved on from a definition of 'no frills' as permission to humiliate passengers.

The Science of Sense

Neuroscience has transformed its approach to the senses over the past two decades. The wave of disruption that has elevated our senses onto the same plateau as visual engagement has been achieved through a growing tendency to question the prevailing dominance of the Cartesian schism. The prevailing belief that the primary function of the brain lays in its ability to translate formal (primarily visual) data into logical deductions by acting as a kind of calculation machine led to the relegation of other sources of embodied intelligence, like touch, taste, aroma, sound and movement, to insignificant nerve reactions.

It is ironic that much of the research that enabled our increasing understanding of the human (and animal and plant) capacity for multi-sensory intelligence was not funded by the businesses that now stand to benefit. The time that it has taken for multi-sensory intelligence to be recognized as a brand opportunity should act as an important reminder not to refuse to consider the improbable just because it is unorthodox.

Multi-sensory Marketing

Contemporary concern to harness the potential of multi-sensory engagement with brand experience was stimulated by a two important books – Schmitt and Simonson, *Marketing Aesthetics: The Strategic Management of Brands, Identity, and Image* (1997) and Pine and Gilmore, *The Experience Economy: Work is Theater & Every Business a Stage* (1999). However, a notable research paper published in *The Journal of Consumer Research* in 1982 could have opened the field two decades earlier if anyone in the business sector had noticed it. In it, authors Holbrook and Hirschman wrote:

> *Many products project important nonverbal cues that must be seen, heard, tasted, felt, or smelled to be appreciated properly … Yet scant research on nonverbal multisensory properties has been reported (hence the need for) a more energetic investigation of multisensory psychophysical relationships in consumer behaviour.*
>
> **(Holbrook and Hirschman)**[30]

The title of their paper confirms how far ahead of the game they were: 'Experiential Aspects of Consumption: Consumer Fantasies, Feelings and Fun'.

Non-Sense

All of these writers and experts made much of the concept of retail as a theatre, in which brands and their customers could participate more effectively if the experience was augmented by multi-sensory cues. By the time that Pine and Gilmore locked down the concept of the Experience Economy, examples like Starbucks and Nike Town were giving substance to the idea of retail and service as a sensorial opportunity – something they defined as a 'fourth economic offering.' Pine and Gilmore argued that 'experiences are a distinct economic offering' that are as different from 'services as services are from goods'. The concept of multi-sensory experience began to be mythologized by the theorists who laid claim to the experiential realm post 2000. The media jumped on the bandwagon and looked to the pundits for quotes. A slew of articles followed that promoted the multi-sensory mythology and before we knew it we were living in the age of full on sensory experience – except that this didn't truly come to pass.

The bland ascetic synthetic reality that still dominates our physical brand experiences would suggest that we're all still waiting for investment in sensory cues to take hold. Wading through the increasingly simplistic, derivative and repetitive body of literature on Sensory Marketing and Branding should confirm to anyone with practical experience that theorists are not the best people to be pontificating about sense. Or maybe they just don't get out enough?

You're likely beginning to think that The Dream Café is cynical about the value of multi-sensory branding. However, we assure you that our cynicism rests at the doors of the available evidence of what some unfortunate translations of theory into contemporary practice have accomplished. We are in fact hugely enthusiastic about the potential of multi-sensory and multi-channel engagement.

Before the Bandwagon

Back in the late nineteenth century, American pragmatist philosopher John Dewy wrote extensively about reflective practices that celebrated 'embodied' encounters with experience as crucial sources of knowledge. Pragmatism had a particular take on the value of sensory experience that was at odds with the consensus of philosophy's history of denial. Rather than accepting the classical prioritization of the brain over the body, Dewy – along with others – recognized opportunities to promote the possibility of a correspondence between our abilities to sense our experience and rationalize it that extended beyond logic.

Subsequent research into the brain has justified the pragmatist position. Specifically, it has identified how different modes of sensory experience excite deductive activity in the brain and the heart. Neuroscience has confirmed the potential of sensorial encounter to profoundly influence our hearts and minds. Now we just need to devise ways of doing that in targeted and economically effective ways.

Multi-Channel

One of the ironies of the post-1999 promotion of multi-sensory opportunity is the fact that the tech industry appeared to be paying more attention to the possibility than the majority of businesses that specialized in developing income out of tangible experiences. Judging by some of the pioneering efforts like 'ISmell' by 'DigiScent', this may be good news. Launched in 2001, 'ISmell' was a computer peripheral device that allowed users to send 'smell-mails'. Despite a conspicuous lack of economic success the techno-determinists are clearly resolved to colonize multi-channel communication. And as the exponential enhancement of software and gadget devices continues to evolve, it is only a matter of time before our mobiles will become platforms for smell-o-vision and haptic encounter. It is just a matter of time, until the right brand concept, before multi-sensory encounter becomes a familiar part of our digital experience.

From Non-Sense to New-Sense

We believe that the task of translating theory into meaningful brand opportunity necessitates a whole new way of thinking and doing. To achieve this requires a fundamental rethink of the way that design is employed in order to supply the solutions to our engagement with and perception of brands. One of the reasons why we added the words 'the Art of' to our book title is informed by our belief that 'design' is a redundant label – and, in many respects, a redundant discipline.

Design has its origins in the nineteenth-century objective to develop reproduction skills in order to answer the need of mass producers to originate forms and images that would help to ensure consumer interest. Since those pioneering days, design has become a catchall label that embraces everything from motion graphics to cars. Despite the proliferation of disciplines and the growth of the industries that they feed, the education, rationales and techniques of design remain largely fixated on the development of repetition rather than origination.

The digitization of most disciplines has short-circuited the design process. It has come to the point where most designs move straight from screen to screen or screen to manufacture without any tactile engagement beyond manipulation of the computer interface. This ubiquity of the computer as tool and medium has introduced new aesthetic styles; however, it has also reinforced the tendency for design to remain focused on reproduction rather than innovation. The computer has done little to encourage design to engage with multi-sensory opportunity beyond experiments with food printing that tend to reinforce the development of 'molecular gastronomy' in the 1990s by Ferran Adrià at the ElBulli restaurant in Spain. Adrià's unpredictable presentation and processing strategies work in a dialectical way to challenge and change food perceptions, but so far the evidence of 3-D printed food seems to focus on the replication of conventional food types. Burgers, or novelty sweets, that look like physical models of mathematical objects are typical. Elsewhere, in areas like furniture product design, style continues to trump content as the definition of function.

All Singing – All Dancing

It's clear that brands need to focus on supplying a 'fourth economic offering'. However, this requires them to find a way of moving beyond the self-reinforcing limitations of design to enter an age of creation more like an applied form of performance art. Performance art is coming into its own at the moment as major art galleries compete (successfully) with retailers for footfall.

Consider the work of artists like Marina Abramovic, who was resident at the Serpentine Gallery in London in the summer of 2014 for several weeks doing 'nothing'. Performance art like this gives visitors an opportunity to become a part of the performance, although it is essentially a hybridized medium that draws on other disciplines and traditions for its forms and means.

It is possible to trace the origins of performance back to the DADA movement. The trace elements of that movement are certainly an important part of the United States' DNA, which has been influential in the evolution of the form. Like so many other creative disruptions, performance owes a debt to the freedom to experiment that distinguished the Black Mountain College from so many other education centres and strategies. Wider awareness of the art form owes much to the development of the 1960s phenomenon of the 'Happening' that drew on the particular stance of artists like Alan Kaprow and George Brecht, and the Fluxus movement.

Means and Ends

Here we will give a brief list of some of our reasons for arguing that we need to take seriously the characteristics that distinguish performance art from conventional design. Performance art:

- Assumes that choreography and orchestration are essential tools and mediums.
- Engages all the senses.
- Involves the end-user in the process of realization.
- Does not prescribe its functionality.
- Invites the end-user to confirm its purpose.
- Creates a multi-dimensional experience.
- Curates objects and environments in dynamic ways.
- Allows end-users to involve their own narratives as a way of determining meaning and functionality.
- Is always in a state of flux and perpetual innovation.
- Develops fluid and hybridized relationships between digital and physical experience.
- Connects with all modes of intelligence.

We could go on, but we hope we've convinced you of the genre's huge potential for helping to define and communicate the future of brands. How we achieve that may be nothing like the 2014 Serpentine performance 'show' that everyone in London has been talking about. Instead, it may involve the development of pre-existing marketing tropes like blurring the lines between public and performer in shared spaces. Or, it may involve more viral events and reimagining retail as galleries. But the underlying point is that performance is multi-dimensional and dynamic – whereas design is still locked into static solutions for a world that is in permanent motion.

Eat Me – Squeeze Me

Embracing sensorial opportunity will vastly extend brands' ability to transform themselves into new typologies and serve neglected needs – as well as creating new ones. However, there are some very obvious areas of branding where sensorial engagement is urgently needed.

Perhaps it should not be surprising that food and drink are ripe for multi-sensory colonization — however counterintuitive that statement may seem. Companies have achieved the industrialization of food by production, processing, distribution, retailing and branding strategies that have focused on efficiency – which has in turn required those industries to compete with the vagaries of nature. However bizarre that ambition might seem, they've overcome nature's 'natural tendencies', by deconstructing and reconstituting food. Processed food and drink dominates our diet – from fast food 'takeaways' to 'microwavable' or 'oven-ready' packets or cans that you buy in convenience stores or supermarkets. The majority is unlikely to contain unadulterated meat or vegetable and will derive their appearance, taste, texture and aroma from the addition of artificially developed flavours, smells, colours and textures for two reasons:

- They allow for greater profit.
- They have longer shelf lives.

The influence of health concerns and longer-term thinking about the impact of industrialized processes on the environment and sustainability have all begun to challenge the traditions of processed food and drink. Although it's still on a relatively small scale, some major corporations are beginning to respond to the competitive threat of emerging ethical brands – by either buying them and developing them as relatively independent brands or copying their approach.

Juice Makes Sense

We visited just such a start-up based in a Bristol UK wholesale fruit and veg market. Led by chef and environmental and social activist Arthur Potts Dawson, The Juice Man specializes in unpasteurized raw juice. The brand represents a combined approach to sustainability and well-being that the monolithic thinkers that still dominate corporate business will continue to find difficult to engage – until they have no choice.

Arthur has an established track record of creating restaurants and even a retail solution, 'The Peoples Supermarket', which promotes zero waste strategy. It was obvious while observing him and his team in action at the Bristol market that his multi-sensory instincts play an important role in developing the business opportunities. The blending of recipes is the equivalent of the perfumer's art involving sniffing, tasting, feeling ingredients and hearing conversations sufficiently – so as not to lose other people's insights. Colour is hugely important too – but like other aspects of appearance, including the brand identity, visual approbation is not prioritized over the other sensorial opportunities. The Juice Man is clearly going to be a player in an emerging category that we call BENIGN BRANDING – that is, brands that prioritize ethics while recognizing that persuading customers (particularly those most in need of better diets or consumption habits) to pay a slight premium for integrity requires the application of sophisticated brand business strategy.

Big Business Sense

Coca Cola's purchase of a majority holding (90 percent ownership at the time of writing) in the independent Innocent smoothies, juice and veg pots brand signals a trend: for global corporations letting independents do their innovation for them. The time has likely come for more evidence of a commitment to internal change to establish long-term brand integrity. Take, for example, Unilever's development of a London-based innovation lab called 'Pitch' that enjoys relative autonomy, with the corporate brand giving it the freedom to seed and grow disruptive opportunity.

Corporations are often described by the use of the metaphor 'juggernauts' to highlight their lack of manoeuvrability. However, scale is less important than the dominance of rationally orientated management and worker culture, and the priority of maintaining short-term capital accumulation for shareholders. Anyone who values fresh and unadulterated food and drink will find the practises that dominate mainstream food perverse at best. Yet the thought of having to accommodate a paradigm shift to natural, beyond printing it as a strap line, is equally abhorrent.

Fortunately, we at The Dream Café have a solution – one that requires engaging in conversations and iteration strategies with some clever people who are really good at applying their imagination and enabling you to apply yours. We know that business is not short of sense; but we also know that we are very good at helping them focus it in ways that make sense.

Some of the Lessons that Contemporary Business Can Learn from Multi-Sensory Engagement

Coming to our Senses

Restoring multi-sensory dimension to brand experience after centuries of neglect may not be as hard as it seems. Re-education is a lot easier when you know that the people who need to learn have all their faculties in place and are fit for sensory engagement.

Participation

One of the reasons why so many innovation opportunities end up underachieving is the physical gap between the decision makers and the creative process. At The Dream Café, we promote a strategy of thinking by doing so; this gives everyone a chance to participate in the creative exploration of possibilities. Our experience has given us the confidence that everyone is capable of much more origination than they assume they are. Often, it's just a matter of breaking old habits.

Your customers have much more sense than you give them credit for

The logic of industrialization is focused on finding the fastest, cheapest way to achieve a given outcome. That ambition has extended from production to dominate the ways in which we design and market goods as well. The emergence of organized global competition has badly shaken the strategy of producing stuff for less and marketing it for more – so much so that it's forcing us to rethink. However, the strategy of dressing up through design and marketing to add value still rules. We firmly believe in the importance of getting the message right at The Dream Café; however, we also maintain that better products inherently give way to better marketing. This is where – and why – the multi-sensory opportunity has so much to offer. The majority of people on the planet is equipped with a full range of sensory connection; yet most have been conditioned by old-school industrialization norms to focus on visual engagement, albeit with a soundtrack (from time to time).

Integrity

Creating brands that have core value is all about ensuring that innovation is based on the level of integrity that we found in The Juice Man start-up. Integrity is the basis of lasting empathy. Even as contemporary style fades, we stay for the long term because of the subtlety of interconnected opportunity that makes each encounter a new one. Think of sensorial integrity through your knowledge of the people who you relate to and you will remember that what makes people attractive is their ability to live breathe and evolve. We may have favourite machines; but unless we have a serious fetish it is the sensorial pulse that keeps us connected.

Sense by Sense

The multi-sensory revolution will take time – and not because of a lack of knowhow. It is almost entirely down to an ideological resistance that is based on the most basic fear of the unknown informing cynicism about the untried and the untested. In other words, anything that does not fit with what we know and expect tends to make us nervous. Gatekeeping multi-sensory innovation has limited the possibility for serious benchmarks. This syndrome of repression and denial will continue for a long time unless someone breaks ranks and shows the way forward. Innovation could be quite simple: just add one sense at a time.

For those who want to find out more about multisensory science we recommend the following books:

Robert Jütte, *A History of the Senses: From Antiquity to Cyberspace* (2004).

Constance Classen, *Worlds of Sense: Exploring the Senses in History and Across Cultures* (1993).

Mark F Bear and Barry W Connors, *Neuroscience: Exploring the Brain* (2006).

Antonio Damasio, *The Feeling Of What Happens: Body, Emotion and the Making of Consciousness* (2000).

N

NOTICING

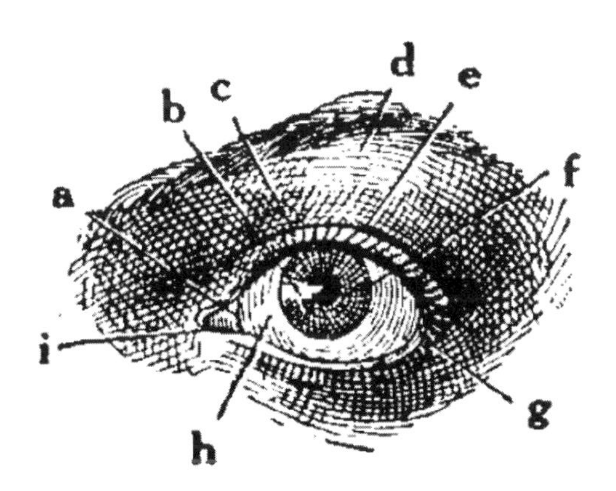

Noticing is at the heart of The Dream Café's difference from the way that conventional agencies operate. Our ability to notice what others tend to neglect is what enables us to leverage the different ways that creative people apprehend the world. When we talk about creative thinkers, the avant-garde, café culture and so on, we don't limit our definition to conventional stereotypes of men in berets with goatee beards or women in French style matelot tops and dark glasses. We are referring to a way of thinking and seeing that is hardwired to the imagination and one of our reference points is Marcel Proust who said: 'The real voyage of discovery consists not in seeking new landscapes, but in having new eyes.'

Noticing plays a crucial role in the menu of services that we offer business. We prototype and create, enabling us to complement and inform each other and our clients' abilities to evolve their understanding while gaining real purchase on innovation opportunity. Our core provision at The Dream Café consists of:

INSIGHT: we investigate and translate into accessible narrative trends and consumers' needs, motivations, anxieties, ambitions and inhibitions.

IDEATION: we work with clients to co-create strategies for building new insights into better products, services and communication strategy.

CAFÉ CONVERSATIONS: we engage our clients and others in conversations that develop their ability to imagine and apply their new understandings to take ownership of the future.

REALIZATION: we involve our clients in a co-creative strategy of prototyping metaphors to enable them to both create and experience solutions to communicating brand value.

However, they do not always come in that order, or all at once. This section of the book will focus on identifying how we use our ability to notice to our client's advantage in each of the three services.

Research or Insight

Delivering research or insight may seem to be a counter intuitive offer from us. After all, we're a confident creative agency that all too often finds itself frustrated by the myopia that permeates most research process and practice and 'creates' alibis for the kind of brand managers who try and maintain their job by avoiding risk. So why – and how – do we conduct research; and why does it really matter?

Our concern to include research in our portfolio is motivated by three primary motives:

- We would rather trust our own research than the kind of limp reviews with which we are often confronted.
- We believe that research pre, during and post any creative process provides crucial learning and enhancement opportunity.
- We are good at it.

Some knowledge of the origins of market research helps explain why it so often hinders rather than advances progress. Marketing began to emerge as a profession and an academic discipline in the late nineteenth and early twentieth century as media, product and service opportunities proliferated. The development of a coherent body of theory and practice was largely achieved in the United States of America and encouraged by the fact that the American business recognized opportunities for mutual benefit by investing in education. During this period, mechanization based on 'scientific principles' began to produce tangible efficiency enhancements, as Ford's factory system evolved into Fordism, and influence domestic regimes as well as factory systems.

Although Market research has its origins in the street surveys of political inclination developed by newspapers in the 1820s, by the 1920s it had evolved into what was proposed as a science that utilized quantitative and qualitative techniques to reveal patterns of purchase habit.

Then, as now, the appeal of a scientific approach to marketing was seen as an insurance policy. However, what we now experience is largely based on the 1950s innovation of the 'Marketing Concept' defined as a 'Management philosophy according to which a firm's goals can be best achieved through identification and satisfaction of the customers' stated and unstated needs and wants'.[31]

Various techniques, ranging from psychological profiling to quantitative questionnaires, have been employed to this end. The majority of them have been designed, enacted, collated and communicated by people who have been employed precisely because they are not regarded as imaginative or creative.

The strict categorization of expertise into professions and disciplines makes all kinds of sense, because it provides opportunity to develop common methodologies and build degrees of trust between users and suppliers. That said, we must remain aware that the majority of market research has the same relationship to science as punters who support their bets by studying form. Studying gambler form would alert you to the fact that the real winners are always the bookies. This leaves a gap in market intelligence that we set out to plug – and then realized that you don't need more science; you need better questions and more imaginative ways of noticing what is going on. This is what led us to develop our own methodology that we call CREATIVE INTELLIGENCE.

The Dream Café Menu

We have a range of choices that enable us to service our clients' brand needs from insight to ideation.

Ten Reasons why the Creative Minds at The Dream Café Tend to Notice Stuff that Others Ignore

- Creative types: Are endlessly inquisitive.
- Tend to ask questions that stimulate respondents to reveal what they really know.
- Don't like predictable outcomes.
- Have an ability to translate abstract concepts into metaphors that allow access.
- Have a passion for spontaneity.

- Connect at an emotional level.
- Love embarking on journeys of discovery.
- Are good at enabling others to takes themselves seriously.
- Are good at noticing the value of stuff that others have relegated to the margins.
- Are more interested in learning than educating.

Creative and Local Intelligence

Creative intelligence is all about combining research rigour with applied imagination. As such, we have gathered a global network of people who represent a wide range of discipline expertise but share a common passion for CREATIVE INTELLIGENCE. This means that we have a slew of intelligent and creative people scattered across the world who not only have a passion and authorized ability to apply their imagination; they also have local intelligence of their own culture. That enables us to deliver up-close, personal and creative insight into where and how to locate, NOTICE, gather and interpret the information that matters.

Primal Stir

Orthodox research tends to focus on the obvious – which isn't usually what creative thinkers do. Rather, they love stirring up the sediment. They get really excited in poking around in it and NOTICING those little nuggets that only begin to sparkle with insight when the dirt is washed off. We bring the stuff that others don't NOTICE into the light and allow it to reveal to our clients the kind of information that they desperately need. It's a bit like reading something in its original language and then reading a translation; the quality of the experience is entirely dependent on the skill and sensitivity of the translator.

The Sieve

One mistake that researchers and its clients often make is to assume that INFORMATION = KNOWLEDGE. But in truth, information only becomes knowledge when it is effectively curated. This is why our SIEVE PROCESS is all about making that vital journey of translation:

GATHERING + NOTICING + CURATION = TRANSLATION
= CREATIVE INTELLIGENCE

Ideation

We came up with concept of The Dream Café when we thought about those paradigm shift moments when creative thinkers and doers gathered around café tables. Then, when they went home and changed the world forever, they were enabled to achieve that disruptive level of innovation by what we can define as a process and, of course, a place:

> *CREATIVE INDIVIDUALS + CAFÉ LOCATION = UNANTICIPATED ENCOUNTERS = ALTERNATIVE VIEWPOINTS = DEBATE = COLLECTIVE INTELLIGENCE = CREATIVE INTELLIGENCE = REVELATION = REALIZATION = REVOLUTION*

We specialize in taking our clients to inspirational locations, where we create a fictional café. We achieve this not just with props and clever art direction, but also with the addition of some extraordinary outsiders. The whole point of getting our clients out of the office is to provide time and space for them to break free of the routines and habits that are limiting their ability to apply their imagination and to set up new and challenging opportunities to do so. As this book is primarily focused on what we are doing right now, the relevant examples of our work relate to the past 12 months. This means that we have to respect our clients' confidentiality, as these projects are still in various stages of evolution.

The Dream Café's work has ranged from new product innovation, including evolving new drink typologies, to creating the future of deodorants. We have also done a lot of work in repositioning brands from healthcare to a plethora of FMCGs (fast-moving consumer goods). These projects typically share a need to identify new market opportunities or find new relevances. While each café is different (and they are always developed to suit the client's brand's specific needs), the principles and the process that we use provides a high degree of assurance for clients who are not used to trusting their imagination. The journey of discovery and realization that we create typically opens up entirely unanticipated opportunities and these include a wealth of self-discovery of latent talent among the participants themselves. We typically require a minimum of three days to achieve this level of transformational opportunity.

Place

As we pointed out in the H = Habitat chapter, creating a 'fun palace' in your headquarters misses the point – as well as a whole raft of opportunities. The great epoch-defining cafés worked because they were in the right place at the right time – which was not at the place where you work on a daily basis. So we take time and trouble to match our location with our analysis of the client's needs. That could mean a chateau in the South of France, an Ice Hotel, or a Bunker in the Bronx. It's all about the energy field.

People

Casting our Dream Café with the right characters is crucial. Again, we determine our selection by what we believe will most benefit our client. The list of personalities we draw on includes all of the professions that we consider to be creative – including people from science and psychology, physics and anthropology. It also includes all of the more stereotypical creative disciplines, ranging from dance to gastronomy. The particular skills are crucial; but the mix needs to ensure a provocative expectation that these individuals' particular insights will take the conversations into new and unanticipated spheres.

Projects

We make our clients work hard and lead them through a variety of activities that ensure they work smart to evolve tangible and achievable dreams. Precedents drawn from a wide range of ideation techniques that we have gathered, evolved and originated inform all the projects that we apply to this end. These include 'Thinking with Your Sleeves Rolled Up', 'Adventures in Unknown Landscapes' and 'The Wishing Tree'. We leave it to our participants' imaginations to work out what might happen during those consciousness raising and changing moments – but they almost always transform ability and outcome.

Confirmation and Consolidation

There is a crucial need to ensure that our clients leave with clarity of their transformational dream and the strategy that will deliver it. This is why we dedicate the last day to making sure that we all agree on what we have discovered and what we are going to do about it – what we call APPLYING YOUR IMAGINATION.

Transformational Realization

One of the most common problems of any creative process is the failure to produce connected and evolutionary outcomes of each stage. Our experience has taught us that the potential for catastrophic and destructive slippage is often caused by the institutionalized habits and structures that involve too many departments and agencies. This not only wastes time by requiring endless and repetitive briefing and re-briefing; it frequently ensures underachievement because the plot gets lost in the whispers of translation.

This is what led us to construct The Dream Café as a location that could manage and deliver the complete journey FROM DREAM TO TRANSFORMATIONAL REALIZATION.

How We Deliver Dreams

We are fortunate to have a network of LUMINARIES that we are able to draw into projects. Rather than being limited by a finite skill base we are able to combine extreme flexibility and precision to deliver precise focus. Our Luminaries are there for us at any stage of The Dream Café Process, because we create opportunities to experience an innovation process that is free of the predictable frustrations of compromise and underachievement.

This synergy provides us all with the liberating potential to offer an assortment of possibilities that range from live performance to prototyping in any medium from food to technological product concepts. We have a list of extremely talented filmmakers, packers, producers, motion graphic artists, writers, typographers and knitters (yes – knitters) who can communicate a client's message in extraordinary ways that will get your customers and the competition NOTICING.

O

ORGANIC

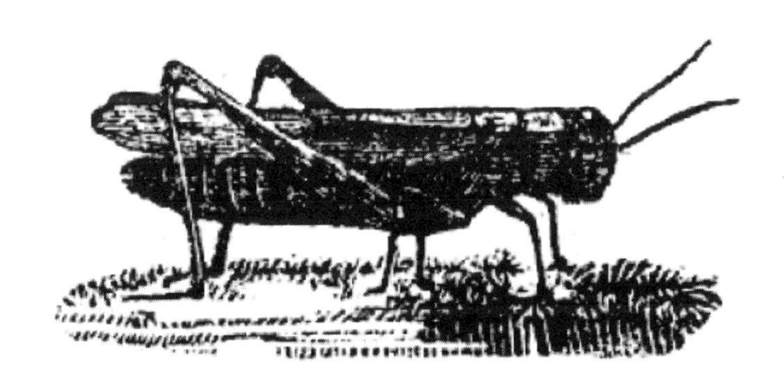

The Dream Café is future focused. We are constantly looking for clues, talking, debating, imagining and dreaming about the big agendas that are going to influence the future of brands. And we are convinced that ORGANIC will become one such major theme substantially influencing the world of brands. This section reveals some of the clues that have informed our forecast.

The *Oxford English Dictionary* gives priority to the predictable association of the word 'organic' with food production. However, it also includes a broader refining ion which resonates with our beliefs at The Dream Café: 'Denoting or characterised by a harmonious relationship between the elements of a whole'.

Our definition of organic is not limited to food or textile sources that are farmed and processed without the additions of chemicals and genetic modification. We also embrace a concept that includes asymmetric aesthetic forms and functions, along with biomimicry. Something organic has the ability to act as a key metaphor for a range of emerging agendas, like integrity, that we have already touched on. We relate to the holistic implications of the term.

Organic is used to reference the existence, or intention, of achieving nourishing links between constituent parts of a whole in a number of contexts. This has countless implications for the future of brand innovation – ranging from the need to manage the various aspects of the innovation process so that they create constructive synergy to the need to accommodate other spheres of innovation so that they become part of an ever evolving healthy organism that is your brand business.

These agendas will ensure that the organic revolution will affect every sphere of brand engagement – with a significant impact on food, fashion, transport, habitat, lifestyle, technology, healthcare, lifestyle and business management.

Dreams and Organic Cafés

The Dream Café provides strategic support for our clients by viewing their brand opportunity as an 'organism' with unlimited potential to evolve. The metaphor of 'organism' is an important one for contemporary business; it implies many of the agendas that have become paramount in a moment where linear theories of evolution do not work. There is an interesting theory, assembled by French philosopher Gilles Deleuze and French psychiatrist Félix Guattari, called the Rhizome theory that deliberately co-opts nature's capacity for organic evolution. It suggests that emulating nature by constantly putting out exploratory tendrils in an ongoing search for new spheres of opportunity offers an antidote to the predictable assumptions of the linear model. Rhizome thinking and doing has much in common with the creative approach in so far as it is contingent, adaptable, inclusive and full of unanticipated opportunity. It reminds us that we need to plant some potatoes and watch them and learn.

Organic Food Business

There is ample evidence for the benefits we can derive from chemical free farming and processing. Though the factory forming lobby continually challenges these advantages, increasing evidence of the side effects of industrialized production has enhanced sales of organic produce.

A proliferation of organic brand retailers and products confirm this growth, with sales of organic products continuing to expand during the recession. Whole Foods Markets provides an interesting brand case study (despite its somewhat questionable reputation as an organic retailer). The retailer and food processor carries an increasingly large range of own-brands and fresh and proprietary health market brands like 'Whole Earth'. Despite criticism for not supporting localism or raising the bar on 'organic certification standards' Whole Foods' stock is more health aware than the major supermarket chains. The company reported revenue of $12.917 billion for 2013, and analysts are predicting that to increase to $14.78 billion for 2014.

The focus on 'organic' credibility can divert attention from the fact that there are considerable dangers attached to the generally high sugar and saturated fat content of many processed 'health foods'.

The health paradox is well illustrated by UK based Green & Black's chocolate to ice cream brand that only produces organic products. Craig Sams and Josephine Fairley founded the business in 1991 as a response to a gap in the market – the lack of a company with concerns about organic and 'green' issues.

The brand name reflects the founders concerns: 'Green' was derived from their 'green' principles while 'Black' refers to the colour of the cacao premium content of their chocolate. Cadbury Schweppes bought Green & Black's in 2005; the brand has subsequently been incorporated into the American owned Mondelez International (formerly known as Kraft). In much the same way that Coca Cola has maintained Innocent as a stand-alone brand, Green & Black's maintains a high degree of independence.

Sweet Success

While Green & Black's environmental record, fair trade policy and organic credibility are significantly better than the majority of confectionary brands, the reality of the brand appeal is still informed by its sugar and fat content, and its appeal to our primal brain. On balance, food producers and processors who promote organic are generally driven by a concern for environmental and personal health. There is evidence that they have done much to anticipate the increasing concern to combat obesity and heart disease through the promotion of a diet that contains natural fibre and a mix of fresh vegetables and fruit.

Design and technology that emulates and learns from natural forms is commonly called biomimicry. Advocate Janine Benyus argues that:

> *In a biometric world, we would manufacture the way that animals and plants do, using sun and simple compounds to produce totally biodegradable fibres, ceramics, plastics, and chemicals. Our farms, modelled on prairies, would be self-fertilizing and pest resistant. To find new drugs or crops, we would consult animals and insects that have used plants for millions of years.*
>
> **(Janine Benyus, *Biomimicry*, 2003)**

Eleven years later, much of Benyus' forecast has either come true or is likely to. Ecological concern has played a role in the evolving status of biometric design; but the realization of business and politics that nature can provide competitive brand opportunities and outstanding efficiencies in the majority of materials, technologies and structures has been the major incentive for innovation investment.

Biomimicry is not a new strategy, as the notebooks of Leonardo da Vinci demonstrate. Velcro, designed in 1941, was inspired by a burr that had attached itself to a dog's fur by hooks at the end of the needles. More contemporary examples range from passive architectural solutions informed by termite mounds, to dust resistant paint based on the minute protuberances that enable lotus leaves to remain dust free. Glues, self-repairing materials and biomimicry databases that hunt and store information like bees collect pollen and materials and forms that reduce drag and energy loss are part of a revolution that is transforming how things are created and used. A 2014 report by the Fermanian Business & Economic Institute predicts $1.6 trillion global output directly attributable to biomimicry by 2030.[32]

Organic Hearts and Minds

The more neuroscience reveals that the human brain is capable of extraordinary levels of multi-tasking and plasticity, the more technology and software will draw on the brain as a system and process model. But at the moment, the application of these 'neural networks' is still limited to metaphors.

Nature has an exquisite ability to evolve self-organizing and adaptable systems. Business is just beginning to learn from these as organizations recognize and try to respond to the collapse of instrumental rationality in the face of chaos. Braungart and McDonough's concept of 'fitting-ness' as a repost to the established belief that the 'fittest survive' (*Cradle to Cradle*, 2008) identifies the need for business not only to learn how to adapt and evolve but also how to anticipate and evolve.

In this respect, the future that biomimicry is creating has the promise of not only being post-classical but also post Darwin.

Wonky (Organic) Aesthetics

Industrialization is all about minimizing difference. The logic of mechanization was predicated on multiple reproductions enabling an economy of scale. Back in the age of Wedgwood and other mass production pioneers, it made sense to promote the perfection of exact reproduction as an asset. Wedgwood was competing with craft potters who created 'crocks' by hand; they did not concern themselves with minute differences as they and their customers were used to variation.

As 'standardization' became the watchword of progress, it was promoted by brand marketing and retailing as an indicator of quality. Policing imperfection through quality control normalized customer expectation and marketing to the point where every kind of product and service was subjected to the measure of modularity. The obsession with exact similarity made sense in product and service sectors where there is an obvious need for commodities like cars and computers to look and perform exactly the same as their promotion promised.

The need for standardization was less obvious for vegetables and fruit. However, the same obsession regularization evolved as farming and food processing became increasingly industrialized. Standardization began to define fresh food and significant investment was poured into ensuring that this could be achieved. Hybrid species were evolved that provided industrial food growers with the ability to predict size and colour along with faster maturation and longer shelf life.

Retail and transport began to approach racking (shelving and display) through a modular strategy that prescribed precise control over the size of the commodities that these systems could accommodate efficiently. This forced farms to impose a metrics approach to selection and classification of size, rejecting any fruit or vegetable that did not fit. Contracts typically insisted that these rejects were composted or used for animal feed rather than sold to other buyers.

Appearance was also part of the criteria that determined the judgement of fit. Asymmetry and blemishes were negatives and the regime of standardization led to further reliance on genetics and chemical control. The obsession with regularity was even enshrined in EU law, which effectively determined that asymmetric and blemished fruit or vegetables were not fit for human consumption.

Thanks to nature's infinite capacity for asymmetry and the growing influence of organizations like Slow Food, the absurdity of legislation to exclude healthy and nutritious food sources purely on the basis of 'wonky aesthetics' was partly repealed in 2008. This said, the sale of 'imperfect' apples, citrus fruit, kiwi fruit, lettuces and endives, peaches, nectarines, pears, strawberries, sweet peppers, table grapes and tomatoes are still subject to prosecution.

The advantages of standardization for big brands used to appear obvious. For one thing, it allowed them to imprint and control consumer values in an area of business open to wide competition, including local and small-scale sources of supply. Encouraging consumers to equate wonky appearance with health and nutrition concerns enabled large scale businesses to exclude sources of competition that were not prepared, or could not afford, to standardize the appearance of fruits and vegetables.

Forget Back Swans – it's the Age of the Ugly Duckling

Lobbying and media condemnation of the absurdity of the attempt to standardize nature's organic inclinations has reduced its impact. As brands begin to recognize the power of ported, there is evidence that global companies are beginning to investigate localism and other alternatives to the one size fits all regime.

A recent example of highlighting the 'value' of asymmetry developed by the French supermarket chain Intermarche shows the prospects as well as the idiocy of legislation based on a potential for endlessly unique appearance. Their strategy of translating prejudice into a 'value' opportunity involved making unique appearance heroic. Intermarche has developed a brand strategy for 'Inglorious' produce to help reduce food waste of 'undesirable' fruits and vegetables. Ugly, deformed or damaged produce has been given an isle of its own that features, 'The Grotesque Apple', 'The Ridiculous Potato', 'The Failed Lemon' and so on. The strategy increased overall store traffic by 24 percent in the first month and achieved strong sticky opportunity in social media and positive PR impact.[33] What next we wonder, vegetarian isle in a French supermarket? Now that would suggest organic evolution.

Organic Futures

Truly transformational innovation is unlikely to occur in businesses that attempt to restrict nature's wealth of organic opportunity. Those that desire to discover more effective ways of taking advantage of it will come out on top. Ironically the culture of standardization is an important reminder of the lingering influence of the cult of instrumental rationality in an age that is busily unravelling it.

Grow or Make Your Own

Fortunately, emerging technologies like 3-D printing will enable the belief that mass production = more profit to be reconciled with consumer desire for individuality. Other initiatives – for instance, buying and selling local to profitable brands that appeal directly to consumers – are allowing big brand businesses to adapt, or at least become aware of the need to.

The collapse of confidence in the 'big and uniform = better' is a reflection of the organic nature of the world in which we now live. Market dominance for bid brands is increasingly driven by two strategies: price and relevance. There is still substantial evidence of big global brands' ability to win price wars. Yet it is also clear that they are competing in a world where the numbers and tenacity of your rivals outweighs your ability to achieve the extra efficiencies required to make competitive price reduction. Cost cutting is no longer likely to deliver sustainable profit, whereas fresh thinking is.

Another aspect of growing your own is personality – although not many people have acknowledged the lack of personality in large corporate business. The evidence of consumer evacuation of anonymous efficiency is likely to become more significant as the legacy of industrialized practice become more visible – and scarier as we learn not to trust machines. Part of what makes organic integrity so attractive is that the customer feels that they're with someone who shares their concerns – who they can trust to deliver a safe and sustainable solution to their evolving needs.

American artisan organic soda maker Chris Reed provides an interesting example of this phenomenon. According to his website:

> *Reeds found that back in the early log cabin days, the pioneers couldn't go to the store and buy soft drinks – [so] they brewed their own sodas ... in their kitchens, directly from roots, spices and fruits ... Each batch of Reed's Ginger Brew is a throwback to these hand crafted brewed sodas and is made with pride ... We choose only the finest fresh herbs, roots, spices and fruits to make our brews. We won't let sugar, preservatives or artificial anything spoil Reed's natural taste.*[34]

Achieving traction at precisely the moment when the dominant soft drinks corporations are losing market share is difficult for a company that – despite its old school values – is a big operator. According to *Market Wired*, Reeds' 'Net revenues increased 10% to $8,950,000' in the first quarter of 2014 compared to the same period in 2013.

Chris Reed is clearly a part of the business success story. He goes out of his way to make his brand personal, appearing in television and social media marketing commercials without trying to disguise his hippie allegiances. Betty Crocker and Ronald McDonald may have worked in their moment; but we suspect that customers in the age of organic require something more substantial than a costume.

New Ways for Old Brains

As consumers' definitions of need are shifting from predictability to originality the potential of organic, strategy becomes increasingly obvious and opportune. The backlash against mainstream food brands appeals to our primal brain's desire for sugar, salt and fat, and has prompted us to take advantage of our instinctual fascination with novelty. The promise of endless originality represents a major competitive advantage for organic strategy. Brands are now operating in a market place that is driven by awareness that a brand's ability to achieve sustainable success is linked to its ability to develop a credible reputation for benign and relevant innovation.

Some of the Lessons that Contemporary Business Can Learn from Organic

Flexing Your Organic Muscles

Outside of its stereotypical associations, organic thinking and doing is all about the flexibility that enables brand businesses to be fleet of foot. We consistently stress the importance of agility at The Dream Café, and we are convinced this flexible response will become a major factor in a competitive world. An organic process is open ended and it promotes co-creation, adaptability and sensitivity to location and individual opportunity. Rather than assuming that colonization is simply down to scale, organic branding takes control by understanding and responding to local opportunity.

Wonky Efficiency

The myths of old-school efficiency mantras still inform the process and practices of the majority of brand businesses. The power of the efficiency myth lies in its ability to draw on the tangible and seductive evidence of cost and timesaving. In an age where a brand can fall out of favour overnight, speed of production is no longer the virtue that it once was. Brands can achieve new market opportunities more effectively by using batch strategies, rather than applying mass production – a new opportunity we have labelled 'wonky efficiency'. You will find numerous examples of wonky efficiency in street food markets, where chefs get creative in a strategy of perpetual innovation in which the unique shapes, colours, textures and aromas of that day's fresh produce inspire them to transform these sensory cues into food servings by a creative process that has more in common with art practice than the conventions of fast food production. The ingredients are celebrated for their difference rather than homogenized into something that conforms to what was served yesterday and this enables conversations and shared delight between chef, server and customer that quickly lead to viral promotion.

The Seduction of the New

The fashion cycle that drove apparel brands to promote style obsolescence through marketing strategies like seasonality is now a dominant factor in most areas of branding. This influence of obsolescence in the brand market has been encouraged by the rapid evolution of software power. Additionally, the miniaturization of its scale has encouraged tech brands to compete on performance enhancement of functional enhancement. The assumption of short shelf life has encouraged a norm of fickle allegiance among brand buyers that is beginning to influence their approach to non- tech brands. An organic brand culture will treat this phenomenon as an opportunity not a threat.

Brand-Mimicry

We've all heard that imitation is the sincerest form of flattery – yet the cult of the 'original' continues to influence consumer and analyst perceptions of value and relevance. When a brand like Apple sets the benchmark, it achieves the kind of kudos that other brands try to clone. But these brands miss the point in doing so; the products they are copying got to where they are by innovating, not merely following. The challenge and opportunity that biomimcry presents is an invitation to imitate nature in order to lead rather than follow.

While Jonathan Ives, who heads up Apple's product and interface design, has clearly learnt from Dieter Rams (the architect of Braun's 'black box' aesthetic in the 1950s and 1960s), he appears not to have noticed that minimalist evangelism is at odds with competitive branding. The argument that one size fits all smacks of an authoritarian and patronizing tone – and fails to grasp the need for inclusive branding. In an age, and a sector, where everyone is waiting eagerly for the next big thing we wonder how long it will be before a wonky communications device renders Apple's minimalist obsession to the redundant style box.

The Wonky Way

The prevailing influence of applied logic is feeling the pressure from the wonky asymmetries of applied imagination – which gives us a great opportunity to rewrite the rulebook. Agendas like spontaneity and flexibility, and local, organic and wonky are replacing the old metaphors and mantras like dominant, monolithic, prescriptive and economic. Efficiency is now an aspiration that we're better able to achieve by creating the most appropriate way – rather than the cheapest and fastest.

P

PREDICTION

Achieving accurate insight into consumers' habits and behaviours has been the aspiration of brands since the first evidence of an exchange of goods and services for income. Before the development and dominance of global brands, regional knowledge helped local businesses keep in touch with neighbours at a level of intimacy that enabled them to service and anticipate need.

Then, as now, the dreamers went further, creating and defining new needs by innovating new and unprecedented products, experiences and services. During the latter half of the twentieth century, political ideology gave way to anthropological and sociological theories about the impact of Western influence – specifically, through a negative depiction of economic infiltration and erosion of indigenous culture. Theory tended to portray an implicitly romanticized Roseau-orientated perception of the 'noble savage' as a victim of global colonial ambition. Levi-Strauss' response is mild by comparison with the conspiracy orientation of many theorists, but nevertheless assumes 'involuntary' co-option as normal:

> *A culture's chance of uniting the complex body of inventions of all sorts which we describe as a civilization depends on the number and diversity of the other cultures with which it is working out, generally involuntarily, a common strategy.*
>
> **(Claude Lévi-Strauss, *Race, History and Culture,* 1996)**

Much has changed during the second decade of the twentieth century, except perhaps in the realm of cultural theory – which, given its tendency to challenge authority, remains surprisingly smug about the authority of its interpretations. We now live in a moment when exporting is no longer dominated by the West. Creating products and services that other cultures want to buy requires brands to engage in a global discourse. Desire is just as, if not more, likely to flow west as it is to travel east or to other points of the compass.

While politically motivated theorists might explain this phenomenon as evidence of capitalism's ability to corrupt the innocent, the global discourse has created a whole new set of hurdles for brands to jump over– or crash through. And it challenges much of what the business of brands thought it knew.

The Media is Messy

Compared to other theorists, Marshall McLuhan managed to remain remarkably objective in his analysis of broadcast technology's impact on the world. McLuhan's ability to concentrate on objective observation and interpretation rather than politically motivated criticism enabled him to predict much of what we are now experiencing in the 'global village' of digital discourse. It led McLuhan to propose that:

> *The tribalizing power of the new electronic media, the way in which they return to us to the unified fields of the old oral cultures, to tribal cohesion and pre-individualist patterns of thought, is little understood.*
>
> **(Marshall McLuhan, *Media Research*, 2014)**

McLuhan analyses a period in communications history primarily defined by a relationship in which broadcasters created content that viewers viewed. While this relationship still dominates, it now has to coexist with a discourse mode that is increasingly defining our relationship with the Internet and will define whatever follows next – which is worth a moment of reflection here:

What will supersede the Internet?

Who will create it?

Is it already being developed?

Will it be organic?

The Cult of NOW-NESS

Although there are still signs of individualism during this moment of NOW-NESS, there is also an emergent global commonality in the digital realm. In this hybrid space our perception of who we are and what we value varies – often between degrees of independence from the normal conventions of narrative that physical locations continue to encourage. Predicting the future of brands will depend on our ability to capture the complexity of the floating digital universe of now-ness. However, as McLuhan pointed out, 'The present is always invisible because it's environmental. No environment is perceptible, simply because it saturates the whole field of attention.'[35]

Here then is the nub of the problem: how do we go beyond skimming the surface to identify the deep underlying themes that shape desire and ambition?

We have already revealed The Dream Café's research process and covered the need for *noticing*. But our insight is not limited to simply identifying the particular set of circumstances that have informed *relevance anxiety*, which most brands are currently suffering from. We also provide our clients with clues to the future through our ability to identify the *zeitgeist shifts* that will inform all of our desires and motives. Most of the time, the future is already here. Identifying the zeitgeist opportunity is partly about where and how you look – and it is always about the kind of questions you ask and the techniques you use to articulate those questions. The characteristics that make creative so good at insight really come into their own when it comes down to the big question of:

What is the next big thing?

Obviously there is a major difference between predicting the future and inventing it; but a creative approach to the world tends to produce insights that are about as close as you can get to a crystal ball. Their inquisitive, eclectic, divergent, narrative instincts approach to information enables them to assemble their evolving awareness into patterns that reveal latent possibilities rather than simply recording what is there.

A Now State of Mind

Penetrating and capturing the syndrome of now-ness that informs our relationship with the digital realm provides a tantalizing opportunity: it allows us to discover the urges and ambitions that determine our unfettered capacity for change and evolution.

Our concept of now-ness is different, but by no means the opposite agenda of the more reflective engagement strategy promoted by The Long Now Foundation, who are perhaps best known for the 10,000 Year Clock. Founded by, among others, Stuart Brand, publisher and activist, and the musician Brian Eno, The Long Now Foundation was established in 1996 to: 'provide a counterpoint to today's accelerating culture and help make long-term thinking more common. We hope to creatively foster responsibility in the framework of the next 10,000 years.'[36] We share their interest and belief in *noticing* and *reflecting*, as well as a belief that understanding our relationship with NOW is a starting point for any evolutionary journey.

NOW-NESS is a busy and eclectic place defined by *hyperactivity*, *multi-tasking* and *temporality*. While we participate in DIGITAL NOW-NESS we are free of the temporal constraints that typically require us to conform to some degree of orthodox progression. Of course, now-ness is not without order; it's simply based on multiple levels and types of order that can be endlessly recombined to suit temporary purposes.

Predicting anything meaningful from a context that is permanently in a state of ferment may seem counterintuitive. However, the underlying syndrome of liberation is a location where *new knowledge* resides. The Dream Café concept of now-ness allows us to access something much more significant and illuminating than the catalogue of momentary enthusiasms that characterize so much of what purports to be insight.

Ironically one of the facets of evidence that we consulted in formulating the concept of now-ness included a website called nowness.com, which provides subscribers with:

> *a daily curated destination for the culturally curious. Premiering video commissions and original series made in collaboration with the world's foremost creative thinkers; we showcase the best in digital storytelling across nine content categories from fashion and music to gastronomy, art and design.*[37]

Now-ness reflects the ability for individuals, businesses, collectives, institutions and interest groups to use the web as a site for curating and inquiry about and into what is new. It is clear that the drive to keep in touch with what is happening in the broad field of aesthetic innovation has become a major global concern for a very broad demographic. It is also clear that the concern to be perceived as an inhabitant of now-ness borders on paranoid for many individuals.

Themes, Dreams and Deep Desires

Our creative intelligence process has led us to believe that we reveal a unique set of underlying desires and needs that influence our engagement with the physical world when inhabiting now-ness. They are as follows:

Digitality

Even if we are 'switched off', the impact of digital everything impacts our sense of self. We are therefore likely to be influenced by the digital sphere's capacity to respond to our underlying needs by co-opting or evolving personas that enable us to achieve something beyond coping. We have a tendency to emulate others who possess (or appear to possess) the kind of character traits, like confidence, that enable them to look at ease in whatever environments or situations they encounter. This desire to participate in unfamiliar situations confidently explains our fascination with film, television and other character-based media forms. It also helps to explain the phenomenon of 'cosplay' and other forms of fantasy participation in which fans dress up and act out a role defined by their favourite fantasy character. Cosplay is a portent of a major zeitgeist shift defined by the increasing opportunity to hybridize our digital and physical experiences.

Access

The digital realm offers us an unprecedented opportunity to eliminate constraints like time, status, comprehension and income (relatively speaking) – barriers that only a short time ago prevented us from gaining the open-ended access to immersive opportunity that the internet now provides. Cynics would argue that our immersions are just an updated version of visiting a library and/or reading a good book or listening to a great story. (If the contemporary concern for libraries and book retailers to invest in low budget screen access are indicative, they clearly still have a lot to learn about exploiting the complementary opportunity that more intelligent integration can open up.)

At The Dream Café we notice a difference that suggests we are evolving into a new space though a strategy of hybridization. We argue that our digital experiences are very different because the addition of social interaction, movement, real-time connectivity and sound (with the promise of fully sensory engagement just around the corner) allows a level of kinetic immediacy and inclusiveness that enables us to engage in a completely different way and at a different level. The concept of 'being there' is appropriate to define this mode of immersion and it gives a whole new meaning to immersion.

Adventure

Our capacity for digital fantasy is endless, as it is what allows us to escape from – the predictability and limitations of the physical world. Participating in now-ness enables us to set out on journeys with high expectations of encountering the characteristics of an adventure including discovery, new relationships, rewards knowledge and so on. We can do things that we would not feel competent or able to do in the digital realm – which is what allows it to reward and even extend our desire for adventure. This is currently mainly owned by the theme park industry but we predict that digital adventure will become a key trope of bricks and mortar retail and eating out.

Control

As the old orders collapse, we are left without the kind of certainties that once framed our sense of purpose (or lack of it). In the digital realm, our ability to access abundant choice creates a powerful illusion of being in control and this is seductive. Gameplay is possibly the most obvious example of digital immersion's potential to transform our personality and assumptions of entitlement from modest to megalomaniac control freaks. It may not be the most positive of virtues or ambitions; however, control is a pressing need – as well as a deep desire that is nurtured and facilitated in now-ness mode that brands need to acknowledge and support. We are, relatively speaking, moments away from the ability to edit our experiences of reality. With innovations like Google glasses and 'go-pro' cameras pointing to 24/7 digital interaction with physical experience, we believe that it will not be long before we can 'rewind' our day.

Curating

In a time where we have access to so much so quickly the desire to impose some kind of order on our abundance is always present. Curating has become an important trope of now-ness. It not only allows us to bring some control to the paradox of choice and the impulse to collect; it also allows us to represent ourselves through our collections and the ways in which we curate and exhibit them. We are always simultaneously talking to friends, strangers and ourselves when we're in curating mode. We are experimenting with our tastes and testing possible lifestyles, as well as trying to impress others. Brands need to either be collection must-haves or support our desire to collect and curate. The culture of curating is at its most visible in trendy city zones. Sit in a funky café and you will see numerous examples of how people wear clothes, jewellery and other adornments in ways that are more like the control switches of an android than a fully functioning human. Observe their ritual of unpacking their technology from their bags, or pouches: this is the ritual of a curator not a user.

Currency

Relevance is a crucial motive for the inhabitants of now-ness because the whole point of occupying the *now* lies in our ability to see and be seen as a constituent of what's happening. Any brand that is pitching for now-ness cred needs 'contemporary currency' – because if you do not belong to NOW, you have no place being there. To be 'current' is the primary ambition of most brands and this is at its most obvious in tech and fashion brands, where the desperate concern to move from trend follower to trend setter defines the difference between ownership and occupation of the future. And, as interactive clothing moves from lab experiments to mainstream, our inner cyborg can soon look forward to more exposure.

Close to the Action

Space and time warping are obvious characteristics of the digital realm but 'being where the action is' is a particular characteristic of now-ness. The concern to be inside rather than outside the 'zone of relevance' is a powerful motivation for the inhabitants of now-ness. In London it is currently the area of the city called Shoreditch. This borough used to be industrially focused, but has been revamped to become the hub of new tech and creative industries and the restaurants, cafés, clubs, bars and fashion, furniture and accessory designers and retailers that service them and the visitors who come in search of cool. In many respects this and other 'cool spots' around the world are more like digital theme parks than conventional destinations. We find them on our digital maps and we report our presence in them on digital media.

Participation

The digital realm has created much more opportunity for the integration of our observation and participation needs. Brands need to engage with this dual mode of observation and participation more effectively. At the moment the dominant strategy employed by fashion brands like H&M is a rather lazy co-option of the language and visual style of celebrity publishing. The reliance on digital screens full of images of models really misses the point and the potential of connecting with our dual personality simultaneously in a way that encourages the integration of our inquisitive and acquisitive inclinations with the degree of fluidity that characterizes our online engagement.

Immediacy

Being there is a matter of urgency in cyberspace as milliseconds can separate us from the possibility of participating in the action. The ability of the digital realm to warp our senses of time and space has introduced an agenda of urgency to our state of now-ness that has the ability to create stress in our physical mode. The paradox of our different relationship with time and space in these different modes of being provides problems and opportunities for brands in equal measure. A passion for perpetual immediacy is one of the defining characteristics of successful start-up brands. The lack of rules about the how, what, when and where of displaying your brands and connecting with consumers continues to leave established brands struggling to compete.

Freedom

Now-ness provides brands with a lab space where they can experiment with servicing the different typologies of desire and need that are particular to our digital personas. When we are in a state of now-ness we free ourselves from constraints that inhibit confidence, financial access and anything else that hinders our physical selves. Testing our desire in digital mode enables brands to innovate faster and further than they might normally consider possible in the physical world. This is where brands that encourage subscription participation are winning. The serial investor Brian Lee appears to have an understanding of how to connect digital with physical by funding and launching businesses that involve celebrity participation with subscription participation. His ShoeDazzle brand represented a co-creation with reality TV celebrity Kim Kardashian. The brand provides online personal styling and retail access and members pay $479 per year, for which they receive one pair of shoes per month to consider as well as feeling connected to Kim. The brand did extraordinarily well from its launch in 2009, but recently it appears to have made a series of mistakes that have led to loss of confidences. This has not prevented Lee from launching another hugely successful start-up brand in the hugely competitive baby diaper sector, but more about The Honest Company in our conclusion.

Titivation

We are conscious of our capacity for voyeurism when we're in a state of now-ness, and are thus caught in a paradox: that is, the voyeur in us competes with our desire to be seen as players in the digital realm. Servicing our dual engagement with the desire to see and be seen offers an interesting playground for brands to develop personas that titivate. The American National Basketball Association (NBA) has invested in building connectivity so that fans get to enjoy closer participation with the players as well as enhancing their ability to engage as an audience. This is a strategy that we call 'brand choreography', which involves a social sharing culture that constantly titivates the fans' concern for competitive engagement by rewarding outstanding performance.

Multi-tasking

Our anxiety to keep up with the culture of now-ness encourages us to become committed multi-taskers. Brands must be ready to service this need to multi-task and our tendency to engage through multiple personalities. Multi-tasking is crucial to the future of media brands and it is no surprise that the Murdoch mega brand that is News Corp has been a pioneer of cross platform, multi-media access. News Corp brands like the British newspaper *The Sunday Times* now exist in a range of media formats that have enabled them to remain relevant to the different modes of participation that our 24/7 lifestyles now demand.

Illusion

The dual habitation of parallel modes of now-ness and physicality encourages us to renegotiate our relationship with illusion. Our expectations of reality are increasingly defined by the inclusion of illusion as a subset of our day-to-day experience. It is therefore crucial that brands service this expectation. Absolut Vodka has developed a series of collaborations with musicians and artists that have enabled the brand to create a perception of benign illusion on which the implications of alcohol consumption are focused on creative experience. From the 41 million views of their collaboration with Swedish House Mafia on their Absolut Greyhound promotion to the development of 'pop-up' 'Art Bars' by artist such as Ry Rocklen, this kind of collaboration allows the brand to invite modes of participation that turn illusion into reality.

Hybridization

Duality is a temporary stage of development. We expect now-ness to become the dominant trope of all of our experiences – which means that our brands need to accomplish the hybridization that will enable them to gain relevance in all modes at all times. This is where the rise of live performance is offering music brands a platform for relevance in the confused and multi-access business arena of twenty-first century music, in which live is one of the few spheres of 'pay to participate' that has not been streamed into relatively unprofitable return on investment.

Novelty

Accessing the new provides the dominant motivation for our participation in now-ness. This means that our primal brain's hardwired enthusiasm for novelty is in a state of permanent alert. Brands need to find ways of enhancing their ability to appear novel and this means that they have to find ways of doing this credibly. Coca Cola has leveraged novelty with panache through a strategy of investing in a fusion of art, technology and current issues that then create immediate media traction. From Coke bottles made from ice served on a beach in Brazil to a solar cooler set up in a remote Indian village, the brand works imaginatively to counter an increasingly cynical perception of the health dangers associated with soft drinks.

Lost in Translation

Brands assume that the old order still prevails. However, the hot news from now-ness is that it doesn't. Time was when you could stimulate desire and provide motive digitally and be reasonably assured that your bit of imprinting would enable you to assume the right response. But this simply isn't the case any longer. The problem with communicating with people who inhabit the digital realm is that the desires and needs that they discover are not exactly the same as the ones that they left behind when they entered. Talking to the people of now-ness requires a new set of cues, a whole new language and a different way of connecting the increasing gap between the digital and the physical.

Q

QUESTIONS

Bullshit and Hot Air

Brands that are serious about the need to engage in transformational innovation are generally able to make decisions without a constant need for verification. They don't question focus groups and seek approval at every stage.

Fast Company recently reported on two brands that tend to be referenced as benchmarks for the belief that 'consumer insight' is 'all bullshit and hot air created to sell consulting projects and to give insecure managers a false sense of security.' One of these was IKEA where 'the unspoken philosophy is: 'We show people the way.' According to the article, 'IKEA designers don't use user studies or user insights to create their products.' They confirmed that: 'We tried and it didn't work.' Similarly, Apple has claimed that: 'We don't waste our time asking users; we build our brand through creating great products we believe people will love.'[38]

We know that this culture of studied indifference is hard for many brand and innovation managers to believe. Those who are serially committed to consumer research make very few decisions without consulting consumer preferences. Consumer insight takes on many forms – and, depending on who is offering what version and who is buying the myriad of manifestations, purports to offer some kind of guarantee of brand reaction. The majority of insight is based on a brand manager's ability to commission research consultancies to develop knowledge about consumers' responses to their brand and its sector. They do this by posing questions that tease out and/or reveal their preferences.

Though we are passionate about questions at The Dream Café, we try to never ask what we consider to be the dumb ones. We are not fans of the research that claims to reveal brand preference based on sampling or simplistic psychological profiling.

We don't try to remain relevant via a quick buff-up based on short-term and innovation resistant insight. We understand and facilitate the need for brands to maintain the shelf life of their existing portfolio; however, we encourage our clients to dig deeper. A client that is prepared to deal with the fact that their brand's shelf life has expired is ready, in theory at least, to create the future.

We've learned from experience that relying on the illusion of contemporary credibility that poor insight affords delays the impetus to move onwards and upwards. Creative Intelligence is capable of reading the consumer's pulse – and it does so in a way that bursts the bubble that leaves so many clients wasting time and resources on futile attempts to breathe life into the dead. We develop the kinds of questions that give our clients the best of both worlds: they get to find out what people *will like* as well as what they *like now*.

Learning from the Avant-Garde

Transformational innovation comes from an ability to frame rather than ask the right questions. The Apples and Ikeas of the brand world are always asking questions. The difference is that they pose these questions to the world that surrounds them as well as to themselves. Like any brand, their various points of access tell them most of what they need to know about contemporary consumer preferences. So rather than wasting resources fretting about now, they focus on the kind of questions that will decipher tomorrow.

When the avant-garde changed the future of art and culture forever towards the end of the nineteenth century, they did so by questioning and refusing to be constrained by a tradition of form and function that had had its origins in Ancient Greece. When they tore up the classical rulebook, they exposed a gap for disruptive evolution that had been contained by habit rather than any absolute sense. They began to perceive classicism for what it was; an archaic aesthetic that had been co-opted by power and politics to represent and promote a particular version of top-down progress. The avant-garde achieved their desire to fracture the myth of timeless relevance by creating a series of questions that could not be answered by the status quo – questions like:

- Does an insistence on tradition inhibit progress?
- Is forgetting as important as remembering?

- Does imitation of the past inhibit evolution?
- Can form and style create new functions?
- Is frustration a legitimate source of innovation?
- Do contemporary forms and solutions help us to realize contemporary opportunities?
- Does resistance to change represent evidence of the need for innovation?
- Is the dominance of heritage a reflection of insecurity?
- Is the future better expressed through flux than the aesthetics of permanence?

Framing Flux

Framing and asking these kinds of questions helped to create a rationale for radical innovation that provided a degree of commonality among those pioneers who dared to challenge the status quo. During the late nineteenth century, the conditions for innovation were as paradoxical as they are today. The context of rapid technological progress was filtered through a very conservative majority view. This view essentially held that maintaining the values of the past would provide stability that would allow the elite to control – rather than be controlled by – progress.

Then, as now, the daring are in the minority – facing opposition and derision. It's therefore crucial for them to derive purpose from questions that enable them to gain purchase on the absurdity of the conditioned tendency to resist and undermine change.

The ability to frame questions that identify and confront the tendency to keep the pause button pressed firmly down is part of a way of perceiving opportunity available to anyone who dares to ask, WHY?

Being avant-garde in the twenty-first century is no longer the province of a few dissident radicals. Rather, it is an essential characteristic of brand culture – one that begins when you can develop your ability to frame the right questions.

And yes – there are right questions. Some may have been what led the most successful brands to gain and maintain their competitive edge. On the other hand, a lack of, or the wrong, questions could be at the heart of the problem that reluctant innovators face. Our experience led us to identify three common problems here:

1 Answers come before questions.
2 The questions are too simple.
3 There is only one question.

We often speculate on the questions that might have informed the evolution of those 'game-changing' brands. We then start to explore the questions that they might (or should be) asking themselves now. Here are some of our conclusions:

Apple: A Questioning Culture

Theodore Roszak – one of the most respected historians and theorists of the evolution of the information revolution – offered some insights into how the origins of the Apple brand lay with the idealist concerns for freedom of information. Roszak explains that these were developed during the counter culture movement of the 1960s and 1970s, and observed in a 1985 lecture that from Satori to Silicon Valley:

> *"many of the inventors and entrepreneurs-to-be of the rising personal computer industry were meeting along the San Francisco peninsula in funky town meetings where high-level technical problems and solutions could be swapped like backwoods lore over the cracker barrel of the general store. They adopted friendly, folksy names for their early efforts like the Itty Bitty Machine Company (an alternative IBM), or Kentucky Fried Computers, or the Homebrew Computer Club. Stephen Wozniak was one of the regulars at Homebrew, and when he looked around for a name to give his brainchild, he came up with a quaintly soft, organic identity that significantly changed the hard-edged image of high tech: the Apple. One story has it that the name was chosen by Steven Jobs in honour of the fruitarian diet he had brought back from his journey to the mystic East[39]"*

If we needed any evidence to support our thesis that radical innovation can be significantly enhanced by sitting some extraordinary creative people around a table, the legend of Homebrew provides it.

Some of the questions Apple posed at the time include:

- Why are computers so big?
- So ugly?
- So expensive?

- Why is the future of telecommunications still attached to a concept that has more in common with a tin can and a piece of string rather than viral access?
- Is functional enhancement more important than the appearance of innovation?
- Is innovation simply defined by doing things differently?
- Do we transform technology into human scale by softening it?
- Should we extend human capability or settle for making it simpler?
- Is the Internet a new species or a new landscape?
- Is mobility the future of communications?
- Should technology have a personality?
- Will the creation of a strong brand personality enable us to enable our adopters to trust in our ability to make their future better?
- Should affordability limit technological opportunity?
- How much innovation should be delivered at each stage of product or service development?

Some of the questions Apple has posed more recently include:

- Is the future multi-sensory?
- Is the 'Internet of Things' the primary location for the next phase of disruption?
- Should Apple focus on creating new functions? New products?
- Is the future of Apple entirely dependent on communication technology?
- Should we provide more content?
- What would make Apple content different?
- Can the Apple brand be extended to create additional opportunities for capital accumulation without compromising the brand's integrity?
- Are we doing enough to support and extend the concept of an Apple lifestyle?
- Are we doing enough to anticipate the tendency to define the future?
- Will Apple be the preferred brand for cyborgs?
- Are we going to develop robotic capability?

- Do we need to develop Apple environments?
- Is our design aesthetic too clinical?
- Has Apple lost its sense of humour?

Big Questions – Simple Answers

Yes, there are a lot of questions – but it's far better to have too many questions than not enough. The trick here is to spot the big question that will allow you to provide the world with something that it does not have.

Innovation that starts with answers rather than questions often gets lost. When the businesses that start their process with the answer realize that it does not match a key question, they often attempt to retrofit their solution to a need. Generally any attempt to post rationalize becomes top heavy and collapses, sprawls or dissolves – not a pretty sight. Tesco, the British owned supermarket to banking retail brand is currently fighting to retain its profitability in a complex battle for hearts and minds driven by low cost European rivals like Aldi and Lidl at one end and more upmarket food chains like Waitrose at the other. The Dream Café believes that Tesco has been partly responsible for sowing the seeds of their own dilemma by not asking (or effectively answering?) the questions of what quality and integrity could add to their brand reputation in an age of discounters, alternative food cultures, food activism and growing public and political paranoias. The brand's failure to comprehend the big agenda of responsibility and sustainability in intelligent ways is indicative of a brand that believes that you just need to display indications of commitment rather than really do it. Tesco executive Tim Mason's explanation of the strategy for a serious but recently abandoned attempt to launch a new food retail brand in the USA called 'Fresh & Easy' in 2007 is indicative of their perception problem: 'The brand is designed to be as fresh as Whole Foods, with value like a Wal-Mart, the convenience of a Walgreens and product range of a Trader Joe's', said Mr Mason. 'That leaves us with a specific edge in the market.' This desire to be all things to all people suggests a real lack of questioning to us. The retailer has continued to demonstrate its lack of awareness, perhaps most embarrassingly with its 'turn your lights into flights' campaign. Tesco customers were incentivized with £2.50 in loyalty points (clubcard) to buy energy saving light bulbs, and turn them into air miles somehow ignoring the fact that the carbon negative impact of flights would substantially outweigh the green impact of an energy saving light bulb. As customers begin to move elsewhere, Tesco is now filling its shelves with organic produce and falling over itself to raise the quality perception bar. Time will tell, but at the moment it looks like a brand trying to retrofit integrity.

Nike: Questions and Answers

Nike is one of the world's leading brands, ranked in twenty-fourth place in 'Interbrand's Best Global Brands' Top 100 list. The business we now know as Nike was launched in January 1964 as BRS, by University of Oregon track athlete Philip Knight and his coach Bill Bowerman. The business was initially focused on distributing for Japanese shoe maker Onitsuka Tiger and would probably have been no more than a way of subsidizing their passion for athletics had it not been for Bowerman's 'eureka' moment of developing a corrugated sole that he prototyped using a waffle iron and tested with Knight.

The evolution of an $8,000 per annum distribution start up to a global brand was a slow journey. However, it was informed by Knight's commitment to daring innovation in product, brand marketing, technology, style and sector at every stage of the evolution.

Nike's approach to brand innovation represents the kind of joined up thinking that makes many brands look like one-trick ponies – that which suggests that they really understand the art of framing the right questions at the right time. In a 2013 interview with *Fast Company*, Nike CEO Mark Parker confirmed that he understands the need to remain wedded to the art of radical innovation:

> *One of my fears is being this big, slow, constipated, bureaucratic company that's happy with its success … Companies fall apart when their model is so successful that it stifles thinking that challenges it.*[40]

'Just Do It'

The same profile draws on a recent example to demonstrate how, despite its monolithic scale, Nike is still capable of innovating like a group of creative radicals sitting around a café table. As its iconic 1988 logo demands, Nike seem to be able to 'just do it'. Referring to the brand's recent innovations into wearable technology, Stefan Olander, who was one of a small team that developed the 'FuelBand', recalled how they pitched an early prototype to CEO Mark Parker in 2010. 'We pulled up [our sleeves] and revealed this', he says, sliding his fingers over the white leathery Velcro bracelet marked with green calculator-like numbers. 'Mark is so consumer-driven that instinctively he said, "Go do this now." His first question was, "How fast can you build this?"'[41]

Some of the questions posed by Nike then include:

- Can a shoe be designed and produced that improves athlete's performance, and experience?
- Can the development of a brand persona support brand extension?
- What areas of human activity can performance shoes enhance?
- Will performance shoes work as a lifestyle brand?
- Can we communicate our commitment to permanent innovation through a logo?
- Will lifestyle marketing damage our reputation for performance enhancement?
- Can we create a retail experience that enables visitors to immerse themselves into the brand ethos?
- Does the adoption of Nike by the hip-hop community provide a brand extension opportunity?

Some of the questions Nike poses now are:

- Are there opportunities for brand extension in the sphere of wearable technology?
- Is it possible to 'mash-up' Nike with other brands in ways that enhance both partners?
- Should Nike do food?
- Are there opportunities for Nike to create virtual presence that will extend its brand reputation for fitness and performance?
- Are there demographic opportunities that are not being colonized?
- Should Nike invent new events?
- Are there new materials and technologies that would enable Nike to reinvent footwear and clothing?

Indeed, Nike has actually achieved that last one with their product the Nike Flyknit. Launched at the London Olympics in 2012, the Flyknit is a seamless knitted sock/shoe. Attached to different soles, depending on the performance requirement and the particular Nike brand of sports shoe. The Flyknit offers significant advantages to the user through its lightness and its ability to conform to the user's foot. Ben Shaffer, studio director at the Innovation Kitchen, Nike's R&D centre explains:

> *What makes Flyknit so truly disruptive is that it isn't a shoe – it's a way to make shoes. As the team members who spent four years developing the technology like to say, they're 'breaking the sewing machine.' The old Nike model involved cutting rolls of prewoven material into pieces, and then stitching and assembling them. But with Flyknit, a shoe's upper and tongue can be knit from polyester yarns and cables, which 'gets rid of all the unnecessary excesses.'*[41]

R

RISK

Fearing – Risk

Risk – or more accurately, the fear of it – lies at the heart of most brands' reason for avoiding the radical. Overcoming risk aversion is a permanent challenge for The Dream Café and we have developed some innovative and effective ways of doing that.

Leaping in Where Others Fear to Tread

We initially learned the art of radical innovation from artists and thinkers who got together round a café table and began to imagine alternatives to the conventions that ruled their area of practice. This inspired us to question some of the myths and rethink the ways in which business takes risks. We instinctively related to perceptions that confirmed the avant-garde as a collection of daring doers who were prepared to leap while others hesitated on the brink – operating according to T S Elliot's maxim:

> *'Only those who risk going too far can possibly find out how far they can go.'*

Learning to Love Risk

Our infatuation with risk taking as a key catalyst for radical disruptive innovation encouraged us to explore the mythology of the artist as loner. However, the more we looked at café culture, the more we noticed the Café's ability to act as fulcrum – a support mechanism that enabled those who were inclined to risk taking to share their ambitions and perceptions with others.

While the majority of brand and business books still emphasize the mythology of heroic individuals the reality of most corporate innovation strategy lies in its tendency to focus on teamwork and discourage individualism. Armed with the knowledge that teamwork can and does play a major part in enabling, we decided to strip out the loner myths and concentrate on how to mobilize teams to become more confident and daring.

Deconstructing Myths

Like his contemporaries, Nobel Prize winning author, journalist and philosopher Albert Camus spent a lot of time sharing his adventures. So when he said, 'On the ridge where the great artist moves forward, every step is an adventure, an extreme risk. In that risk, however, and only there, lies the freedom of art', he failed to acknowledge the safety net that we might call a team today.

The problem with replacing these loner myths with evidence of collective activity lies in the danger of eradicating the need for the kind of individualistic behaviour that is essential for effective innovation. Individuals bring elements like personal motivation, passionate belief in personal perception, refusal to listen to naysayers, a lack of conventional inhibitions and an ability to derive energy and commitment from negative response to innovation.

The current approach to team building tries to iron out the individual – and in doing so fails to acknowledge that behaviour often dismissed as arrogant or selfish is actually important. Replacing individual zeal with teams may achieve 'on-brand' behaviour patterns. While it can help to avoid the worst kind of belligerent behaviour, it can also create a lot of alibis for risk avoidance.

The Dream Café's Top Ten Alibis for Risk Aversion

Some the best excuses we have heard so far include:

- We need to get some more insight.
- We do not have the budget.
- Incremental innovation is less risky.
- We let our competitors take the risks, and then come in strong.

- Risk is OK for artists; they have nothing to lose.
- This does not fall into our five year plan.
- I have seen these kind of market gaps before and they go out of fashion while you're thinking about them.
- We need to know if it will work before we invest.
- 'Disruption' is just one of those buzz words.

Ownership?

When you work for a big brand, its reach – and the complexity and scale of the infrastructure that supports it – often overshadows your line of sight. Working as a cog in the wheel of brand maintenance can impede your ability to see both opportunities and threats. Corporate myopia is partly a bi-product of scale – but it is often driven by the inertia that reconciling conflicting and/or parallel interests encourages.

New brands frequently evolve with hope rather than confidence – which frequently make the entrepreneurs who started it acutely sensitive to market conditions. However, they also have a heightened sense of their responsibility. Those who actually own a smaller brand that they launched themselves tend to step up to the plate. But there are plenty of places to hide and lots of reasons to avoid taking ownership in a large brand business. Employees at big corporations will hide in the insight team, the financial planning department, the innovation team – even in the toilet – to hide from risk.

They will come up with countless reasons for avoiding ownership and not taking risks, including (but not limited to):

- It might not work.
- We do not have enough budget to test it.
- No one has heard or seen anything like it.
- Early testing identified two really negative responses.
- We would have to establish the market for it.
- You are damned if you do and damned if you don't.
- I have more to lose.

Some of the Lessons That Contemporary Business Can Learn from Other Histories of Risk

Although we focused on a particular aspect of innovation history to create our café culture thesis, we are very conscious of the other more dominant histories that continue to inform how teams are managed and the fact that they exist at all.

Our ability to facilitate teamwork begins by deconstructing some of the beliefs and practices. It continues to ensure that many teams simply do not deliver the opportunities for disruption that are organized and trusted to deliver. We are deeply suspicious of any strategy that tries to create coordinated teamwork. Teams are collections of individuals that have an ability to work together to create more than the sum of the parts. Trying to imprint your collaborators with manual mantras breeds conformity and is not likely to encourage a revolution anytime soon.

Enabling the kind of teamwork that delivers dreams requires that you accentuate individuality. You must let your team know that they can trust in your permission for them to take risks.

You are not in the Army Now

The ways in which teams are conditioned by contemporary team building strategy betrays the origins of the majority of team building theory. American mechanical engineer Frederick Winslow Taylor evolved the theory and practice of Scientific Management as a direct response to meeting the need of automated mass production in the 1880s and beyond. 'Taylorism' became inextricably linked to 'Fordism' as applied to Henry Ford's automobile assembly line strategy. Taylorism was based on the application of scientific method to identify opportunities for efficiency in all aspects of production and led to the regularization of employees' behaviour at all levels.

An extract from Taylor's *Principles of Scientific Management* confirms his belief that uniformity is the key to efficiency:

> *Under scientific management the 'initiative' of the workmen (that is, their hard work, their good-will, and their ingenuity) is obtained with absolute uniformity and to a greater extent than is possible under the old system … in the past he chose his own work and trained himself as best he could.*
>
> **(Frederick Taylor, *Principles of Scientific Management*, 1911)**

There were obvious parallels between Taylorism and the techniques used by the armed forces to imprint predictable reactions in any situation. Teamwork became obsessively focused on coordinated effort, and individualism was not encouraged. Many would argue that the ghost of Taylor no longer haunts contemporary team strategy. Yet its presence still lurks in the DNA of management thinking and doing to create a conflict of interest in enabling innovation. If you strip away the contemporary rhetoric and styling gloss of brands that are lionized as innovators, their ways of doing and thinking still reflect many of the basic tenets of Taylorism – including:

- Shared values.
- Prescribed working practices.
- Regular progress monitoring.
- Suppression of individuality.
- Specific time frames.
- The manager is the hero.
- Predictable working relationships.
- Fitting the dominant model.
- Delivering against prescribed expectations.

Lean and Keen

The notion of 'small equals beautiful' is counter-intuitive to big business. The ability to control a market through the scale of your operations has brought significant success to the global brand world's giants. Unfortunately, scale does not always work as a guarantee. As new technologies and alternative economic models and opportunities allow smaller scale operations to become increasingly competitive, large-scale operations will find themselves unable to cope with the speed of change. The solution is to set quasi-independent groups in the large-scale business so that they have the ability to act in much the same way as a start-up. Small scale does not leave anywhere to hide; in fact, it's likely to foster a greater sense of personal ownership.

Keenness is a characteristic that has gone out of fashion in big business because it can suggest naivety or immaturity – perhaps worse. In the great big manual of predictable management, a keen employee is not a team player – because they may be perceived as someone who is not operating according to the team's interests.

However, we like keen people at The Dream Café because of their ability to radiate energy, positivity and a can-do attitude. All of the above offers a great antidote to contemporary cynicism. The tendency to educate all members of staff to become team-players has made it harder to think of a small cluster of people as a team – yet we do. Small teams are one of the most efficient structures available to any business that is serious about enhancing its ability to engage in disruptive innovation. Advantages of small teams include:

- Accountability.
- Cooperation.
- Flexibility.
- Flat hierarchies.
- Shared responsibility.
- Synergy.
- Efficiency.
- Multi-tasking.
- Clarity of purpose.
- Rapid approval.
- Shared perception of success or failure.
- Shared commitment.
- Equal exposure to risk and reward.
- Rapid response.
- Common ownership.

This is why our Dream Café tables are rarely overcrowded. We think of them as *dream sized tables* – big enough to gather enough people to get into dream mode, but not big enough for anyone to hide.

Risky Teams

Size may be promoted as the answer to everything – but a mix of skills, cultures and experience really matters in creating great teams. However, we need to rewrite and rigorously edit the rules to enable teams to become more effective.

Creating an innovation team that can deliver *risky outcomes* depends on the ability to create *risky teams*. Beat poet Lawrence Ferlinghetti was not just a radical artist. He was also an entrepreneur who created and maintained the City Lights Bookshop in San Francisco in 1953 that functioned, like any great café, as a crucible. Ferlinghetti was a collaborator who was also prepared to stand up and be counted as an instigator of the risks of being a poet. His insight, in *A Coney Island of the Mind* (1958) that, 'Constantly risking absurdity and death whenever he performs above the heads of his audience, the poet, like an acrobat, climbs on rhyme to a high wire of his own making', summarizes many of the characteristics that we think are essential for a great team:

- An ability to overcome negative response.
- An ability to understand that being ahead of the game is risky.
- Tenacity.
- Humour.
- An ability to define your own vision.
- A preparedness to keep developing and promoting it until it sticks.

Developing a team that can drive an innovation process does not begin from a 'you', 'you' and 'you' selection process, and it does not start from evaluating compatibility. In some circumstances, the right disruption team should consist of one person. We recognize that we are stepping on the toes of decades of theory and practice on how to create great teams – but then again, that's what we're known for.

The Dream Café Team Recipe

Some variations on the 'traditional recipe' include an imperative to select people who:

- Have little in common.
- Possess different skills.
- Are better at thinking by doing.
- Are better at thinking than doing.
- Excel in communication skill.
- Appear to have no connection with the area that you need to innovate in.

Future Team Recipe

The key steps are as follows:

- Create an innovation strategy based on divide and rule.
- Identify someone who is a free thinker and give them some time off.
- Meet them when they are ready to suggest something.
- Do not dismiss it.
- Give them a seed fund and let them make the rules.
- Facilitate their strategy; be prepared to question it and suggests other versions but let them make the final decision.
- Let them know that they can continue to work on their own, but if they need a team you are willing to second or buy in at least four other people (as long as they are not all loyalists).
- Stand back and wait for something to smoulder.
- Catch it as soon as it begins to and do everything possible to help to fan the flames – all the while remembering that petrol is not the opposite of cold water.
- Do not undermine ownership once the idea begins to get some legs.

S

SYNERGY

The *Oxford English Dictionary* defines synergy as: 'The interaction or cooperation of two or more organisations, substances, or other agents to produce a combined effect greater than the sum of their separate effects.'

The American engineer, inventor and full time innovator R Buckminster Fuller, who coined the term 'synergetics', refined the term in the following way:

> *A dynamic state in which combined action is favoured over the difference of individual component actions.*
>
> *Behaviour of whole systems unpredicted by the behaviour of their parts taken separately, known as emergent behaviour.*
>
> *The cooperative action of two or more stimuli (or drugs), resulting in a different or greater response than that of the individual stimuli.*

Fuller understood that the myth of the lone artist, or inventor, limited the potential to discover that co-collaboration offers a more productive strategy for ensuring that the questions you define, answer and eventually develop are more likely to be relevant if they emerge from a dialectical process. Fuller's acknowledgement that stimulants can help suggests that he was aware of the avant-garde tradition of lubricating, or otherwise stimulating and encouraging, participants to share their imaginations.

The gaps in any brand strategy are the locations for lost energy and opportunity. At The Dream Café we focus on creating opportunities for synergetic connectivity that ensure our clients can expect to achieve more than the sum of the parts.

Philosophy and Synergy

Post Descartes, scientific method was generally adopted as the organizational logic that would enable rationality to rule areas that may otherwise be considered affairs of the heart – and business was one of them. This philosophical position can be broadly defined as 'modernism' (not to be confused with modern art) and was focused on reducing any opportunity for unanticipated events.

The extreme rationality of the modernist philosophy proved to be effective during the first phases of industrializations. However, as the world moved into what philosophers defined as the 'post-modern' period, it became clear to many that the attempt to predict and control limited – rather than enhanced – opportunities for innovation. For example, as Peter Engholm, a manager for Dell, the technology solutions brand, suggests:

> *Globalisation inevitably meant the fall of true modernist principles, as corporations now faced the interaction with different cultures that did not fit into the modernist paradigm with its assumptions of rationality and legitimacy.*
>
> **(Peter Engholm, *The Controversy Between Modernist and Postmodernist Views of Management Science: Is Synergy Possible?*, 2001)**

Philosophical pondering on the nature of reality began to acknowledge that the attempt to 'modernize' was doomed to failure. It neglected to acknowledge the ability of alternative versions of reality to negate, frustrate and demonstrate more effective alternatives. Post-modern theorists recognized that synergy was an essential characteristic of the state of permanent flux that they believed was a truer representation of reality.

The post-modern position may be depressing for those large scale businesses that are clinging to the wreckage of instrumental rationality. However, synergy offers a key to a future of endless opportunity for those organizations that have embraced flux as an alternative.

The Science of Synergy

Neuroscience concluded some time ago that the majority of life forms are dependent on somewhat complex synergies between sensory information and reactions.

Recent research has begun to identify an even more complex explanation of synergy – one that recognizes that human negotiation of manufacturing experiences, including hybrid digital–physical encounters opens up different needs and opportunities. A brief summary of Oxford University neuroscientist Charles Spence's research reveals the emerging awareness of cross-modal synergy:

> *His research focuses on how a better understanding of the human mind … for a radical new way of examining and understanding the senses that has major implications for the way in which we design everything from household products to mobile phones, and from the food we eat to the places in which we work and live.*[43]

Breakthroughs in the science of the mind are representative of the gradual breakdown of the inheritance of Descartes' insistence on the primacy of logic. Thankfully we are beginning to recognize the importance of synergetic engagement and celebrate the fact that the human brain is capable of multi-modal engagement and the kind of plasticity that allows us to keep in learning as long as we continue to challenge ourselves with new experiences.

Audrey Steele argues that:

> *The first fundamental state of engagement is immersive. Immersive environments provide guided, sequential experiences of stories that draw viewers into a new world where someone else serves as the producer and director of the experience. Highly immersive environments provide dynamic experiences typically involving multiple sensory pathways.*[44]

Unfortunately there appears to be a substantial gap between theory and practice, as most of the experiential marketing that we encounter leaves us wondering if anyone out there understands the difference between display design and immersion. A recent promotional strategy to promote Surf, a Unilever laundry soap brand, attempted to use shopping malls as a location to engage consumers in a digital–physical multi-sensory experience that was designed to promote the launch of new aroma choices. The temporary installation included elevators that were imbued with scent and sound and video screens. This kind of initiative is typical of the literal attempts to create immersive environments that range from the sophisticated; like the creation of a boating lake and cocktail bar on the roof of Selfridges, to the 'scratch 'n' sniff' encounters that you endure in shopping malls.

At The Dream Café we are passionate about multi-sensory opportunity, but we are also very conscious that bombarding consumers with sensory overload quickly leads to confusion and alienation.

Psychology offers useful insight into the role of synergy and cognition, particularly by its ability to demystify the process of developing innovative concepts. Psychology professor Dr Robert Epstein provides an objective appraisal of the creative process as largely a matter of reassembling fragments of knowledge that already exist. He argues that we can take 'control over the pieces of knowledge that are available to become interconnected ... in other words, discovering the opportunity for synergy.'[45]

The Nature of Synergy

Anyone with an open mind will likely connect his or her understanding of the concept with the Darwinian theory of evolution. Peter C Corning from The Institute for the Study of Complex Systems argues that:

> *Synergy – a vaguely familiar term to many of us – is actually one of the major organizing principles of the natural world. It has been a wellspring of creativity in evolution and has played central role in the evolution of complexity, from the subject matter of physics and chemistry to human societies.*
>
> **(Peter Corning, *Nature's Magic*, 2003)**

As we identified in our brief reference to biomimicry and organic opportunity in the O = Organic chapter, nature's ability to self-organize and maximize limited opportunity provides a constantly evolving source of inspiration for creative thinkers and doers. Successful brands need to act and think synergistically; the same is true for the businesses that own and develop them and their market opportunity.

Of course, this thesis is not new. Synergy is a permanent agenda for management curriculums and plays a key role in the theory and practise of marketing. Stephen R Covey has explored synergy in some detail in his book *The Seven Habits of Highly Effective People* (2004). Covey describes synergy as 'The combined effect of individuals in collaboration that exceeds the sum of their individual effects'. The basis of his argument stems from a belief that we fail to exploit our full potential, although he does not explain how most of us have been educated out of doing this.

Marketing Synergy

Walt Disney is widely accepted as being the first individual to develop synergistic marketing techniques in the 1930s. Disney licensed large numbers of manufacturers the right to use his Mickey Mouse character in products and ads. This created a win-win as it provided an important income stream while ensuring that Disney received substantial, effectively free, promotion of his films.

Digital Synergy

With the rise and rise of digital media, synergy has become a crucial feature of encouraging multi-platform engagement and it is called 'stickiness'. Stickiness is all about creating reasons to linger in the digital realm. An obvious example is offered by fashion retail websites where you are encouraged through a banner or 'popup' window to 'try' something that could coordinate with the item that you are currently browsing. The concept of stickiness has significant implications for the hybridization of digital physical engagement and intriguing potential for choreographing our journey through the Internet of Things, as digital interconnectivity between the gadgets we own, or utilize, become normalized.

Café Synergy

One of the obvious advantages of café culture lies in our ability to provide a catalyst for synergetic interaction. The fourth space concept encourages and accelerates meaningful collisions and cooperations by creating unanticipated connections. However, the nature of those connections is also important. Roger Shattuck wrote in *The Banquet Years* (1968) of the influence of socialization (fuelled by food, drink and merry making) on the invention of avant-garde innovation. The examples he quotes are full of synergetic engagement - history has confirmed that this opportunity can be endlessly reinvented.

Lori Waxman's analysis of the relationship between café culture and the development of the SoHo focused New York art scene in the early 1970s identifies how synergy made stuff happen. She quotes from the autumn 1971 issue of the vanguard art magazine *Avalanche*:

On Saturday, September 25, to mark the unofficial opening of Food, an artist-run restaurant at 127 Prince Street, free garlic soup, gumbo, chicken stew, wine, beer, and homemade breads were served to friends, gallery-goers, and passers-by until late in the evening. … FOOD, the 'restaurant commune' – as it would be dubbed by reviewers for the New York Times *and* New York *magazine – that in its heyday was a centre of life for a diverse group of artists who called Manhattan's then- gritty SoHo district their home …As artist Suzanne Harris recalls: 'We didn't need the rest of the world. Rather than attacking a system that was already there we chose to build a world of our own'.*

(**Lori Waxman,** 'The Banquet Years', 2010)

Creating Synergy

Anyone who has ever been involved in a creative process that entails embodied participation will know the difference between theoretical projections and active prototyping. When you engage in any creative activity where degrees of origination are involved, the development and application of the participant's imagination is usually fuelled by a fully sensory interactive engagement with the immediate environment. Synergetic engagement includes your interaction with the people sharing the space that you are occupying, it involves your own and others' memories and may well draw on media and a variety of other sources of potential inspiration. These active strategies typically inform a continually evolving iterative process in which tentative combinations and assemblages are constantly improved upon, because they can be evaluated in ways that theory excludes you from.

Dream Café Synergy

Synergy is fundamental to the principles and processes we embrace at The Dream Café. Indeed, Dream Café synergy:

- Underpins our ability to create unexpected and unanticipated connections between people, places, processes and projects.
- Is defined by taking people out their conventional locations and exposing them to inspirational opportunities to make new connections.

- Is discovered where food, drink, conversation and collaboration begins to happen.
- Is the point of connection between unrealized opportunity and transcendent achievement.
- Is a magic moment when disruptive concepts and strategy start to make sense to the gatekeepers.
- Is moving beyond the predictable into a destination that no-one knew existed until they discovered it.
- Allows your imagination to be applied to achieve tangible breakthroughs.
- Always takes our clients to somewhere that surpasses what they were anticipating.
- Becomes a lifetime habit so that nothing is ever the same again (in a good way).

Some of the Lessons that Contemporary Business can Learn from Synergy

Maximizing Opportunity

Rationalists and their detractors both tend to reference Aristotle positively, since many of his conclusions are open to interpretation. As an architect of applied logic, Aristotle's famous assertion that 'the whole is greater than the sum of its parts' appears to endorse his core belief in objective analysis. It could equally support the thesis that Aristotle was conflicted between the mystical traditions that still influenced thought and practice in the fourth century BC. Perhaps even more importantly, it recognized that magic depends on allowing that transformation will happen if you allow yourself to trust that it will.

Mash-UPS

One of the most effective ways of triggering a synergy opportunity is to create space for serendipity in your process. One of the numerous ways to do this is to bring like into a relationship with unlike, then allow the mash-up to draw you into combinational concepts that will inspire you to think in very different ways about the innovation opportunities that are waiting for your brand to occupy them. For example, Nike's and Apple's 'mash-ups' led to the 'fuelband' and confirms the power of culture clashes where two brands that appear to operate in very different domains reveal potent commonality. The 'fuelband' is a digital wristband that allows users to monitor their fitness. The combination of functionality and wearable technology draws on the separate heritages of Apple and Nike, while serving to extend awareness and build credibility for their individual brand extension ambitions, a win-win.

The Art of Unpredictable Outcomes

We mentioned in our advocacy of alternative approaches to team building that trusting your collaborators is a vital starting point for anyone who is serious about the need to disrupt them in order to be road ready to disrupt the marketplace. Trusting others begins with the trust to say yes to strategies that appear to be counter-intuitive, like one-person teams.

It's simple. If you really trust your own and your team's dreams, just light the touch paper, stand back – and watch the magic of synergy happen.

T

TRIPPING

The Urban Dictionary defines tripping as: 'To travel with the goal of meeting local people, as popularized by social network.' They offer other examples of usage that amused us, such as: 'We went tripping through Europe last summer and met some locals who invited us to their house parties and took us to cool underground bars.'

We have to admit that we wondered for a bit about the folks who compile these definitions. They had one we really liked: 'Going tripping beats being a tourist.'

Brands can learn a lot about the art of innovation from the various actions, practices, processes and provocations inherent in the term 'counter-culture'. The term is used to define a complex, multi-faceted and loosely connected phenomena that emerged in the United States of America during the late 1940s and began to dissolve and dissipate during the 1970s (or not, depending on how you interpret history).

We have already discussed the counter-culture's influence on Apple's evolution – and much of the importance lies in the word 'counter'. The Dream Café is fond of this word, because it summarizes the need for brands and the businesses that own them to start acting and thinking counter intuitively. Creating your own counter-culture begins with questioning everything that you thought you knew and deliberately and perversely evolving and testing concepts that your intuition tells you that you do not empathize with. This takes you into the 'risk zone' because you may well find that when you test these possibilities the target demographic does not get them either. The typical response to perceived negativity is to put the dream back in the box and close the lid. The reason why *perseverance* is crucial for breaking conventional habits lies in the fact that it gives you the opportunity to discover that its often not what you are selling but how you are selling it. The complex negotiation of the difference between what 'I say' and what 'you hear' creates the opportunity for connection. This takes us right to the heart of what branding does and why it so often under achieves, because the conversation was misunderstood long before it reached the real world.

Big business was a major catalyst for the development of a counter culture. It was seen as driving force for a top-down solution that limited choice and the adoption of alternatives. While the majority of Americans were extremely enthusiastic about the post second war explosion of material opportunity, a percentage were alienated, and it was in the fault line that counter-culture emerged in its many guises from beatniks to Hell's Angels.

Biker culture is one example of counter-culture in play. It translated the outsider and journey mythologies that evolved around the exploits of the pioneers who colonized the United States into a contemporary outlaw stereotype. It was one aspect of a much more complex rebellion that brought together the emergence of youth culture with a range of dissenting groups. The folk music revival that we have referred to as a touch point in the history of café culture was an example of how political protest against capitalism could become a major economic opportunity.

Rich Folk

The folk revival has various sources, but one major catalyst was focused on the aggressive disenfranchisement of 'Oakie' farmers by banking interests during the 1930s. That sad moment of American history spawned the hugely influential Woody Guthrie, pioneer of the 'protest song' whose mantle was taken up most successfully by Bob Dylan – a legend who needs no further discussion.

Performers, their managers and the labels who owed their popularity to their adoption of counter culture aesthetics and associations have indeed earned phenomenal amounts of money. This is compelling proof of the thesis that doing things in a way that challenges your own – as well as others' – status quo pays dividends. Bands like the Rolling Stones, who honed their bad boy image through the co-option of counter-culture iconography and mythology, have long joined the establishment. Yet they continue to cash in from music and style that was constructed to deliver an anti-establishment message. Understanding counter-culture as a business opportunity requires brands to do more than emulate the style and embrace the ability to challenge convention. Commitment that is perceived as more than a pose equates to counter culture integrity and that is where the best of both worlds lies, because it enables you encourage mainstream adoption from 'wannabe' rebels while maintaining a base level of buy-in from hard core rebels.

In 2014, the Rolling Stones band/brand are estimated to still be earning a combined income of £88 million per year, while lead singer Mick Jagger is reckoned to be currently worth $328 million. While the music business is suffering revenue loss its brand presence is still substantially dependent on the aesthetics and themes of counter culture. Our list of dependencies includes:

- Open air festivals.
- Mash-up festivals: particularly food and music.
- Fashion.
- Performance style influenced by the development of open air events.
- Alternative political values.
- Independent labels.
- Multi-platform access.
- Personal excess.
- Media reportage.
- Lifestyle dependency.

Ironically the contemporary problem of the music business may be due to too much dependency on its counter-culture heritage. The music business may just be in need of a new 'culture quake' that jolts it into an alternative future. At The Dream Café, we believe that the major shifts in strategy that have been driven by technological disruption are a reflection of a paucity of new thinking rather than innovation.

The Merry Pranksters

The Merry Pranksters provide a bridge between the beat generation and the hippie movement. Their influence helped to establish surrealist practice into everyday life. The Merry Pranksters are largely associated with the author Ken Kesey, best remembered for the novel *One Flew Over the Cuckoo's Nest* (1962). Kesey is widely cited as a major influence on the spread of LSD psychedelic experiments in performance, experiential events and art production.

In the early 1960s, San Francisco based Kesey became associated with Neal Cassady, Allen Ginsberg and Hugh Romney (better known as 'Wavy Gravy') all of whom had been regulars at the Gaslight Café. This association informed the creation of the Merry Pranksters and led to the development of experimental performances called 'Acid Tests'. As you might imagine, these involved LSD use to accentuate a 'tripping out' response to installations that incorporated strobe lights, fluorescent paint, music from a band that later became the Grateful Dead and poetry performance.

Far Out

These experiential events were enfranchised to a wider audience by a legendary bus trip that Kesey organized in 1964 with Cassady, Wavy Gravy and others from San Francisco to New York. 'The Magic Bus' trip extended the Prankster's concern to create 'art out of everyday life'. Kesey and his compatriots were incredibly influential in the development of 1960s counter culture and its impact on brands today.

They achieved this level of influence with a preparedness to explore potential beyond the boundaries of convention – which enabled them to connect with a latent need. Cynics and moral purists would argue that their promiscuity and deliberate pushing of LSD was the main factor in the adoption of their values by the wider community; however, this misses the point of the lesson that they offer innovators today.

> *Neuroscientist Gregory Berns argues that stimulants have played an important role in facilitating innovation. It is difficult to argue with his insight when he identifies what he considers to be three critical characteristics of the individuals that he terms 'iconoclasts' and their ability to productively interact with others: 'perception, courage and social skill'*
>
> **(Gregory Berns, *Iconoclasts*).**

The Electric Kool-Aid Acid Test

The Electric Kool-Aid Acid Test was the title of a book written by Tom Wolfe (1968) that documented the Magic Bus Tour. Wolfe's book was a major influence on the development of a style of reportage called the 'new journalism' that involved immersive participation.

The Electric Kool-Aid Acid Test became a kind of hippie bible. It is credited with huge influence on the enfranchisement of counter-culture lifestyle. Our drug free alternative at The Dream Café offers a version of the Merry Prankster's initiatives that could have a similar level of impact on brand innovation today.

The Dream Café's Electric Kool Test (Note Acid Free)

Step 1

Create or hire in a 'Prankster Unit' consisting of at least six different disciplines that are partly hired in and partly home grown.

Step 2

Provide them with a budget to create events that disrupt your culture.

Step 3

Make sure that the events involve immersive participation.

Step 4

Make sure the events will enable participants to have fun.

Step 5

Hire or appoint a documentary reporter to record these events.

Step 6

Review this distillation to identify clues that will allow you to connect your brands with latent needs.

Step 7

Prototype these concepts.

Step 8

Set up a 'Magic Bus' to take them out on the road and throw a party at every stopping point.

Step 9

Harvest and apply everything you learn to your brand vision.

Tripping into Your Brand Future

Our co-option of 'Merry Prankster' disruptive strategy is primarily focused on shaking up and shaking out old conventions – specifically, those that prevent you from developing and applying your imagination. *The Electric Kool-Aid Acid Test* achieved impact primarily because Kesey understood the value of personal and cultural disruption.

A simple principle of disruption is to start with you. Unless you challenge your own modus operandi you will be forever prescribing to, rather than learning from (and with), your collaborators. Kesey understood that everyone has the potential to be a collaborator – and insight that made him able to anticipate as well as influence the evolution of a whole new set of needs and practices.

When you create a disruptive event, everyone – including you – must confront something outside of his or her experience and conventional mode of engagement. This allows participants to be free – which adds to the potential for mayhem. And throwing off our inhibitions is a powerful catalyst for uncorking our imagination. At a basic level, breaking down conditioned inhibitions is the main alibi for the undeniable influence of drug taking on the creative process. However, we can achieve this effectively – and with much less destruction – by employing creative techniques, including benign humour.

The Prankster period was driven by a desire to unlock conventional behaviour in order to release individual and collective potential to think and act differently. The codes that defined and conditioned behaviour in the 1960s were a lot more oppressive than most of the ones that we have to overcome today. Nevertheless we are all victims of conventional education and professional practices.

The formality that dictates our working lives is largely a construct of learnt behaviours. Many of these habits are driven by a culture that still believes that mechanistic efficiency is the route to competitive success. The 'theme park' approach that brands are adopting only proves that many of those conventional norms are still lurking behind the scenes.

We urgently need to break down those conventions. The concept of tripping is profoundly important in doing so, because – like a vacation – we can experience it in short-stay format rather than relocating. Let's return to the 'being a tourist' definition of tripping to remember what a good vacation does: liberates us from our routine, introduces us to new experiences and unanticipated encounters, unfamiliar terrain and a multi-sensory overdrive. It gives us the time to savour the moments – and suddenly, we start to *notice*. Different experiences liberate us for a higher and holistic level of participation that can quickly achieve transcendent level of awareness.

Think about it – when was work that good? All of the joy you encounter when you go on a great holiday will occur when you undergo an 'electric kool test'. The difference is that you will come back wired to change your future, and you'll stay wired – because good disruption is as addictive as bad drugs.

Some of the Lessons that Contemporary Business Can Learn from Tripping

Do Something Different Everyday

We are all creatures of habit – with our imaginations often imprisoned in a predictable event calendar that does not leave space for 'brain exercise'. Breaking one habit a day can have a remarkable impact on our consciousness and help us to achieve Kesey's ambition of moving from objective to subjective state of awareness.

Challenge Everything

Our habitual routines generally surround us with things and people that are familiar to us – and, to a certain extent, predictable. While predictability is often a desired state, it frequently gives way to logic in lieu of imagination. Challenging the value of all that we know can be the first step to an altered consciousness. You only need to reflect on the shifts in the way we do things and the evolution of new things to do that have been created by technological innovation during the past decade to comprehend the impact of disruption. From the displacement of physical and other physically distinct interfaces with touchscreen interaction to the rise of social media we are confronted with conspicuous evidence that old habits can die.

Immerse Yourself

Experiences can be vicarious unless we are prepared to commit to them. So whatever you engage in, whether it's creating live brand experiences or dismantling the barriers that limit trans-disciplinary and cross-cultural interaction, do it at an immersive level. We feel that so many examples of experiential branding we have encountered that simply fail to deliver must have been signed off by someone who did not bother to sample them. Perhaps they were persuaded that their failure to connect was due to their inhibitions rather than a fundamental weakness in the strategy and/or execution; but whatever the alibi our experience tells us that immersion is a very effective measure of effectiveness. Participation by sitting on the edge of the pool dangling your toes in to test the water is never going to teach you how to swim, let alone win races.

Get on but Remember to Get off the Bus

Literally taking a trip away from the office to break your routine and expose yourself to the possibility of unanticipated encounters can do wonders. Of course, you have to remember upon your return to get off the bus and do something that is informed by what your experience has alerted you to.

Have Some Fun

The Merry Pranksters were not engaging in anarchy for the sake of anarchy. They really believed that humans were capable of achieving a higher level of consciousness if they could be released from the monotony of conditioned habit. The key to the jail door was fun. Fun liberates us by bringing us to back to what 'education' had tried to educate us out of – learning more about ourselves and others – because there are fewer rules.

U

UNDERSTANDING

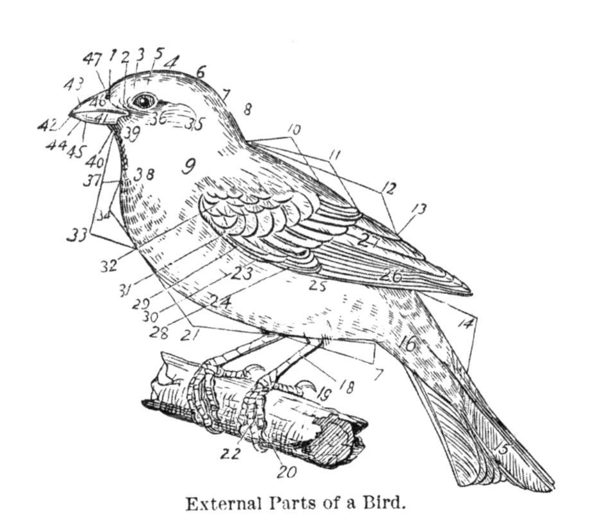

External Parts of a Bird.

One of Einstein's insights that we take to heart at The Dream Café is:

'If you can't explain it simply, you don't understand it well enough.'

We realize that daring to quote this maxim will mean that we will immediately be hoisted by our own petard for the more obscure sections of this book. All we can say in our defence is that at least we tried hard to *understand* first before we then tried hard to *explain* some pretty complex ideas.

So try as hard as we might, we recognize that defining the future requires a preparedness to grapple with abstract, obscure and even esoteric concepts, as the artist Paul Chan recently wrote in *Selected Writings 2000–2014*: 'A new world demands a new language and we are all equidistant from the potential to imagine a new language for this new world'.

Understandings

Remember – if radical innovation was easy, everyone would be doing it. So one way of reading this list is to treat it as a rehearsal. You can use it to prepare yourself for the fact that once you press the disruption button your biggest problem will be deciding which concepts to run with rather than how to create them.

We have attempted to create a list here that captures some 'understandings' essential for successful brand innovation. It is a very long list and by no means comprehensive; but our strategy here is merely to get you thinking:

- Understanding that your future may initially appear esoteric to you and your potential customers and investors.

- Understanding that innovating brand opportunities is not just about new products and services; it is about the creation of new places in which customers will need them and new reasons for needing them.
- Understanding that it can take time to develop new connections between what you know and what you need to know.
- Understanding that freedom to explore what may seem like obscure concepts.
- Understanding that any significant original concept will generally be hard to grasp.
- Understanding that when we try to gain purchase on tomorrow, our only reference point is today or yesterday.
- Understanding that our personal resistance to the untried and untested is not particularly relevant.
- Understanding that we can manage innovation, but not in conventional ways.
- Understanding that maintaining the value of our brand equity exists in what we are good at doing tomorrow rather than what we did yesterday.
- Understanding that being radical is often just defined by doing things differently.
- Understanding that teamwork is not a formula that we must endlessly repeat.
- Understanding that you already have – or can access – the knowledge you need to invent your future, if you take time to notice it.
- Understanding that the new is actually another variation of what we already know.
- Understanding that disruptive innovation begins with challenging ourselves.
- Understanding that imposing conventional rules over any activity is likely to produce conventional results.
- Understanding that if we do not invent the future someone will do it for us – and it will be theirs and not ours.
- Understanding that our reservations may be the only thing standing between us and a new and better brand future.

- Understanding that evolution often involves dismantling established ways of thinking and doing.
- Understanding that change is often painful.
- Understanding that innovation is a lifetime habit.
- Understanding that demand is now evolving faster than supply.
- Understanding that NOW-NESS is a place that we need to inhabit if we are going to own a slice of it.
- Understanding that sense is not just logic.
- Understanding that we may be able to sense the future faster than we can see it.
- Understanding that metaphors help us to reimagine what we thought we knew, and to visualize what we do not yet know.
- Understanding that the best ideas may be the hardest to recognize.
- Understanding that research is essential to innovation.
- Understanding that empirical research often requires physical contact.
- Understanding that conversations are a vital form of research and development.
- Understanding that new thinking comes out of connecting with new people and unfamiliar spheres.
- Understanding that our future may be residing somewhere else.
- Understanding that combining what we are good at with what others are good at creates new possibilities.
- Understanding that making prototypes sooner rather than later helps you to share and involve others in the development process.
- Understanding that creating the future may require you to access skills that you never though you would need.
- Understanding that new knowledge tends to be easier to develop when you are not stuck in the office.
- Understanding that the freedom to do things differently requires a different perception of time, place and responsibility.
- Understanding that difference involves getting used to alien concepts.
- Understanding that creating the future depends on your ability to explain what you have discovered to people who were not there.

- Understanding that trying to attach economic value to an idea that is not yet complete is likely to act as a disincentive.
- Understanding that the future often does not work in the same way that today does.
- Understanding that creating new needs is informed by your ability to evacuate today's needs.
- Understanding that whatever form and function your future colonizes, humans are incredibly adaptable.
- Understanding that connecting the gap between the digital and the physical NOW is a crucial location for innovation opportunity.
- Understanding that human capability has been informed by the same primal desires for the entire length of our existence on the planet.
- Understanding that humans are fascinated by opportunities for more effective engagement with the route from basic to transcendent existence.
- Understanding that the need for meaning is the permanent imponderable.
- Understanding that our need for meaning will demand and respond to new answers for as long as our species survives.
- Understanding that everything that we do not yet know about what will happen tomorrow is an opportunity waiting for us to define an answer to.
- Understanding that we only need to change our perspective by a very few degrees to get an entirely new point of view.
- Understanding that thinking is just as important as doing.
- Understanding that if you are not having fun you are doing it the wrong way.
- Understanding that if the people you are working with don't keep surprising you, they may be doing something wrong.
- Understanding that if you are not surprising the people that you work with, then you may be doing something wrong.
- Understanding that if you are not all surprising yourselves, then you may all be doing something wrong.
- Understanding that collaboration is much more than a buzz word, but is also an old fashioned concept that may need innovating.
- Understanding that there is rarely gain without pain.

- Understanding that there is no such thing as too many ideas.
- Understanding that editing is just as important as imagining.
- Understanding that a sustainable innovation culture is supported by transparency.
- Understanding that innovation is as much to do with knowing when to let go of an idea as it is to do with creating one.
- Understanding that most new ideas take time to stick.
- Understanding that a healthy innovation is committed to learning from failure.
- Understanding that the future is a strange and unfamiliar place to everyone who was not there on the day it was created.
- Understanding that most of what we need to know remains to be discovered – and understood.
- Understanding that the inquisitive part of our primal brain provides the permanent and indisputable rationale for investing in a disruptive innovation strategy.

Our brain's need for novelty is insatiable. However we may choose to intellectualize our innovation process, we are essentially in the business of supplying demand. The search for the new, untried and untested is a key source of motivation for creators as well as consumers. Artists, inventors and thinkers are always in search of a new fix; that's what keeps them innovating.

Here are some of the important things that you need to understand about employing creative people:

- It is important not to exploit their need for adventure; otherwise they will burn themselves out.
- Creative people tend to be sensitive and can easily become resentful if they believe that they are not respected.
- A lot of creative people are unorthodox and do not like to be squeezed into a modular rule-dominated environment.
- Creative people do not like to be told 'no' without a careful explanation.
- Creative people are often not good at explaining what they are thinking and can benefit from working with sensitive translators.

- Creative people often work better out of the office.
- Creative people are not great at time management and require gentle steering that allows both sides of the relationship to recognize each other's realities.
- Creative people often rush into blind alleys – and should be encouraged to do so.

Rethinking Innovation Strategy

A quote that has been attributed to both Leonardo da Vinci and Tom Peters tells us a lot about the value of understanding: 'Life is pretty simple: You do some stuff. Most fails. Some works. You do more of what works. If it works big, others quickly copy it. Then you do something else. The trick is the doing something else.'

'Doing something else' is the name of the twenty-first century game that we call business. Our current market place demands that brands who want to survive invest in perpetual innovation of their greatest asset – that is, their store of human ingenuity. As psychologist Mihaly Csikszentmihalyi has pointed out, the act of creation is essentially an act of re-creation, with ourselves as the subject of perpetual reinvention:

> *It is when we act freely, for the sake of the action itself rather than for ulterior motives, that we learn to become more than what we were. When we choose a goal and invest ourselves in it to the limits of concentration, whatever we do will be enjoyable. And once we have tasted this joy, we will redouble our efforts to taste it again. This is the way the self grows.*
>
> **(Mihaly Csikszentmihalyi, *Flow*, 1991)**

Recognizing that innovation is an essential part of the human need to create, and acknowledging its beneficial impact on the participants, offers intriguing evidence for the potential of the opportunity for brand businesses to rethink their innovation strategy.

The volatility of the contemporary market demand confirms that humans need the endless titivation that creativity can supply. As small-scale producers demonstrate the potential to feed that need from local and sustainable sources a win-win opportunity for permanent imaginative renewal for makers and users had begun to challenge the tradition of big is best. Their example suggests the possibility of a very different approach to innovation that is not obsessed with mechanistic efficiencies. The legacy of industrialization and the heritage of instrumental rationality have left business with a machine mentality in an age of organic opportunity.

Understanding the Consciousness Gap

Comic Book artist J H Williams summarizes the dilemma of creating under the clock: 'Furious activity is no substitute for understanding.'

At The Dream Café we are always exploring the potential of finding different ways of doing things. We combine our excitement with alternatives with a very pragmatic approach to business and therefore we recognize the dangers of getting carried away with romantic idealism. A critic of the 'small is beautiful thesis' may immediately shoot holes in the notion that local small-scale business can cope without the support system of big business.

What gets lost in the rush to defend the 'big is best' thesis is the fact that so many of the brands that we are in awe of began with one or two people following their inventive and entrepreneurial inclinations. Their ability to scale up their ingenuity to global might is open to anyone – which is why they now have to spend a lot of time looking over their shoulders to see who or what is coming up from where they left off. The big brands are busy buying up their small-scale competitors, but they do not necessarily understand that their competitive edge may lay in their ability to return to their roots. This is why innovation works better and faster when it operates on a human scale with a human rhythm.

Some of the Lessons that Contemporary Business Can Learn from Understanding

Understanding Takes Time

The classic 'need to innovate' wake up call for large corporate brands is provoked by the realization that a start-up has stolen a chunk of their market by doing something that they could have easily done. If they were not so busy basking in the superior track record of your brand reputation that is. This is the moment when the need to innovate suddenly becomes urgent and organizations start to throw people and money at it to take back what they have got used to considering to be their territory. Of course they often get it wrong, because their strategy is informed by panic rather than understanding.

There is worrying evidence that these businesses do not learn from their increasingly frequent failures. This may well be because the failures are a bi-product of institutionalized processes that are so normalized they are never questioned. Perhaps the problem is not the lack of innovation strategy but too much of the wrong kind? Most big brands that have been around for a while tend to treat innovation as a rational science and their process leaves very little room for risk, which means that it is concerned with removing rather than encouraging the opportunity for serendipity. Beyond a tendency to prioritize instrumental rationality as the hallmark of good innovation process you will find tiers of management that want to hear precise answers that they can pass up the chain, and that means hunches are definitely not welcome.

It's easy to understand that the chain of command finds it hard to change a way of thinking and a set of processes and protocol habits that have served them well and we are not suggesting they should because it is clear that when they try they can get it wrong. The Dream Café believes that innovation needs to develop from an environment that is geared up to develop, welcome and listen to the kind of questions that can lead to new understanding. Changing established habits takes time but once you accept that there is more than one way to innovate it is likely that you will start to think and do things differently because you have the best of both worlds: an efficient maintenance pipeline combined with fresh thinking that is not weighed down with history or protocol.

Learning by Doing

We do spend a lot of time at The Dream Café sitting at tables talking, because creating inspirational cross cultural and trans-disciplinary conversations is a very effective way of inspiring the imagination. But we also get up a lot, roll our sleeves up and encourage our participants to think by doing. We understand that you do not need to have masses of making skill to think by doing, it's just a matter of giving dimension to your dreams. Because brand managers are not encouraged or even recruited because of their ability to literally create stuff, our 'sleeves rolled up' strategy can appear either scary or irrelevant or both. Our experience tells us that provided that you have the right kind of support in the form of people who have the skills and empathy to enable others to overcome their creative hang-ups that we get quickly into the play zone. This is where the doubters suddenly find themselves having fun as they realize that giving dimension to an idea is not about creating shining objects it's all about give form to your imagination. The point at which you experience that feeling of thinking through your hands, or other moments of sensorial immersion, is where understanding of innovation opportunity really begins to gel.

Provisionalism

One of the ways that we differentiate ourselves from other agencies is through our concern to practise what we preach by exercising our own capacity to apply our imaginations. Our own creative engagement plays a big role in our strategy of creating spaces and processes that enable us and others to turn innovation into an art form. Duncan tends to do this through music and has enjoyed a parallel career as a musician and producer so look out for The Smoking Mirrors at a venue near you. In keeping with the principles of The Dream Café, Duncan's band represents a meeting of minds and discipline expertise as well as musical talent. The line-up includes a writer, an inventor and a psychotherapist. Geoff tends to make stuff that is a reflection of his commitment to provisionalism and that movement's advocacy of questions as a starting point for better questions. The provisionalist ethos is also enshrined in the beliefs that inform The Dream Café. Check out the manifesto and some examples of Geoff's collaborative practice with fellow artist Peter Jones at www.crookandjones.co.uk.

Connectivity

As Dr Robert Epstein suggests creating new knowledge involves connecting the knowledge that is out there in different ways. The reach of the Internet has encouraged everyone to believe that all the new thinking and new benchmarks you will ever need already exist in the outer reaches of the universe. The speed at which we can now access stuff that we were not aware of has had an unfortunate tendency to suggest that fulfilling our quest to be part of NOW-NESS is just a matter of logging in. At The Dream Café we spend quite a lot of our time reminding our clients that the next big idea may be already in the room. This is not to suggest that we eschew data searching, but we do encourage understanding that data are only ever one source of the need to turn up the volume on your capacity to develop and apply your imagination. We have yet to see any convincing evidence that copying what has already been done leads to a sustainable innovation strategy. The point of connectivity lies in your ability to assemble a rich and diverse set of clues, conversations and possibilities, and then to combine those together in ways that allow you define the underlying possibilities rather than copying the surface noise.

Artists do it Sitting Down

We are endlessly fascinated by the extraordinary change of consciousness that our clients achieve when we get them to sit down at our Dream Café table. It should not come as a surprise when you review what artists have achieved just by sitting down with other great thinkers. Engaging in the art of conversation is an essential component of the art of radical innovation, because it takes you out of the particular version of your sphere of knowledge that you have spent a long time developing and encourages you to compare and contrast what you know with what others know. This is the point at which you have an opportunity to understand that your knowledge is not the source of the answer of what to do, or even how to do it – but it can be a very useful starting point.

Your knowledge is a point of view and it can be liberating to recognize this because that moment of revelation can transform you from knowledge defender to a collaborator who is able to recognize that others have other ways of arriving at solutions. Somewhere in the 'collaboration zone' unpredictable combinations exist that individuals would possibly not have evolved on their own. Investing time in the art of conversation may appear to be an unnecessary indulgence to people who are programmed to think that efficiency is all about coming to the outcome in the most direct way, but anyone who has participated in our Dream Café conversations will be able to testify that 'talk is not cheap', it is a crucial strategic investment.

V

VERIFICATION

Critic and theorist Walter Benjamin stated that: 'Ideas are to objects as constellations are to stars.'

Seeing is Believing?

Walter Benjamin was driven by a concern to establish a relationship between the everyday stuff that surrounds us and the big historical markers that we use to make sense of our reality. To Benjamin the minutiae were a crucial component of how to understand the bigger picture. Rather than stripping them away, he raked through them and reconstructed a more complex and arguably more accurate depiction of reality, or its history. In order to make sense of the abundance that surrounds us, we must develop of a set of skills that are harder to apply than they are to develop. Confronted with an endless stream of data and the paradox of choice, we're apt to complain that life was simpler in a pre-technological and industrial world. But we would be kidding ourselves. In reality, our contemporary dilemmas are no different from the ones that confronted (or confront) traditional arable farmers. It just comes down to the experience that we develop into the rigour that enables us to separate the wheat from the chaff.

The Paradoxes of Choice

Though we clearly live in an age of choice, much of that choice is illusory – or so inconsequential that it uses our valuable time and cognitive ability on making decisions that we really should not be bothering with. Part of our job in writing this book is to help you focus on the bits of innovation opportunity that really matter – and guide you in making judgements about them. Verification of what to develop and what to shelve or dump is crucial in any innovation process, and verification requires decisions based on some kind of comparative judgement. The obvious problem lies in our highly imperfect ability to make unbiased and accurate judgements. As American psychologist Barry Schwartz has pointed out:

> *Our evaluation of our choices is profoundly affected by what we compare them with, including comparison with alternatives that exist only in our imaginations.*
>
> **(Barry Schwartz, *The Tyranny of Choice*, 2005)**

The Lebanese-American statistician, theorist and writer Nassim Nicholas Taleb provides a useful explanation of our tendency to misjudge when making decisions about future potential. We assume that if our actions and intentions have followed a familiar process, then the results should be predictable. But as Taleb confirms:

> *When you develop your opinions on the basis of weak evidence, you will have difficulty interpreting subsequent information that contradicts these opinions, even if this new information is obviously more accurate.*
>
> **(Nassim Taleb, *The Black Swan*, 2007)**

Collaborative innovation is beginning to challenge the false efficiency of specialist and stat driven process, because the presence of others raises the probability of divergence of opinion and evaluation criteria. Schwartz laments the increasing tendency to accelerate decision making by limiting the time for discursive reflection and a reliance on digital information rather than conversation:

> *As the number of choices we face continues to escalate and the amount of information we need escalates with it, we may find ourselves increasingly relying on secondhand information rather than on personal experience.*
>
> **(Barry Schwartz, *The Tyranny of Choice*, 2005)**

As we become more deluged with information, we tend to shore up our expertise by quoting form precedents that loosely relate to the areas of engagement that we are making judgements about. This has the advantage of making us seem knowledgeable and hints that we 'knew from the get go' that this or that example was bound to happen – and equally bound to succeed. Google will feature highly in any dot.com innovation strategy meeting and will lead to lots of hindsight awareness posing as predictive ability. In reality the only thing that we would have known then is the only thing we know now – namely that Google was entirely unpredictable as a concept and as a success story.

Asking is Not as Easy as it Seems

If we are sensible, we turn to others for verification. But we don't always react sensibly to their opinions. From our personal experience here is a typical scenario:

Us: What do you think?

Respondent: Tell me more?

Us: Well I am really just interested in whether you think it will work.

Respondent: So can I try it?

Us: No, it's still at the prototype stage.

Respondent: Well it looks OK.

Us: OK thanks.

This scenario represents some of the common mistakes that we make when we seek verification. Here is our shortlist of the things that we know we are doing wrong:

- Our first question is way too general.
- Our first question invites the need for explanation that we should have provided before we began to look for verification.
- We ask for opinion on something that cannot be verified.
- Our respondent has to default into meaningless platitudes.

How could we do this better?

- Set a timeline for each stage.
- Provide a clear introduction to what we are seeking verification on.
- Explain our criteria.

- Identify any deficiencies that will inhibit the ability to test the concept in its present state of development.
- Make sure that there is more than one respondent.
- Make sure that the respondents reflect different areas of knowledge.
- Manage the feedback process so that we are not blocking by defensive justification.

What You Get

How you obtain verification will vary according to what you are verifying and what you need to know. But of course, the more robust the feedback, the more you will learn. You must avoid setting up circles of self-congratulation; even obvious negative bias is useful as it will help you to anticipate issues that you were not aware of or did not consider to be important. This is why we deliberately create Dream Café scenarios where we involve expertise that is outside of the conventional specialism involved with a given brand. Sometimes breakthroughs come from a simple WHY question that no-one who was close to the brand would have been likely to ask.

Where You Get it

The place or places in which you locate your feedback session/s will have a profound impact on the quality and relevance of the insight that you gain. We invoke the café metaphor because it allows us to represent a climate of conviviality, socialization, constructive debate and fun. If you have ever had to suffer one of those feedback sessions sitting on a plastic chair in a cramped space with migraine inducing lighting and heating that was not designed for human comfort, then you will know why most innovation never leaves the room. Every city has an abundance of 'rent-a-room' facilitation spaces that typically come with a white board as standard. Wipe-clean laminate tables and plastic chairs complete the budget solution that appears to have been designed to ensure that imagination is unlikely to enter the room.

How You Get it

Our experience tells us that the quality threshold for the locations where you develop feedback in is crucial. That awareness has involved us taking our respondents to far-flung and provocative destinations so that everyone is out of their norm, everyone is relaxed and the experience cranks up the imagination. The other crucial aspect of feedback is doing it live whatever you are testing – and that it is witnessed, explored and verified in the zone where you intend to apply it. Architects are famously criticized for designing buildings that they would not want to live in. Anyone who has visited an architectural practice will see connections between people who develop brands that they want real people to empathize with on computer screens. Unlike the 'shift work' factory system of creative practice, architect Sunand Prasad's approach to fuelling his imagination and understanding touches on many of the habits that distinguish artists and other creative practitioners from those who think that formal process is all.

> *Immerse yourself in the worlds of the people who will use and encounter the building or place.*
>
> *Forget the building for a while. Focus totally on what people will be doing in the spaces and places you are designing – next year, in five years, in 20.*
>
> *The most inspiring thing is to see human ingenuity in action – it is all around us.*
>
> *Ask off-piste questions. What if this library were a garden? If this facade could speak, would it be cooing, swearing, silent, erudite?*
>
> **(*The Guardian*, 2 January 2012)**

Gather inquisitive and reflective people around you. The rapid bouncing back and forth of an idea can generate compelling concepts at amazing speed.

Verification Can be a Form of Collaboration

It is vital to enter any verification scenario with an open mind; it's truly the only way you will learn more. A good feedback session will simply be an extension of your collaborative process, causing some respondents to typically become part of the team who evolve the next stage of iteration.

How Artists do it

One of the reasons that we draw on the mythology of art and involve artists in our innovation processes is that artists verify differently. Although there are a lot of successful brand artists who think and act like hard-nosed entrepreneurs, others are useful to the innovation process precisely because they do not fit the norms.

Some of the Lessons that Contemporary Business Can Learn from Verification

Reflective Practice

Reflection is a well-studied process with parallels in the empirical process in science. It plays a vital role to play in any effective verification process. The simple but reasonably accurate stereotype of an artist engaging in reflective practice is captured by the artists who keep stepping back, literally, from the work that they are creating and staring at it for a long period of time. While this activity may appear to confirm the negative impression of artists as work-shy layabouts with too much time on their hands, that impression is simply wrong. The artist's time spent observing allows them to engage in a multi-faceted verification process that involves making a series of judgements that will have a profound effect on the next stage of iteration. These judgements will range from issues of colour, proportion, function, materials, techniques and form at the very least. The reflective process will also involve the artist making decisions based on their ability to imagine the piece at a further stage of development, so that they will be able to track innovation opportunity by a comparison between 'then' and 'now'. Conceptual artist Marina Abramovic confirms the potential of reflecting on tangible experience: 'After walking the Chinese Wall I realized that for the first time I had been doing a performance where the audience was not physically present. In order to transmit this experience to them I built a series of transitory objects with the idea that the audience could actively take part.'

Artists are Social Animals

We know it's a shallow stereotype but some artists seem like the typical 'party people' because they know how to relax, or appear to. But artists who are adept at verification know that their passion for capturing and translating experience lies in their understanding that if you do not fully participate, then you do not fully experience. This is what pushes them to spend time hanging around with other artists who enjoy finding out about what's going on. As dancer and choreographer Akram Khan says:

> *Go on a journey with someone who is as different to you as chalk and cheese. I am inspired by the dialogue between two different bodies, two different minds, two different ways of expressing a single idea.*
>
> **(*The Guardian,* 2 January 2012)**

Artists NOTICE

Artists who are really good at verifying excel in bringing a new perspective to the table. It may appear irrelevant, esoteric or just downright weird initially; but once you reflect on it for a bit you will recognize the value of an alternative point of view. If you are lucky you may get a multi-faceted view – but this can depend on when, where and what is being served. As contemporary artist Polly Morgan confirms: 'One of my favourite new ideas came about when I stopped to examine a weed growing in the forest I walk in' (*The Guardian*, 2 January 2012).

Artists are Practical

Artists are endlessly inquisitive, because they are driven by a desire to translate experience. This tends to lead to an awareness of how to do quite of lot of practical things – which in turn enables artists to evaluate a lot of stuff from a practical perspective. The English conceptual artist Chris Dobrowolski takes practicality to a whole other level in a career that has included the construction of a boat, plane and pedal car to explore the theme of 'Escape'. His recent book on that theme, *Escape* (2014), was reviewed as documenting 'a lifetime of ingenuity and "inner need" that will change your view of what's possible'.[46]

Artists put things in a different setting. They can be very good at taking things out of a predictable context and locating them somewhere else. This can suddenly challenge everything that you though you knew about what you have been working on. As Director Goold confirms: 'I always try to reshape my ideas in other forms: dance, soap opera, Olympic competition, children's games, pornography – anything that will keep turning them for possibilities' (*The Guardian*, 2 January 2012).

Artists work in different time zones. One of the stereotypes of artists that we have found to be kind of true – at least in some cases – is their instinctive resistance to modularity in any shape or form and that applies to time. This is likely to mean that if you go with their flow you will find that you are working better in the evening that you did in the day. Artist Susan Philipsz steps outside of conventional time frames by: 'Daydream[ing]. Give yourself plenty of time to do nothing. Train journeys are good' (*The Guardian*, 2 January 2012).

Although it may seem to be counter-intuitive, learning in the way that an artist is likely to sheds new light on what you are trying to achieve, how to achieve it and crucially how to verify it. It may take longer than you anticipated or involve working in locations that you would normally associate with relaxation – and it will probably involve unsociable hours. But the results will be worth it.

The Moment of Verification

Daniel Kahneman effectively summarizes our limitations as verifiers: 'We have a very narrow view of what is going on.' He also points out that we still have a capacity to be 'generally overconfident in our opinions and our impressions and judgments' (*Thinking Fast and Slow*, 2011). This is precisely why we deliberately extend the field of consultation and collaboration – to ensure that we know as much as we can possibly know.

W

WONDER

When was the last time you just sat and wondered?

When was the last time your mind and heart were full of wonder?

Is your brand full of wonder?

Is your Innovation strategy full of wonder?

Is your business full of wonder?

Will the world be more full of wonder when you get your next big brand innovation to market?

These are some of the questions that we ask ourselves and the clients of The Dream Café. We believe that any brand or individual that has lost the ability to possess and inspire wonder is unlikely to be a stakeholder in defining the future.

Our obsession with wonder began when we were thinking about the underlying concept for The Dream Café. We knew its role would be to act as a crucible for innovation that was built on the great disruptive historical moments inspired and facilitated by cafés. The idea of an 'Age of Wonder' is based on that revolutionary period during the late seventeenth and eighteenth centuries, which saw the birth of modernity that challenged – and substantially altered – almost every area of human endeavour.

It is no coincidence that the original 'Age of Wonder' was fuelled by the socialization opportunities and facilitation of British coffee houses, where art met science and wonder was born as the makers and shakers: 'congregated in the coffee house of London where they drank, ate, smoked and did experiments' (Jungnickel and McCormmach, Cavedish, 1996).

Historian Richard Holmes' analysis of the connection between science and romanticism during the age of scientific revolution provides a helpful portrayal of an age when people in all fields literally decided to set sail and find out what was there and what was possible. For some of them it was a journey into uncharted physical waters; and for others the space they navigated was in the lab: the studio.

Somehow voyaging on the digital realm does not quite cut it (YET!). Fortunately there is still a lot of physical landscape left to explore. Every brand needs to inspire a sense of WONDER. The Dream Café is committed to establishing a new 'Age of Wonder', providing the brands we support with a new landscape of opportunity.

The significance of the coffee house lay in its ability to attract and facilitate different individuals with the requisite knowledge, skills, ambition, confidence, tenacity and in some cases the money that enabled them to combine their DREAMS and translate them into a NEW REALITY. As such, the coffee house became the connecting point – a location for the synergies and sense of collective wonder that enabled an evolving and ever-changing interaction between thinkers and doers that inspired them to dream and deliver a new furture.

This level of commitment and daring to set sail into uncharted waters seems to be lacking in many of the brands that need to reinvent themselves. Part of our impetus in creating the Dream Café is to help to re-establish the spirit of wonder. We want to enable our clients to have those new and inspirational interactions that will allow them to take the risks that their forefathers did.

Every age has its excuses for not taking risks. But the concern about setting sail into uncharted territory in the twenty-first century hardly compares with the deep breath required in the eighteenth century. The first Age of Wonder was a period when exploration and colonization of land, sea, aesthetics, science, botany, manufacturing and transport (to name a few of the areas that were transformed) required a level of belief, tenacity and daring that is at least the equivalent of leaving a launching pad today and flying off in search of a new planet.

How to Create Wonder Brands

We cannot create 'wonder brands' simply by making a few tweaks. It requires a radical process of transformation that affects every aspect of your business. The wonder agenda begins when executives and others get their heads out of the screen and get their bodies out of the office.

As such, the first step of the journey to wonder involves freeing your mind of everything that you thought you needed to do next – and, within reason, what you did in the past. Committing to doing things differently is a good place to start. The voyages of discovery that led to the invention of the modern world were essentially journeys into the unknown. The possibility of being the first to arrive and the first to KNOW outweighed the huge risks involved.

Creating some kind of map that is comprehensive enough to accommodate an arrow that points in the direction of wonder is a four-stage process at the very least. DREAMING is a good place to start. It can provide the powerful motivation you need to break all those risk-averse habits that stand between you and a sustainable future. The best kinds of dreams are the ones that embrace those fantasies that fall into the 'IF ONLY' category.

Revolutions nearly always begin when someone asks 'why?' and tries to do something different; or utilize a different way. People who are used to following an innovation process that is created by an accumulation of carefully researched incremental awareness are beginning to find that their goals are always predictable in a good and BAD sense. The problem lies in wanting to know the answer before you set sail. On the other end of the spectrum are people who are proud not to know exactly what they want to find (and how they will use it) – they will own the future. What matters to those open-minded adventurers is their blind belief that there is always something new to find as long as you are prepared to let go and WONDER what might be there, wherever that might be.

Searching with an open mind and heart is crucial at the first stage. However, it is always important to remember that turning what you find into a brand that makes a difference is where you encounter moments where you need to get really focused. It was exactly this approach that enabled the coffee house to become the cradle of the industrial revolution, the scientific revolution and the romantic movement (to name a few of the major upheavals of tradition that started or were refined through coffee house catalyst conversations).

The conditions that most of us confront today are very similar to those that our eighteenth-century counterparts engaged with. Like the majority of them, we are locked into habitual repetitions. We operate in an environment where we believe in and continue to utilize combinations of experience, theory and habit, because they have been enshrined into the processes and conventions that are our norm.

Unlike our eighteenth-century counterparts, we have access to extraordinary resources. This means that we can go faster and further into the unknown with a much greater assurance that we will be able to return and apply what we have discovered.

Dreams and Perceptions

We always know far more than we think that we know about brands and their markets. However, we are not always aware that the depth of our knowledge may be the very thing that is blocking us from defining and grasping our future.

This is why it's so important to share our dreams with other individuals who may well know little about the precise nature of our business. Locating people who have profound knowledge and experience in other spheres can help you discover your next destination. Informing your process by chance is crucial; if we try and double guess and play it safe, we simply reinforce the journeys of predictability that we are trying to move on from.

Replicating the climate and culture that enabled coffee houses and cafés to fuel those constructive revolutions that disrupted what the world thought it knew and ushered in the future that we now occupy is a strategy that can only benefit from unanticipated encounters.

To use an eighteenth-century metaphor, you need to 'gather a head of steam' before you release the throttle and head into the unknown to discover somewhere that none of us have been to before.

New Locations and New Perception

Despite Proust's reservations, journeys to unique locations can really transform your point of view. We frequently make an analogy of the different ways in which you understand your experience of the iconic Manhattan architecture when you are standing in it and when you are viewing it from the shoreline of Brooklyn. Your immersive experience is complex and, if it's the first time, often overawing. You focus on the visible and iconic landmarks like the Empire State Building or the Chrysler Building and just marvel at the WONDER, or cringe at the CHAOS.

Midtown is a bit like the marketplace today: unpredictable, intimidating, potentially scary to the faint hearted and always chaotic. Cross the bridge and only a couple of miles way order is imposed. You can trace the archaeology of the buildings, see the symmetry of the street plans – and if you get creative, you'll notice the gaps for innovation.

Mapping Your Imagination

Giving dimension to the products of your imagination is the first step to fully applying it. Consulting a map is a classic way of confirming the route that you intend to take. But when you make a journey of the imagination the map has to be a retrospective act of clarification. In other words, you cannot define the route until you know where your imagination has taken you.

In a world where the old orders and predictabilities have broken down, or are in danger of doing so, we urgently need new maps. The maps that we have been relying on are a fiction that was designed to reassure us that the world was measurable by the laws that classicism had given us. The world is exactly like our imagination and once we understand it we can establish purchase and empathy. The landscapes of our imagination should be as fertile, exciting and open ended as the world in which they will deliver our ambition.

Script Writing

In addition to maps, storytelling is another way of capturing the potential of the journey into the future. We have affection for scripts, rather than just stories, because scripts lend themselves to performance. And when you perform a journey of ambition many of the gaps and opportunities that you have not grasped become visible.

Turning your disruptive ambition into a performance also provides you with an opportunity to give some kind of dimension to your brand concept, your territories and your communication strategy. We are not suggesting the need to create a detailed prototype of your wonder brand, but a prop that represents it can be in the form of a metaphor if it helps the plot to make sense. Acting your way into the unknown will allow you to simulate many of the opportunities and hurdles that were typical of the great Age of Wonder.

Developing a 30 minute performance with a day's preparation may appear to be a fairly shallow simulation of the age of daring do but we know that it will raise some of the key problems and key questions that only emerge when you actually 'cast-off' (or 'cast') and take the journey into the unknown.

Some of the Lessons that Contemporary Business Can Learn from Wonder

Measuring and Moving Onwards and Upwards

It's essential to create a tightly structured audit of outcomes and evaluate how far you have gotten on your journey of creating a revolution. This will enable you to become a credible player in the New Age of Wonder. The extent to which you take the art of enacting the potential of applying your imagination will determine how much you are capable of learning before you embark on that journey in real time.

Do not expect to conclude a definitive strategy. However, you can expect the key stages to be announced and put into the right order so that the future of your wonder brand is much clearer.

If it Fails, Start Again

The force of negative reaction and the strategy of suppression is usually what transforms 'velvet revolutions' into the violent upheavals that all too often follow the 'why' question. The history of brands is littered with 'riches to rags' and back again stories that include major players like Ford, Disney and FedEx. The secret of recovery appears to lay in a combination of an ability to combine self-belief with the humility of learning from your mistakes. Wendy's, the American fast food chain, went into massive decline during the 1980s as customers rejected breakfast innovations and sloppy service standards. The recovery was informed by the appointment of a 'hands-on' franchisee James Near as CEO. Near used his customer facing experience to reengineer the whole approach to service at Wendy's and developed innovations, ranging from smaller portions to an expanded salad bar, that were developed from listening to and observing customers. Ultimately the turnaround from loss to profit was driven by an obsessive commitment to quality control that was built on recognition that the people who produce and serve the food are the only ones who can translate protocol to practical outcomes and the people who eat are the only ones who can confirm if you are getting it right.

There are Other Ways of Wondering

Evoking wonder is just one of many strategies that we have developed and employ to uncork our clients' innovation potential. Time and content decisions will always begin with an analysis of our client's perception of their needs, and our view of what is possible for them – which is usually limitless.

X

X-RATED

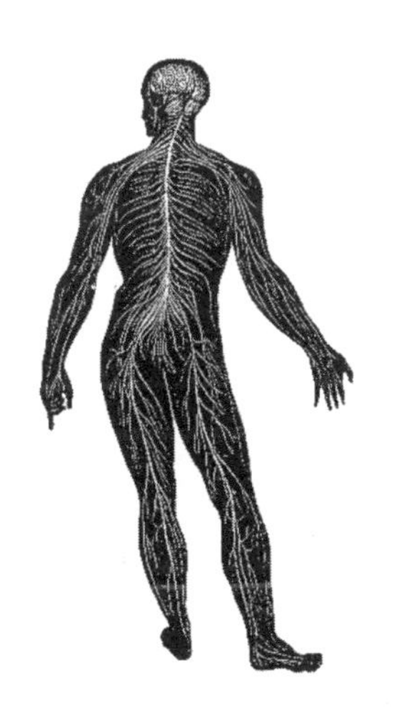

Shaken and Stirred

Shock was the most common response to the disruption that came out of the radical disruptive challenges that emanated out of those café culture moments when the world of convention was shaken, stirred and eventually transformed. The avant-garde shocked the status quo because of its willingness to cross boundaries of decency, morality and tradition. Resistance to the assault on tradition was the common spark for the defensive stance that underpinned the desire to protect and defend continuity and all that it stood for.

It wasn't difficult to offend the contemporary mores of society in the nineteenth century, as the establishment were deeply concerned about the corrupting potentials of access to new ideas and new opportunities for engagement that industrialization created. An attempt to superimpose religious piety over human instinct dominated the official institutions' response to the threat of licentious seduction.

We run into more problematic terrain where aesthetic innovation inspired a backlash. For example, the opening night of Stravinsky's 'Rite of Spring', in 1913, provoked a 'riot' – in much the same way that the deliberately provocative 'Sensation' art show in Brooklyn, in 1999, evoked an attempt by New York Mayor Rudolph W Giuliani to cut funding for the museum. Moral indignation inevitably swelled visitor numbers, but the outburst of concern confirmed the dangers of deliberate confrontation.

Bringing shock value into the realm of lived history the period from the 1950s to the present that shaped the contemporary world of branding could be seen to be just as repressive and orthodox as the nineteenth century (without even attempting to include the rise of fundamentalist positions). From the moral outrage against that 'good-ole gospel' boy Elvis doing a bit of pelvic manipulation on the *Ed Sullivan Show*, to the contemporary concern about Miley Cyrus 'twerking', the moral 'majority' does its best to remain in the driving seat.

Despite the perpetual prevalence of the moral panic button, it is clear that creative innovation that appals one generation frequently becomes the new norm. It is also clear that the time scale that it takes to translate from 'offended' to 'fan' is getting shorter by the second.

Branding with disruptive intention will always involve walking a tightrope between the conditioned concern to play it safe (usually by offering an update of the tried and tested – or risking negative response by challenging tradition).

The issues for brand innovators fall into three main territories:

1. Is it possible to build awareness by leveraging controversy?
2. Does the negativity created by the backlash negate the advantages of the spin-off of viral and largely free publicity?
3. Is there a connection between the knee-jerk capacity to be offended by art that confronts social mores and the immediate response to radical innovation?

The answers to the first two questions are provided by the history of the Benetton brand's marketing strategy and its development of 'shock advertising' in the 1980s. The 'United Colours of Benetton' campaign was devised and executed by photographer Oliviero Toscani, who was given free license by the Benetton board. The campaign that emerged under Toscani's direction used large billboards to depict images that were intended to court controversy.

Rather than featuring products, they showed images that confronted big themes like racism, AIDS and execution. The campaign both attracted record numbers of complaints and won numerous awards from the advertising industry. In 2000, an image of an execution in the state penitentiary in Missouri created a backlash that led to Toscani's resignation and Benetton's prolonged departure from 'shock advertising'. However, the brand has recently reignited their commitment to themes that matter. They launched an 'Un-Hate' campaign in 2011, which focused on challenging the tendency for global diplomacy to be led by narrow self-interest and featured ads that depicted unlikely scenarios like President Barack Obama kissing his Venezuelan counterpart Hugo Chavez. One image of Pope Benedict XVI kissing a top Egyptian imam was quickly withdrawn after a complaint from the Vatican, but not before it had confirmed Benetton's restoration of its credibility as a brand that is not afraid to cause offence by challenging negative conventions.

Luciano Benetton explained the shock strategy as evidence of corporate citizenship: 'We did not create our advertisements in order to provoke, but to make people talk, to develop citizen consciousness'. Benetton explains how he sees himself as a 'radical': 'I believe this is the only way one has in my position - to be an example myself. I paved the road trying to make people aware of participating in problems' (*The New York Times*, 16 October 2006).

The decline in the brand's USA sales following the death row execution images controversy in 2000 clearly dented Benetton's bottom line. However, the fact that their turnover was 20 times higher when Toscani resigned than it was at the time of his first shock image – and that they have returned to controversy – suggests that attention grabbing can overcome negative backlash.

The Continuity Gap

The answer to question 3 can also be partly provided by referencing the strategy of 'shock' marketing developed by Benetton. Toscani, who was quoted shortly after his resignation, felt no need to apologize: 'Art represents the edge and of course the edge can make people feel uncomfortable' (AdAge.com, 2001).

The fact that the Benetton brand is not known for its radical fashion styling raises an important issue for anyone considering brand innovation strategy. It can be argued that a brand that focuses on radical communication, rather than the development of a brand range that reflects its concern to be perceived as radical, has a persona continuity problem.

There is a widespread tendency to believe that innovative communication is representative of brand innovation. However, there's real danger of developing a rebel identity if you lack the courage to follow it through as a core ingredient of the brands that you bring to market. A joined up brand will always aspire to coherence between the perception that it promotes and the reality of its brand experience. In short: brands need to practise what they preach.

The Strategic Value of Disruption

Any brand that sets out to challenge its own and/or the market's habits and conventions is taking a risk. That said, as we have made it clear, brands do not have a choice any more: we have reached a moment where the games is called DISRUPT OR DISAPPEAR.

This chapter's theme has focused so far on the examples of brand and avant-garde strategy that have provoked relatively extreme reaction. But 'shock value' is just one part of a very diverse range of provocations that are available to brands that are not risk averse.

When we asked if there is a connection between the knee-jerk capacity to be offended by art that confronts social mores and the immediate response to radical innovation, we were deliberately highlighting the fact that the shock of the new is not reserved for intentionally shocking provocations. Rather, it is a common perception of anything that challenges convention. The first home domestic computers followed by mobiles and then smartphones have all shocked conservatives who clung to a habitual relationship with communication. However much we believe in Steve Jobs' preparedness to not ask people what they wanted but give them more than they knew they needed, the fact is that Apple has consistently redefined what we understand the limits of our ability to create and communicate.

Despite the evocation of the liberation through an escape from an Orwellian dystopia with the 1984 launch campaign, Apple has erred on the side of titivation rather than confrontation in its brand communication strategy. Reaction has ranged from cynical sneering, through indifference to, as Arthur C Clarke's summation of adoption rituals prophesies, 'I told you so' confirmations from the safety net of hindsight should never be mistaken for foresight.

Apple is now a familiar part of the communication landscape with a significant reputation for transformational innovation. The brand is defined by its commitment to perpetual innovation and has thus created its own need to continue on this path. We are more likely to be shocked by the Apple brand if it fails to innovate than we will be by what it does next to reframe the market.

The self-conscious creation of art and the promotion of an artist as brand were influentially achieved by Andy Warhol's projection of a monosyllabic persona who existed in a decadent alternative world that was populated by deviants during the early 1960s.

Warhol's engagement with creating films and video and performance enabled him to use his brand savvy to promote others most notably the rock band The Velvet Underground, who personified Warhol's brand theme of OTHERNESS and gave it a new level of attitude.

The development of Warhol's studio into what he called 'The Factory' anticipated much of what now forms the physical location ambitions for innovation brands like Google and many agencies. Warhol used the Factory as a location where the physical production of art works, performances, media production and lab like experiments could cross fertilize each other while serving to promote Warhol as an avant-garde art brand. Events like the 'Exploding Plastic Inevitable' (1966) that featured live rock music, exploding lights and film evidence his far sighted understanding that a radical brand persona, once committed to, needs to be maintained by constantly experimenting and not being afraid to fail.

Being Japanese

Fashion is an area of branding that can reasonably claim to understand the profit potential of avant-garde strategy as a loss-leader promotional tool. Fashion brands are constantly looking for designers who can provide them with NOW-NESS currency. The basic formula involves creating extreme runway collections that may never be sold but will give style direction to a mass-produced range for each season and provide brand credibility through degrees of shock factor.

Although each decade has its own crop of enfants terribles who are herded willingly from art school to the spotlight, the broader implication of using avant-garde reputation to promote national credibility remains relatively under-used.

At the start of the 1980s, Japan had no significant fashion brands in the global market place. The 1980s was a period when avant-garde style became synonymous with youth culture. Yet Japan remained so outside of the fashion hierarchy that it was not even referenced. However, this began to change as Japanese designers, who had long ago begun to think and act like artists, started to establish a foothold in the West. The emergence of a small number of new designers created the brand equivalent of a seismic shift as they began to demonstrate their unique aesthetics. Eventually, this led to a provocative design strategy that rethought and represented fashion as a means of redefining the human form. The 1981 launch of a collection by Rei Kawakubo's brand Comme des Garçons, designed by Yohji Yamamoto, was challenged in the Paris Fashion Show and reported as the equivalent of aesthetic anarchy:

> *The rigid Paris fashion crowd who was used to the glamorous haute couture long-legged runway shows was now woken up by a new, thought provoking and revolutionary vision. The models, all in radical asymmetric black garments and flat shoes, were now looking more 'like the boys'. The silhouettes that were sent down the runway were far away from the current body ideals where the norm was to accentuate the female body shape, not to hide it. The garments were deconstructed, oversized and loose fitted leaving the models to move without restraint … The collection of Comme des Garçons, was named the 'Hiroshima chic collection' by the critics … closer to conceptual art than fashion.*[47]

This was the avant-garde strategy Comme des Garçons used on the establishment by entering the fashion business's epicentre and challenging everything that has been established as the measure of 'good design'. It worked; suddenly fashion was not about style but concept!

Sell-Buy Dates

Fashion has also led the way into what is commonly known as the 'fashion-cycle', which focuses on constantly refreshing desire by promoting the concept of aesthetic redundancy. Today's shock becomes tomorrow's cast-off. In branding terms this represents an extreme form of survival strategy that would be the equivalent of killing your young to make sure that the next generation has something to feed on.

As the fashion-cycle has been adopted by or forced on almost every sector of branding, it has become problematic for the wider concern to achieve a sustainable future. The problem with a strategy of style redundancy is the impact that it has on perceptions of value as style becomes content and vice versa. As food and technology brands find themselves caught in the paradox of needing to look as if they are key components of now-ness they are also required to deliver functional guarantees at the basic level of performance and legislation compliance.

While a new campaign and/or pack design can achieve short-term relevance, the expectation of consumers for connectivity of style, content and functionality are difficult and hugely expensive to maintain. Many brands that rushed into style redundancy now find that they are the victim of emulating a strategy that works best for brands that rely on materials and production techniques that are relatively cost effective to restyle and repurpose.

Some of the Lessons that Contemporary Business Can Learn from X-Rated

Shocking Functions Have a Longer Shelf-Life than Shocking Styles

Tesla, the electric car, is currently successfully demonstrating that the redefinition of functional capability and purpose is one of the great integrity opportunities for brands. The advantage of shocking enhancements of functional capability relate to the ability to set the bar so that the new-normal falls outside of your competitors' reach for some time to come.

Tomorrow is not Today

When Comme des Garçons took on the world fashion elite they demonstrated that attempting to shock and provoke by buffing up what's already available rarely works to a brand's advantage. In fact, it can quickly alienate loyalists as well as limiting appeal to new consumers. Creating shock is and should be about thinking and doing differently. Shocking by using what makes you different will get you NOTICED and REMEMBERED – which is a good thing.

All that is not Solid Melts into Air

Brands that try to trade off notoriety that they've achieved via form without content are the equivalent of 'one hit wonders'. If you are going to go to the trouble of creating a disruptive response then it is a good idea to make sure the payoff lasts long enough for you to recoup your investment. Examples include the mobile phone brand Sony Ericsson, which had its time in the sun but simply failed to invest in maintaining its lead as competitors emerged who offered more. Sony eventually bought out Ericsson in 2011 and has re-launched as 'Sony Mobile'. Saab, the

Swedish car brand, used to have an established niche in the USA market, but its failure to innovate led to its complete loss of presence there.

Beyond NOW-NESS

The cult of NOW-NESS tends to encourage the kind of eclecticism that makes it difficult to get clarity on direction. In a brand world where retro is the next big thing meaningful shock is hard to achieve. Being prepared to challenge now-ness agendas that stylists have an endless ability to promote requires confidence and tenacity. The Spanish fashion brand Zara has developed a nimble design and supply chain that has enabled it to manage its relationship with trends. Zara has reached a point where a combination of quick response and test runs of new styles have created the potential to set their own style agenda.

Conceptual Engagement

The arts have always done better in the 'shock stakes' with conceptual work that challenges the status quo norms and values. A concept is essentially a metaphor that is waiting to be attached to something that does not yet exist, because we do not yet understand it and therefore cannot register it. Swarovski crystals have invested in creating conceptual value through commission artists and designers to create experiential instillations and one off pieces and this has leveraged the perception of the brand as the default luxury badge for a slew of products ranging from a limited edition Rolls Royce car to fashion.

YEARNING

You'll wonder where the yellow went when you brush your teeth with Pepsodent.

(Pepsodent Toothpaste, 1953)

As commercial television became a viewing option from 1955 in the UK onwards, this tagline to promote the American toothpaste brand became one of the most memorable jingles introduced. Yearning for loss of yellow plaque may not have been the theme – but the commercial appeared at a time when both sides of the Atlantic were buying into the complex cocktail of desire for fictional pasts and fantasy futures that still informs branding strategy today. The presence of an audio-visual screen in the home and aggressive but very inventive marketing accelerated the British population's widespread and relatively rapid adoption of American brands and American brand strategy.

Modernity and Nostalgia

Yearning for a golden age of innocence and achievement was a key theme of media and politics on both sides of the Atlantic. One possible influence was the need to heel the scars that the disruption of the Second World War had created; combined with the search for comfort as the new threat of the Cold War loomed. The UK's event horizon in the 1950s was initially dominated by the crowning of a young queen – an occasion harnessed by royalty and politicians as a source of pride and motivation. However, by the end of the decade, a cocktail of the optimism and the pessimism that at the time defined the 'American Dream' was mixed up with existentialist angst and kitchen sink realism.

Many people in the brand business (as well as vast numbers of consumers) yearn for what they perceive as a 'Golden Age' of branding, a nostalgia fuelled by the popularity of the American produced HBO series *Mad Men*. As fiction has an ability to do, *Mad Men* becomes part of the ever-expanding web of references that contemporary yearning is constructed from. And as our access to digital media expands, so does the opportunity to personalize our relationship with it. Even a brief review of social media sites like Facebook and Pinterest would confirm how the theme of nostalgia dominates our attempts at acting out self-definition in a public medium.

Given this level of self-election, it should come as no surprise that many contemporary brand personas reflect a similar level of reliance on nostalgia for a fictional past as means of building value connectivity.

Programmed to Learn?

Neuroscientist Dr Sedikides has pioneered a field that today includes dozens of researchers around the world using tools developed at his social psychology laboratory, including a questionnaire called the Southampton Nostalgia Scale.

According to Sedikides:

> *After a decade of study (launched in 1999), nostalgia isn't what it used to be – it's looking a lot better. Nostalgia has been shown to counteract loneliness, boredom and anxiety. It makes people more generous to strangers and more tolerant of outsiders. Couples feel closer and look happier when they're sharing nostalgic memories ... Nostalgia does have its painful side – it's a bittersweet emotion – but the net effect is to make life seem more meaningful and death less frightening. When people speak wistfully of the past, they typically become more optimistic and inspired about the future.*
>
> **(*The New York Times*, 8 July 2013)**

Jack Daniels, the American 'Tennessee Whiskey' brand, has become the world's best-selling American whiskey brand by creating a nostalgia narrative that focuses on the mythology of the founder Jack Daniels. The strength of a strategy that connects craft production heritage with contemporary relevance has enabled the brand to incorporate key moments in the history of American culture. For example, referencing Frank Sinatra's enthusiasm for the brand gave Jack Daniels access to another timelessly cool legend. This particular strategy was extended with the launch of a special edition connecting the brand to Sinatra's hundredth birthday. The signature edition was launched at Las Vegas airport with interactive stations for tasting, viewing and listening to all things Frank.

While Sinatra had a Jack–Frank relationship with the brand for over half a century the ability to connect Jack Daniels is now informed by the ability all things Rat Pack to act as shorthand for the mythology of a Golden Age. The capacity of recycled myths to sell contemporary brands underlines the power of nostalgia as brand trope.

Retro Yearning

Fashion is the most obvious example of a the brand market that is contently recycling its own history to the point where it has become increasingly difficult for teenagers to use fashion as a statement of rebellion when they are likely to be wearing the style that their parents used to try and alienate their parents. Music, transport and clothes all successfully boost their profitability by returning to retro styling. We are clearly not averse to pulling on a few heart strings ourselves at The Dream Café, as evidenced by our self-conscious allusions to avant-garde precedents that disrupted culture and society. Our reasons for alluding to the past are informed by our understanding of the deep significance of the human tendency to yearn for a Golden Age.

Deep Yearning

Our tendency to yearn for moments of our or other people's past – as well as other ages – is accelerated by the ubiquity of multimedia access that enables us to visit and experience some version of pretty well anyone, anywhere, at any time. While we could be forgiven for assuming that nostalgia is a by-product of media access, history shows us that the relationship between narrative and nostalgia is much older. The origins of the word evolved through a combination of a Greek compound, consisting of νόστος (nóstos), meaning 'homecoming' and a Homeric word, and ἄλγος (álgos), meaning 'pain, ache'. This reminds us of the primary trope of Greek mythology and the Ancient Greeks' tendency to weave fact with fiction for therapeutic effect. Later definitions attached nostalgia and yearning to melancholy, a medical concept.

The romantics seized on yearning as key trope and their sentimental imaginings about the meaning of landscape and ages of innocence in which bucolic collaborations between benign individuals anticipated socialism all contributed to our contemporary fixation with nostalgia.

Marcel Proust's monumental exercise in inventing a particular genre of 'memory fiction', 'Remembrance of Things Past', has become a primary source for our contemporary fascination with sensory memory. Neuroscience is slowly acknowledging how our multi-sensory discourse with experience acts as both a repository and a catalyst for memory and yearning fictions.

Brands' failure to understand and exploit the ways in which these stimuli are passing through the emotional seat of the brain, the amygdala, remains a mystery that we intend to resolve. Our research has confirmed a range of compelling links between the human need to yearn and a brand's need to connect at a deep emotional level. Our concern as an agency of imagination to break down the tired clichés upon which so many brands are encouraged to rely does not represent a compromise with our enthusiasm for the power of nostalgia. The true power of yearning lies in our ability to connect function with fantasy to help to develop brands that enable users to connect with therapeutic experience through the conduit of pleasure.

Luxury Yearning

Luxury branding is full of examples of the potential to weave facts and fictions into functions. The majority of luxury brands that now dominate the market trade off of faux heritage allusions. That doesn't mean these brands don't have heritage and/or integrity; it's just that they utilize the tropes of nostalgia and yearning to connect with their customer base and new adopters.

As new markets like China and India open up, the tendency to develop access by utilizing associations with nostalgia has increased. The British traditional kitchen range manufacturer Aga has successfully traded off of heritage to penetrate other European countries and is now turning its attention to emerging economies with a big push into China. Marketing theorists Atwal and Bryson's summary of the branding strategies of luxury restaurants in emerging markets rings true for a wider spectrum of brand personas:

> *They attempt to reveal the luxury in their brand through authenticity, nostalgia, exclusivity for the culturally rich segment, and also with commercial components of sensory pleasure, ambience, and décor for the socially inclined circle.*
>
> **(Atwal and Bryson, *Luxury Brands in Emerging Markets*, 2014)**

The common strategies utilized by luxury brands in all sectors to connect customers with a romantic reinvention of a fictional version of the past involve the simulation of qualities that are associated with a craft tradition of making. The classic ingredients include 'hand-made', natural materials, expensive and rare materials, and traditional forms often reference style icons from the past and/or decades that were associated with classic style like the 1920s. These allusions are enhanced by aroma and textures that summon up nostalgic associations with heritage as we demonstrated in the O = Organic chapter through our example from Chris Reed's Ginger Beer branding.

The choreography of sensory experience has been an important factor in the development of car interiors at all levels of the market, but the top-end 'luxury range' tends to be led by obsessive attention to brand experiences. Pat Oldenkamp, vice-president of design and marketing for Eagle Ottawa, a major supplier of leather for the automotive industry, confirms how nuances of aromatic detail have a major impact on customer impressions:

> *The beauty of leather is that it is very sensuous … We spend a lot of time making sure that the touch of the leather is right, the smell and colour. It's all important. It is Eagle Ottawa that provides Nuance leather for those sexy Cadillacs.*
>
> **(Sheri Daley, *Viral News*, 5 April 2014)**

Appropriated Yearning

The luxury fashion market's abundance of nostalgia has led to an interesting process of international heritage exchange. In short, different designers build their brands by co-opting another country's heritage. Armani's signature unstructured style borrows from American style legacy, while American designer Ralph Lauren draws on English classics and American heritage and heroes. An extract from the online Ralph Lauren magazine reveals the extent to which brand equity is manufactured by appropriation and association. Roberta Newman, a professor at New York University who has researched the history of baseball in advertising, explains Ralph Lauren's salute to Babe Ruth:

> *Ruth was a smart dresser. He was often depicted in well-cut suits and beautiful fur overcoats ... today all-American style is a mainstay for Polo Ralph Lauren, and the shawl-collar sweater is a staple of its spring 2014 collection. Yet many details about the sweaters worn by baseball greats past remain a mystery.*[48]

Heritage has proved to be important for emerging markets as Gilbert Ghostine, President of Diageo Asia Pacific, comments about the importance of their decision to open 'the world's first Scotch Whisky embassy', The Johnnie Walker House, in Shanghai. Ghostine said:

> *Diageo is the leading Scotch business in Asia Pacific. With the launch of the Johnnie Walker House, we are bringing Scotland to China by creating a flagship home for Scotch whisky ... Our ambition is to help Chinese consumers discover the status and rich heritage of Scotch whisky ... This is a game-changing moment for Johnnie Walker in China as we open the ultimate luxury venue for our consumers and demonstrate our commitment to building the Scotch category in China.*
>
> **(Deadline, 3 July 2009)**

Some of the Lessons that Contemporary Business Can Learn from Yearning

Authenticity

'Authenticity' is a key word for the 'back to the future' brand strategy. While it is particularly associated with the luxury movement there is a fetish level of concern in a range of areas from clothing and footwear through music to cars. Verifying and buying into retro at the authenticity level involves and is informed by 'anorak' levels of research and detail. The culture of authenticity has particular resonance for youth culture where owning, listening to and wearing examples of authentic 'retro' act as a sub-cultural signifier and allow individuals to assert their independence from the mainstream. Taylor Goddu highlights the example of JanSport who:

> *flirted with Reddit [an entertainment, social networking service and news website where registered community members can submit content, such as text posts or direct links] as a way to engage new fans as part of its 'Live Outside' campaign, including deploying street artists to literally bring its products to the streets. Those products include a refresh of a classic silhouette in its modern Heritage Series backpacks. Inspired by the original 1960s design … the product not only highlights the brand's endurance and relevancy over time, but also deftly pulls consumers back to a point of connection. Instead of running with the masses and capitalising on fads, they recognised the value in consumer rediscovery.*
>
> **(Taylor Goddu, 2014)**

Yearning for a Slice of My Action

Perhaps the last reference for faux heritage and yearning for the past should go to the Italian artist Giorgio De Chirico, who became associated with the surrealist movement. At the end of the Second World War, De Chirico's early works began to fetch stratospheric prices. Unfortunately, however, the master no longer owned any so he began to copy his own style, replicating numerous works from his youth. For instance, there are 18 known versions of his 'Disquieting Muses'. He even started backdating the copies, forging the date they were painted.

The most obvious example of imitation not amounting to flattery is the 'own-brand' phenomenon, in which leading supermarket chains create their own version of established brands that look and perform like the original but are cheaper.

Z

ZEITGEIST

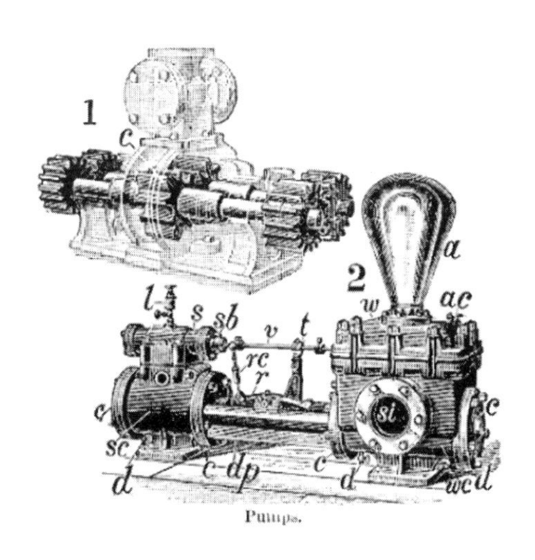

Pumps.

The *Oxford English Dictionary* defines Zeitgeist as 'The defining spirit or mood of a particular period of history as shown by the ideas and beliefs of the time.' But what makes a zeitgeist brand? We at The Dream Café believe that defining the zeitgeist should be the paramount ambition of every brand. The process involves careful balancing of consumer motivations and needs with creative strategies that enable a brand to understand and define what everyone knew they needed – but could not quite articulate.

In order to achieve zeitgeist status, companies must create a narrative – a story enables the customer to perceive your brand as the answer to their need to reconcile the paradox of their desire for security and adventure. You can achieve this by building in touch points that allow the customer to trust the brand's reliability while at the same time revelling in its ability to signify and unlock the future. The narrative must make customers feel both safe and edgy by building in balance to the brand promise. For example, coherence between the promise and mythology of the brand and its functionality is crucial. And while that need may be obvious, too many brands fail to achieve that balance – because they are obsessed by rational benefits.

The brands that define the Zeitgeist in 2014 are an eclectic mix of products and services. We've already discussed some – tech brands like Google and Apple and sports and fitness brands like Nike that use technology as a key facilitator of performance enhancement. The brands that capture and communicate the zeitgeist demonstrate an interesting set of commonalities; however, they also highlight the extraordinary level of complacency in other sectors that continue to rely on formulas developed in the twentieth century or earlier.

The failure of a number of bricks and mortar retail brands to fully comprehend the implications of online shopping is a useful reminder of the ongoing tendency for a number of established brand sectors to treat start-ups as evidence of naivety rather than threat. This failure to innovate competitively offers a shocking insight into how juggernauts can freeze in the glare of their own headlights. Online shopping has redefined the point and purpose of traditional retail; but that sector has largely not stepped up to the challenge beyond setting up their own online channels. Music retailing became of the most conspicuous casualties of the rise of online competition. The disintegration of global brands like HMV and Virgin Music Stores are indicative of the danger of failing to comprehend the nature of the future and offer lessons to other brand sectors that are currently still hanging in there. It is easy to dismiss the demise of established physical music retail brands as a combination of downloading and Amazon's and other online competitors' discounting, but the real issues was a failure to reimagine purpose and value and to innovate. It is ironic that the closure of so many major music retail stores coincided with the increasing popularity of live music performance, suggesting that customers are still looking for physical interaction with their favourite brands.

Dreaming of the Opportunity

The Dream Café has yet to work with a traditional retail brand, but we find it difficult to suppress our enthusiasm for doing so. We see huge opportunities for disrupting this sector's strategies. The following list offers a selective but indicative insight into our palate of possibilities:

- New materials.
- New functional enhancements.
- New emotional touch points.
- New narrative opportunities.
- New multi-sensory modes of establishing brand empathy.
- New values.
- New kinds of access.
- New levels of integrity.
- A hybridization of physical and digital persona.
- Capture and allow access to adventure.

The problem with reviewing what is, rather than what could be, is complicated by the need to understand that innovation is more about a state of mind than resource availability. Because tech brands are driven by the need to respond to the exponential enhancement of computing power, they tend to focus on innovation. However, that does not mean that they are going to employ radical strategy. The failure of brands like Nokia, Blackberry and Motorola to continue to define the future of mobile communications after such promising starts is a story of unhappy endings.

Our consideration of what makes a zeitgeist brand begins and ends with the theme of sustainability. In other words – once you start to innovate, you can never stop.

Coherence

Much of what we do at The Dream Café involves finding new points of connection by discovering and tuning the ways that established brands communicate their relevance to the communities that they are or could be targeting. Any business's goal is to achieve their clients ambitions for them; but our hearts and our heads tell us that the process of 'rearranging the deck chairs' is at best a holding stage. Our Creative Intelligence Process, detailed in the N = Noticing chapter, enables us to delve much deeper into consumer concerns than the 'insights' that many agencies claim. We keep discovering that the restlessness that is driving the search for the new is informed by a growing belief that the pseudo-innovation strategies many brands have adopted are merely evidence of a lack of zeitgeist commitment.

To Thine Own Self be True

Brands like Samsung become increasingly successful when they live up to their stated aims rather than cloning the competition or offering style as content solutions. The following quote, derived from Samsung's corporate website, offers a laudable example of disruptive ambition: 'Samsung is taking the world in imaginative new directions.'

When Samsung and brands like it dare to disrupt, they connect the consumer's neural network to a conclusion of coherent integrity. That is the point at which we move from price point promiscuity to a serious opportunity to develop the kind of brand loyalist empathy that Apple has been so good at creating.

Daring Do

The mythologies that inform our perceptions of the avant-garde tend to romanticize the cult of the outsider by glorifying the rebels who lived hard and died young before they achieved the success that they observed. This fixation on the tragic consequences of anti-establishment daring-do has helped to perpetuate the myth that taking creative risks leads to penury. Additionally, this mythology tends to obscure the fact that the majority of mega-rich artists and the returns achieved from investing in art have been gained from work that was produced with the intention of disruption.

There is a clear connection between daring to do things differently and long-term profitability. While the success of brands that have redefined their market rarely involves the level of personal suffering that many artists endure before their work is accepted, risk is at the heart of taking ownership of the market as opposed to being a victim of its unruly forces. Although we advocate risk taking as a safer strategy than not taking risks, we are also pragmatic enough to acknowledge the importance of experimenting before betting the bank. The Dream Café has been very successful in enabling brands to re-imagine the business they are in by working on giving dimension to metaphors. These metaphors help them see who they are and what they really are good at doing in new ways.

How Nivea Got into the Metaphor Business

Global skin and body care brand Nivea illustrates how finding out how to express the value of your brand in a new way can totally transform your stakeholders' perception of the business that they are really in. We believe that once the doors of perception are unlocked and opened, the opportunity for innovation can be let into the room.

As the summer of 2014 began, one brand that characterizes safe in its functionality dared to re-imagine its functional role as an emotional touch-point in a narrative of care. Nivea created a perfect summer storm by appearing to exist as the cutting edge of digital technology while remaining a tried and trusted old-school brand. They achieved this with a magazine insert that enabled readers to pull off a paper wrist band that had a printed radio frequency tag that could connect the wristband to a smartphone app. Attaching the paper bracelet to a child's wrist allowed parents to monitor their children's movements and even set up a safety zone that set off an alarm once their child strayed further than they thought was safe.

Although their product remained the same, Nivea dared to do something different. As such, they engaged in the kind of applied imagination exercise that is central to the processes and promise of The Dream Café. We hope for the brand's future that, now they have discovered that a physical brand can have digital functionality and a whole new narrative opportunity, they will get radical about 'Nivea The Zeitgeist Brand'. Nivea is not noted for its track record of mould-breaking innovation; but it has revealed to itself and other brands that it could become radical by reimagining its functionality. It can do so by developing and exploiting the emotional touch point opportunities waiting to be discovered. This is what defines a zeitgeist.

Some of the Lessons that Contemporary Business Can Learn from Zeitgeist

Foresight

Foresight has been prized and feared, probably in equal measure throughout history as savants have been worshipped or persecuted. The fate of the savant or seer depends on the ability of the ruling majorities to deal with an alternative point of view. Most of the time you only need to know that telling powerful people what they want to hear is risky; but people who are prepared to risk the wrath of the ruling classes have achieved most of the benchmarks that define progress.

We've had moments at The Dream Café where we have been midway through a predicative presentation and sensed the temperature in the room drop as clients' minds and hearts appear to close down. While some of these moments of negativity may well be a by-product of our failure to connect effectively, our post-mortems suggest that clients can perceive any opinion that does not reinforce their own as a threat.

However well we prepare to promote the thesis of radical innovation, we have no time for the belief that foresight is a gift that just happens to evolve in a limited number of individuals. Seers or savants are just people who do and use research techniques more effectively. They apply their skill in this sphere as an adjunct to an evolving ability to NOTICE discrete opportunities and extrapolate that potential creatively.

As notable avant-garde pioneer William S Burroughs said: 'The best way to keep something bad from happening is to see it ahead of time … and you can't see it if you refuse to face the possibility.' What made Burroughs so influential was his ability to not only see but also make the future. He did that because he refused to accept the possibility that he couldn't.

Too Much – Too Soon

It may come as a surprise to anyone who has heard us rant about the limitations of insight-led innovation strategy; but if they are surprised, it is because they did not wait long enough for us to finish our point. The position of the Dream Café is not anti-insight. However, we do despair at innovation cultures that research opportunity to death in order to create an alibi for risk aversion.

We believe that research can enable strategy to become more rather than less radical as long as the research is creatively led. Part of the problem with innovation strategy lies in pundits and practitioners' tendency to focus on the result rather than the journey.

Even a mild excursion into the history of radical innovation in the arts will lead to the conclusion that the majority of the iconic works and moments that we now cherish as evidence of paradigm shift potential came out of an accumulation of knowledge that was constructed by a slow and reflective learning process. We suspect there are examples of people who are not fools rushing in and succeeding first time, but we have not encountered any that we think are worthy of serious consideration.

The trick of successful innovation appears to lie in the ability to choreograph the contradictions of risk versus opportunity into a state of flow. Mistaking learning as an end in itself is a real issue that needs to be better managed; but the patience to wait for that moment of optimum outcome is something that has to be learnt. And that knowledge is nearly always the outcome of better iteration strategy.

Ten Reasons Why Creatives are Good at Research

There are a lot of reasons why The Dream Café calls itself an 'Imagination Agency'; but our principal motivation grows out of an absolute belief that creative individuals see the world differently from the people who have been programmed to impose order on everything they encounter. This section identifies some of the reasons why we bring the kind of edge to insight that enables innovation opportunity to be discovered and realized.

Creatives:

- Are endlessly inquisitive.
- Tend to ask questions that stimulate respondents to reveal what they really know.
- Don't like predictable outcomes.
- Have an ability to translate abstract concepts into metaphors that allow access.
- Have a passion for spontaneity.
- Connect at an emotional level.
- Love embarking on journeys of discovery.
- Are good at enabling others to take themselves seriously.
- Are good at noticing the value of stuff that others have relegated to the margins.
- Are more interested in learning than educating.

Now Versus Then

We admit that we are not great fans of retrospective in our professional lives. We feel that we have accumulated enough experience of the lazy approach to creativity that involves revamping or stitching together second hand ideas to know that it stifles originality. This said, individually we have infatuations and recurring fascinations that include old motorbikes, cars, music and people that are informed by their capacity to continue to excite our imaginations.

So are we victims of the paradox of choice? We think NOT!

We may just want it all; but we regard ourselves as beneficiaries of the PARALLELISM OF OPPORTUNITY and believe that is one of the benefits of the hybrid future.

The conflict of interest in facilitating the undoubted short-term economic expediency of recycling the past by posing it as the future is best understood by focusing on the phrase 'short term'.

CONCLUSIONS

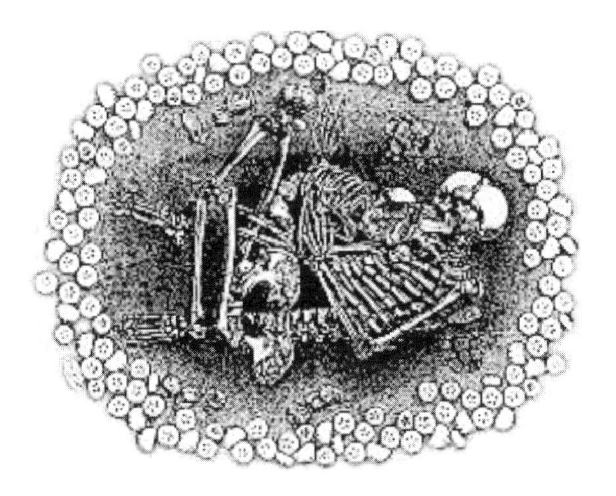

Reaching conclusions in a book that is about the future is not a good idea – as the future is always open and we want our readers to treat this book like a developing conversation rather than a panacea solution. Like any great Dream Café conversation, your ability to engage in challenging discussions with an open mind is likely to lead to enlightened conclusions, whereas entering the journey with a conclusion already in mind will take you back to where you started. The art of radical innovation lies in your ability to compare what you know and need with what others know. To us a great conclusion is more than the sum of the parts so here, for the record, is our part.

The range and calibre of people that you include in your café conversations will have a profound influence on the scope and quality of the outcomes. The kind of prejudices that dominate the worst kinds of institutionalized innovation process include simplistic stereotypes that lead to the exclusion of individuals or disciplines that are assumed to be incapable of comprehending, or adding to, a journey of logical engagement.

When the musician, poet, writer, artist, fashion icon and political commentator Polly J Harvey described herself she concluded: 'I'm an artist. I'm a creative, imaginative artist. I explore what I want, to wherever it takes me, and I don't let anything compromise that.' We have met a lot of senior brand managers who would see no point including such a maverick in their corporate strategy. Chances are, they would automatically label her as unqualified to make a valid contribution = BIG (BUT PREDICTABLE) MISTAKE.

Brands that want to lead rather than follow need to learn to do things that seem counter intuitive. They must embrace a process of learning by doing that permits you and your colleagues to make mistakes. This book has taken us on a learning journey, which has taught us more than we anticipated through its ability to introduce us to a set of questions that continue to resonate and in many ways have led to us revising the basic assumptions that underpinned what we thought we knew. We hope that it encourages you to go on a similar journey of your own.

Our book is intended to provoke reactionary feedback and we are conscious that our use of terms like 'The Age of Wonder' challenges the dominant rhetoric of branding and business. We suspect that our thesis is likely to be cynically dismissed by the gatekeepers of conventional brand innovation process but we hope that it will provide reassurance to those fellow travellers who are trying to create opportunity for alternative strategy. We were reminded in a recent conversation with a creative who had been hired in by a major global brand to stimulate new thinking that it is important to respect the fact that the 'sausage machine' is still the dominant source of income for corporate business. He had arrived from a successful career in launching disruptive digital start-ups and admitted that it took him a few years to recognize that real opportunity for change lays in the development of parallel initiatives, rather than dismantling the status quo simply because it is established and conventional. The Dream Café is not the enemy of well-honed efficiency; we know from our own business experience that the rational approach to sustaining profit has an important role to play in any well run business. Our concern to fuel debate and challenge convention is informed with a belief that any brand business that allows 'the appliance of science' to dominate all aspects of its thinking and doing is likely to fail to notice the opportunity for new growth. There is too much evidence that 'well-honed' machines are quite adept at driving off cliffs because the 'fast forward' button was permanently pressed down. The Dream Café enables brands to explore the landscape that lies beyond the straight route and our experience tells us that it is those odd diversions that are likely to provide inspiration for alternative opportunity.

As we considered the need for brand custodians to apply their imaginations to creating new market opportunity, we became more convinced than ever that the future is waiting to happen. Any learning journey involves some reflective moments – points where you take the time to notice what you have actually discovered. We don't offer our conclusions as a recipe; however, they do constitute a set of very serious recommendations. We are painfully aware of how much we have had to leave out of this book. But we are also acutely aware that our passion for addressing the need to challenge risk-averse behaviour in the branding world has been enhanced by our research and reflection process. We conclude with some 'don't do' and 'think about' suggestions for brand businesses that want to seize the mantle of the avant-garde.

The Dream Café is in the branding business for the long haul. While we delight in our ability to provide a range of brands with sticking plasters, we are always up for the risk of alienating our clients by insisting that the level of innovation that they need cannot be achieved by massaging their existing brand portfolio, which is not likely to lead to sustainable growth.

Reconciling the paradox of THEN versus NOW by investing into creating TOMORROW depends entirely on our ability to change our conditioned behaviour. We believe the main rationale for perpetuating old ideas comes by making the following mistakes:

- Excluding different points of view.
- Excluding different types of people.
- Excluding discipline expertise that does not seem to fit your norm.
- A failure to notice that prioritizing style over content leaves you vulnerable to consumers' tendency to flip from adoption to style boredom in seconds.
- A lack of understanding that creating brands that become the object of imitation is a more sustainable strategy than copying your competitors.
- Mistaking personal taste for informed judgement.
- Always prioritizing consumer perceptions over intuitive hunches.

- Believing that investing in the untried and untested is more of a risk than trying to sustain brands that are well past their 'use-by' date.
- Confusing a yearning for retro values with innovation.
- Using the past to act as a digital crib-sheet while failing to notice that the real advantage of heritage lies in its potential to reveal what has already been done so that you don't need to waste your imagination and budget on reinventing it.

Global Disruption: How Threats Become Opportunities

We are at a moment of great seismic shift in the global economy. Despite the fact that all the seismometers have been registering the kind of trembles that we should worry about, we continue to believe that the balance of power will remain with established brands. We say: THINK ON! The power brand players are going to develop in emergent (BRIC) economies like China and Mexico.

The first thing to notice about recently emerged or emerging economies that are likely to start to take control of global and local brand opportunity is that they do not look or behave like Western economies. And the difference in aesthetics, behaviours, values and other nuances that linger in these indigenous cultures is the very source of their opportunity. As we have suggested the trick of competing globally while thinking locally is to go beneath the surface and clarify what is unique, then find new ways of dimensioning that which is really different.

Art is Where the Heart is

Passion is the single most important motivator for change. It was passion for a different world with different values and different opportunities that gave birth to the original avant-garde – and it will be the same kind of passion that gives birth to the next wave. The great advantage of PASSION BRANDS is that passion is catching.

You can achieve maximum effect when customers' latent passion for meaning and relevance meets your passion for applying your imagination. This explosive combination creates definition for creator and consumer and that is the perfect feedback loop for further innovation opportunity.

We are conscious of the fact that disruption implies that shock precedes adoption. We are not suggesting that the passion model is devoid of shock value. The way to understand the shock created by a passion brand is the equivalent of meeting someone that you know you are going to have a relationship with. It is the shock of recognition of unanticipated opportunity.

Split Personalities and Hybridization

The immediate future will be owned by brands that manage to recognize and respond to the fact that the average person has at least two personalities, one that they have developed for their increasing occupation of the digital realm and the other that they have more slowly evolved to cope with their physical experience. The brands that learn to be bi-lingual and manage to communicate relevance in digi-speak as well as physi-speak will be the winners in the battle for hearts and minds.

Biospheres and Buy-Buy-Buy

The assumption about caring about our impact on the future is that it is inextricably linked to anti-capitalist ideology. However, we find this to be a very limited perspective on a win-win opportunity. There is a huge untapped market for BENIGN BRANDS that offer new and more diverse POSITIVE PARTICIPATION opportunities.

The future of well-minded business is a long way removed from the ongoing tendency to clone the language and iconography of 'counter-culture' strategies. Gone are the days when supermarket-owned brands can pretend to have anything to do with 'whole foods'– unless they can demonstrate provenance and values that have genuine integrity. The Dream Café believes that do-gooding is a WIN-WIN for the brands that dare to question the declining returns of industrialized food.

Big Worlds and Small Brands

One of the assumptions that still haunts the DNA of big business is the myth that BIG = BEAUTIFUL. At The Dream café, we believe that SMALL = THE NEW BIG. The tendency for big brand businesses to buy start-ups or small-scale businesses that point to new competitive opportunities is typically driven by the belief that some of them will open up new global potential.

The tendency to think global limits the ability of business to recognize potential and to apply it if it discovers it. We ask why big business cannot make a profit from creating and/or nurturing brands. We argue that the kind of thinking that puts global potential as the default measure of relevance dates back to an age of colonial ambition that is rapidly evaporating.

Creating Innovation Opportunity

The real art of radical innovation lies in our, and your, ability to take a range of possibilities and assemble them in a way that creates competitive opportunity. Innovation for the artist involves a process of collage in which separate elements, including pre-existing technologies, functions and strategies, are placed together in a way that enables insight into something that does not yet exist.

Noticing and Not Just Seeing

If you look at the history of radical innovation it invariably starts with someone noticing a gap in the market and this will often be influenced to look at familiar processes, rituals, experiences, objects, habitats and so on in a different way from the groups or individuals that are the typical users. This fresh perspective will inform some oblique thinking that will be likely to begin and evolve with the framing of questions around WHY, IF, WHEN, BUT agendas. These questions will help the observer reframe the familiar and beg to test its veracity against relatively uncomplicated evaluation criteria.

How Incrementalism Encourages You to Believe that Jumping on the Bandwagon Equates to Radical Innovation

At The Dream Café we are constantly reviewing what is going on out there and we thought it would be interesting to share some recent discussions. We do not want these to be read as recipes, but we provide them as evidence of the problems that anyone faces when they try to anticipate the future. We are confident that the art of radical innovation always lies outside of the trend rather than in it.

Printing Your Own

Transforming 3-D printing to £-D requires a far broader adoption of the technology by domestic consumers. We are excited by the potential of 3-D printing, but it is important to recognize that it is unlikely to become the location where the next big example of the art of radical innovation happens. Our research tells us that the relationship between big brand business and 3-D printing is still at the stage of the music industry's denial of the impact of streaming. We believe that every brand sector needs to start viewing its future through 3-D glasses. Once they see the danger of doing nothing, or not enough, they need to start thinking and doing in 3-D. Yet at the same time, every brand needs to be paying as much attention, or more, to discovering or creating the next big thing. 3-D will become a self-fulfilling-prophecy, but the leap of faith that led to its development as a technology was achieved quite a long time ago and now everyone is trying to apply it. Like a gold rush there will be few winners, but there will also be a lot of losers, the people who bet everything on hope rather than strategy.

Stimulants and Opportunities

It would be an oversight to conclude a book on The Dream Café without mentioning coffee and other stimulants, but our interest is not limited to the concept of refreshment as an innovation lubricator we believe that refreshment provides a significant sphere of innovation opportunity. When it comes to defining examples of the art of radical innovation it is clear that coffee has a lot to teach us. From a position of relatively complacent stasis it has gone through a series of disruptive moments during the last two decades. Compared to other beverages, coffee still leads in the re-imagination and re-invention stakes; beer, spirits and soft drinks still have a lot to learn from coffee. That said there is evidence of some complacency creeping back into the coffee sector as brands that have ridden the storm start to sit back and capitalize on their assumption that coffee has established the new normal. We say BIG MISTAKE! The future of coffee, like any other refreshment solution, will be driven by a whole set of new technological, political and social innovations that are only just beginning to evolve like new understandings of the body clock. The more that technology becomes a key source of the criteria that we consult before we make a choice, the more it will be programmed to influence of choice of refreshment on the grounds of wellbeing as well as habit or fashion.

Borrowed Time

The tendency to hire, borrow and swap access to anything from cars to skill will have a huge impact on brands in the twenty-first century. The brands that will succeed in this new moment of access will be the ones that can provide sharable opportunity. Building trust as a SHARE-WARE source will encourage users to buy into experience enhancing add-ons. This a very different future from the one that early generations experienced with laundrettes and Internet cafés, which was driven more by affordability than lifestyle choice. While there is plenty of evidence to suggest that economic and space access are major determinants of the average person's ability to own or store stuff, the desire to rent rather than buy appears to be driven by other determinants like the paradox of choice or short-term need. The arrival of rentable bicycles in London in 2010, known as 'Boris Bikes' after the mayor who was in office at the time, has confirmed the attraction of sharing transport systems in cities. Car sharing brands that utilize apps like zipcar are now beginning to proliferate and open up all kinds of opportunities for brand promotion that extend well beyond the obvious transport associated links.

Mood Brands

The potential of developing mood brands interests us a lot because it provides a number of interesting spaces into which we can focus our passion for embodied thinking and doing. We believe that the lingering influence of instrumental rationality has led to obsessive focus on brand experiences that assume that greater efficiency is the only sensible human need. The growth of 'wellbeing' brands should long ago have convinced most brand sectors that we humans are multi-faceted individuals with a complex range of emotional needs and capability.

The open-ended nature of our emotional identities creates an endless opportunity for brands that are created to appeal to and service our ever-changing moods.

Benign Brands

The phenomenal success of The Honest Company, the eco-friendly baby and household products brand, co-founded by actress Jessica Alba, Christopher Gavigan and investor Brian Lee, is a perfect illustration of The Dream Café thesis that creative intelligence is the key to a sustainable future . The Honest Company was established in 2012 to plug a market gap for families who wanted affordable organic products for their babies. According to interviews, the inspiration came from Alba's concern that her search for organic products for her new born child produced limited success. The fact that a creative artist responded to the limited opportunity for organic choice in the baby market by creating a new brand is an exemplar of the power of applied imagination and the need for the perceptions of people who bring new perspectives to business. The fact that The Honest Company achieved a market valuation of $1 billion in August 2014 demonstrates that challenging market inertia by thinking and acting differently creates business opportunity.

Daring to be Different

The brand that comes closest to the principles and practices of the avant-garde for us is Tesla Motors Inc., an American business that develops, manufactures and markets electric cars and electric vehicle powertrain components. Tesla CEO Elon Musk announced in 2014 that the brand would share its technology in open source 'in good faith' to encourage other developers to contribute. Musk's logic is based on encouraging fellow travellers to share his passion for a sustainable future for transport through a strategy of co-creation. He explains the need to accelerate the emergence of the electric car:

> *The unfortunate reality is, electric car programs (or programs for any vehicle that doesn't burn hydrocarbons) at the major manufacturers are small to non-existent, constituting an average of far less than 1% of their total vehicle sales.*
>
> **(*Fortune*, 12 June 2014)**

Our assessment of Musk is that he represents the personification of APPLIED IMAGINATION that is vital for developing a sustainable future for brands. His strategies of utilizing open-source, co-creation opportunity to support Tesla's mission to create beautiful and highly efficient transportation sources is exactly the kind of approach to café culture creativity that enabled the avant-garde to invent the future.

We can't wait to meet Elon Musk in a Dream Café sometime soon.

Building a Brand through Applied Imagination and Creative Intelligence

Writing this book has caused us to research, analyse and overview a broad range of brand endeavour. The search for brands that demonstrate the liberated thinking that characterizes avant-garde practice has led us to NOTICE the dominance of brands that try to cope with chaos by clinging to the pseudo-science of incremental innovation. It is no surprise to us that this has led us to the sea of mediocrity that dominates brand thinking and strategy.

Like all the other books that purport to offer insight into brand innovation, we have found ourselves returning to the usual suspects like Apple, Google and Virgin. While we have tried to augment those clichés (with the encouragement of our editor) by considering a range of start-ups and other less obvious examples, we are excited to reach a conclusion that the best is yet to come – and we intend to be involved in ensuring that the future of brands is avant-garde.

ENDNOTES

1. Leonore Thomson, Personality Type: An Owner's Manual, 1998.
2. http://archive.wired.com/entertainment/hollywood/magazine/1609/ff_starwarscanon?currentPage=all.
3. http://www.cwhonors.org/archives/histories/lazaridis.pdf.
4. http://www.nps.gov/nr/twhp/wwwlps/lessons/walker/wafacts1.htm.
5. http://www.worlddreambank.org/L/LOEWI.HTM.
6. http://www.fastcompany.com/51547/fords-escape-route.
7. https://plus.google.com/+PrayagUpd/posts/KtWFuGdbR4y.
8. http://www.world-of-lucid-dreaming.com/famous-lucid-dreamers.html.
9. http://www.forbes.com/fdc/welcome_mjx.shtml.
10. http://www.theguardian.com/sustainable-business/nike-history-sustainable-innovation.
11. http://www.telegraph.co.uk/culture/film/8143834/Robert-Rodriguez-for-far-fewer-dollars.html.
12. http://www.virgin.com/entrepreneur/richard-bransons-top-20-virgin-inspirational-insights.
13. http://www.biography.com/people/henri-cartier-bresson-9240139.
14. http://www.huffingtonpost.com/brian-honigman/35-tech-entrepreneurs-failure_b_5529254.html.
15. http://voices.suntimes.com/business-2/grid/curse-open-office/.
16. http://farina-group.co.uk/build-collaborative-office-space-like-pixar-google/.
17. http://www.modernamuseet.se/en/Stockholm/Exhibitions/2012/PicassoDuchamp/More-about-the-exhibition/.

18 http://syndiscovery.com/does-the-imagination-age-make-synaesthesia-more-attractive/.

19 http://www.wired.com/2012/04/bezos-letter-shareholders/.

20 http://www.greenleaf-publishing.com/content/pdfs/af06anse.pdf.

21 https://twitter.com/GoldenWonderUK/status/332057107144790017.

22 https://m.youtube.com/watch?v=eywi0h_Y5_U.

23 http://www.moma.org.

24 http://www.independent.co.uk/life-style/food-and-drink/news/horsemeat-discovered-in-beefburgers-on-sale-at-tesco-and-iceland-8453040.html.

25 Peter Zackariasson and Timothy Wilson (eds), The Video Games Industry: Formation, Present State, and Future, 2012.

26 http://www.slowfood.org.

27 http://longnow.org.

28 http://www.electronicsweekly.com/university-electronics/university-of-bristol/sensabubbles-float-mid-air-display-systems-2014-04/.

29 http://www.treehugger.com/clean-technology/six-sidewalks-that-work-while-you-walk.html.

30 http://www.dies.uniud.it/tl_files/utenti/crisci/1982%20Holbrook.pdf.

31 http://www.businessdictionary.com.

32 http://www.forbes.com/sites/rebeccabagley/2014/04/15/.

33 http://m.wimp.com/allsupermarkets/.

34 http://reedsinc.com/.

35 Mademoiselle, Volume 64, 1966, p. 114.

36 http://longnow.org/.

37 http://www.nowness.com.

38 http://www.fastcodesign.com/1663220/user-led-innovation-cant-create-breakthroughs-just-ask-apple-and-ikea.

39 Alvin Fine Memorial Lecture at San Francisco State University, 1985.

40 http://www.fastcompany.com/most-innovative-companies/2013/nike.

41 http://store.nike.com/gb/en_gb/pd/fuelband-se/pid-886061/pgid-886058?.

42 http://www.nike.com/gb/en_gb/c/innovation/flyknit?.

43 http://www.psy.ox.ac.uk/team/principal-investigators/charles-spence.

44 http://thearf-org-aux_assets.s3.amazonaws.com/jar/steele.pdf.

45 https://www.youtube.com/watch?v=SR71m0HgdAo.

46 Derek Horton, Artist, writer, curator and ex-head of Research in Contemporary Art at Leeds Metropolitan University. See http://www.jardinepress.co.uk/books/Escape.html.

47 http://muusings.muuse.com/japanese-avant-garde-fashion-revolutionary-influence.

48 http://global.ralphlauren.com/engb/rlmagazine/editorial/spring14/Pages/baseball.aspx.

INDEX